Other books by the author

Workers' Worlds: Cultures and Communities in Manchester and Salford, 1880–1940
(edited with Andrew Davies)

Class and Ethnicity: Irish Catholics in England, 1880–1939

The Wilson Governments, 1964–70
(edited with Richard Coopey and Nick Tiratsoo)

Labour: Decline and Renewal

'England Arise!' The Labour Party and Popular Politics in 1940s Britain
(with Peter Thompson and Nick Tiratsoo)

The Labour Party since 1951: 'Socialism' and Society

The Labour Party

Continuity and Change in the Making of 'New' Labour

Steven Fielding

First published 2003 by
PALGRAVE MACMILLAN
Houndmills, Basingstoke, Hampshire RG21 6XS and
175 Fifth Avenue, New York, N.Y. 10010
Companies and representatives throughout the world

PALGRAVE MACMILLAN is the global academic imprint
of the Palgrave Macmillan division of St. Martin's Press,
LLC and of Palgrave Macmillan Ltd. Macmillan® is a registered
trademark in the United States, United Kingdom and other
countries. Palgrave is a registered trademark in the European
Union and other countries.

ISBN 0–333–97392–5 hardback
ISBN 0–333–97393–3 paperback

This book is printed on paper suitable for recycling and made from fully
managed and sustained forest sources.

A catalogue record for this book is available from the British Library.

Library of Congress Cataloging-in-Publication Data

Fielding, Steven, 1961–
    The Labour Party : continuity and change in the making of new labour /
Steven Fielding.
        p. cm.
    Includes bibliographical references and index.
    ISBN 0–333–97392–5 (cloth)
        1. Labour Party (Great Britain)—History. I. Title.

JN1129.L32 F457 2002
324.24107'09'04—dc21   2002072127

10   9   8   7   6   5   4   3   2   1
11   10 09 08 07 06 05 04 03 02

Printed in China

*This book is dedicated to Abby, Jack, Tom and Anna
in thanks for making an old man very happy*

Contents

List of Tables and Figures

Preface

This book is a historically grounded introduction to the Labour Party; it is designed for students of politics and contemporary history, as well as more general readers. The central concern of the work is to explore the relationship between what is today described as 'New' Labour and that which came before. For different reasons, supporters and critics of Tony Blair's 'modernization' of his party – as well as many less partisan commentators – have mainly stressed its novelty. One of the main purposes of this book is to show that the present-day party actually embodies much continuity as well as change. It therefore suggests that in order to go beyond the rhetoric of 'New' Labour and more accurately assess the impact of Blair's leadership we need to understand Labour's past.

The Introduction surveys the most significant attempts to define 'New' Labour and in so doing criticizes the prevailing view that Tony Blair's party is simply the result of an accommodation with 'Thatcherism'. It advances the proposition that while Labour under Blair's leadership has not been untouched by the consequences of earlier Conservative success, a proper understanding of the contemporary party entails looking beyond the 1980s. Thus, instead of thinking of 'New' Labour as a deviation from the party's past it is better understood to be a reworking of Labour's dominant 'revisionist' tradition. One of the main problems with the very notion of 'New' Labour – and its antithesis, 'Old' Labour – is that it promotes a largely mythical and dichotomized view of the party's past. Thus, to help further an appreciation of the wider argument advanced in this work, Chapter 1 includes an outline of Labour's history and sketches the main means by which it has been interpreted. The subsequent four chapters survey the party's problematic relationship with the Liberals, as well as the development of its ideology, electoral strategy and organization. These chapters are each concerned to investigate the extent to which 'New' Labour can be said to represent a radical break or an essential continuum with the party's past. Having established the historical context, Chapters 6 and 7 look in more detail at the contemporary party's economic and social policies. These make particular reference to the notions that Blair has abandoned the party's long-standing commitment to using the state to intervene so as to both check the failure of the market and promote a more equal society. The concluding chapter recapitulates the basic argument that underpins the book and casts a sceptical eye over claims that somewhere between the end of Blair's first term as Prime Minister and the start of his second period in office 'New' Labour – as understood by many analysts – 'died'.

The genesis for this work was a paper delivered as part of a seminar series on Socialist Ideas and Party Politics at the End of the Twentieth Century which was held under the auspices of the European Studies Research Institute, University of Salford, during the autumn of 1997 and organized by Martin Bull and Jim Newell. I am particularly grateful to Alice Brown for her supportive comments on this paper.

As is written somewhere (see Chapter 3), 'by the strength of our common endeavour we achieve more than we achieve alone'. Unfortunately, writing a book is largely an exercise in individualism. Nonetheless, this book has benefited from the assistance of a number of friends, colleagues and people I was uncouth enough to ask for help. Those of particular aid have been: Andrew Adonis, Stefan Berger, John Callaghan, Ben Clift, David Coates, Jocelyn Evans, Declan McHugh, Eric Shaw, Duncan Tanner, Jon Tonge, Stephen Ward and Mark Wickham-Jones. I should like to make special mention of Nick Tiratsoo whose support over the years has been far beyond the call of duty and is greatly appreciated.

Steven Fielding

Introduction: What is 'New' Labour?

On 7 June 2001 'New' Labour, led by Tony Blair, achieved its second General Election victory in a row. This was an unprecedented achievement: hitherto, in all its 101 years of existence, Labour had failed to secure two back-to-back full terms in government. Such was the scale of the 2001 result, some commentators even believed the party was guaranteed at least one further period in office. Yet, despite Labour's sustained electoral success and over four years in power, the character of Blair's party remained uncertain. What exactly was 'New' Labour: was it basically the same as the historical Labour Party, albeit updated to meet present-day needs, or was it a genuinely distinct political phenomenon?

There are two basic means of assessing Labour under Blair between which all observers oscillate: one emphasizes how far the party has changed and the other stresses its continuity with the past. Probably the most commonplace view has it that when, during the autumn of 1994, Blair first referred to his party as 'New' Labour he described something real. The majority of observers considered that in trying to compete with the electorally successful Conservatives, Blair turned Labour from a keen critic of capitalism into one of its champions, abandoned its commitment to reduce inequality and cut most of the party's ties with the manual working class. Thus, by the time of the 1997 General Election it was widely believed that little distinguished 'New' Labour from the Conservatives under Margaret Thatcher and her successor, John Major. As a consequence, if Blair formally held office after 1997 many considered 'Thatcherism' – and so the assumption that the pursuit of the free market should be at the heart of policy – remained in power.

In contrast, commentators less inclined to condemn the party's direction after 1994 considered that Labour under Blair remained committed to policies designed to offset some of the worst consequences of the free market and so could hardly be described as Thatcherite. These measures included enabling trade unions to achieve statutory recognition from employers and establishing a minimum wage. Such proposals were implemented after 1997, while Blair's Chancellor Gordon Brown modified

1

taxation rates to facilitate a modest redistribution of wealth from rich to poor. On this reading 'New' Labour marked more of a continuation than a break with the party's past. This stress on continuity was also embraced by some of Labour's long-standing left-wing critics. Like those who saw 'New' Labour as a break with the party's traditions, they thought Blair to be in awe of capitalism, but considered he shared that disposition with most previous Labour leaders.

The present work aims to shed further light on the 'New' Labour enigma by directly questioning the extent to which it represents change or continuity with the party's past. It is motivated by the belief that those wishing to fully understand Labour's contemporary nature need to place the party in its historical context: they need to historicize 'New' Labour. This means looking beyond the 1980s and the impact of Thatcher's Conservative governments. It also implies focusing on the thoughts and actions of the party's 'revisionist' thinkers, who influenced Labour's course for most of the period after 1945. It would nonetheless be wrong to see history as the equivalent of the 7th Cavalry riding over the horizon to rescue us from error: historical 'facts' are as shrouded in subjective interpretation as other forms of evidence. However, by properly historicizing 'New' Labour we should be more able to understand the course undertaken by Blair since 1994 and better equipped to assess how accurately students of the party have interpreted that journey.

The purpose of this chapter is to introduce some of the concerns and concepts to be developed during the course of the book. Its particular aim is to make the reader familiar with some of the most salient means by which academics, journalists and other contemporaries have attempted to understand 'New' Labour. It needs to be indicated at this early stage that the present work is primarily concerned with Labour's internal ideological and organizational character, electoral performance and economic and welfare policies. Thus, while constitutional matters are to be discussed, this is done only in so far as they were relevant to 'New' Labour's rapprochement with the Liberal Democrats. Foreign policy is in contrast virtually ignored, except in relation to the influence of the European Union (EU) on the Blair government's ability to manage the economy. Neglect of these issues is due to the fact that they are not central to the 'New' Labour debate as presently constituted, rather than a reflection of their intrinsic unimportance. Those with an interest in Labour policy in relation to such matters are therefore enthusiastically referred to works that in their different ways put contemporary policy into its historical context (Foley, 2000; Little and Wickham-Jones, 2000).

'New' Labour

Before proceeding further we need to define the term 'New' Labour for, of all the problems encountered in analysing Blair's party, one of the most basic is the problematic significance of that label. Reflecting the differential weight placed on the term's substance, those debating the nature of change within the contemporary party cannot even agree how best to transcribe it. Thus authors have at times employed a cautious 'new Labour', an assertive 'New Labour', a wholly qualified ' "New Labour" ', or, as here, a sceptical ' "New" Labour'.

As will be indicated in more detail during the course of this work, when Tony Blair first added 'New' to 'Labour' his intention was clear: to demonstrate to voters that the party had fundamentally and irreversibly changed with his election as leader. Blair wanted to highlight his claim that the party was no longer that which many imagined it to have been during the late 1970s and early 1980s: that party he described as 'Old Labour'. Blair insisted on the reality of change because as late as 1992 a significant number of key voters apparently still thought that, despite the many reforms introduced during the 1980s, the party under Neil Kinnock was too much like the one he had inherited in 1983. So far as they were concerned, Labour remained dominated by the unions; it was only interested in representing the interests of the poor and a variety of minorities; it was economically incompetent; and it was preoccupied with raising income tax. Blair and other 'modernizers' (such as Brown and Peter Mandelson) believed Kinnock's failure to persuade voters that he had transformed the party was the main reason Labour lost the 1992 General Election, its fourth defeat in a row.

That many electors saw Labour through the distorting lens of a hostile popular press was very much a moot point, for in 1994 Blair's objective was to get elected, not debate the shortcomings of public opinion. This meant he had to take the people's flawed perception of his party's past and present as it was: Blair did not believe he enjoyed the time or resources to alter it. Therefore, just as the Labour leader emphasized his ostensible admiration for Thatcher to attract voters easily impressed by a claim to her mantle, so he deliberately made the party's break with its past appear more apparent than it actually was. As some analysts now appreciate, as a result, the 'New' with which Blair prefixed 'Labour' is highly contentious and should be viewed with some suspicion (Rubinstein, 2000; Larkin, 2001).

The Conservatives certainly argued at the time of the 1997 General Election that 'New' Labour was a con trick perpetrated on the electorate, one designed to obscure the party's real antedeluvian character. Yet, while Blair's terminology is questionable, we would be misguided if we threw the baby out with the bath water and dismissed the idea that Labour has changed in the recent past. Instead, we should doubt that Labour has been transformed at quite the pace and scale its leader was wont to suggest. Blair's 'Old'/'New' Labour dichotomy after all reflected the ill-informed prejudices of wavering Conservative voters. As such it was initially conceived to serve as rhetoric. Only subsequently did the Labour leader suggest the 'Old'/'New' division should be taken to be an intellectually rigorous and historically accurate means of conceptualizing the party's development. Nonetheless, supporters, critics and the media gave those changes introduced after 1994 an inflated significance by reflecting in their analysis Blair's bifurcation of Labour history. To take one example, after making a speech to the Fabian Society in June 1994, a newspaper headline declared: 'Blair ditches Marxism for market economy' (*The Independent on Sunday*, 19 June 1994). There is not enough space here to tackle the misconceptions contained in that headline; these should become fully apparent as the reader progresses through this book. Suffice to say, its dual assumptions that Marxism exerted a pronounced influence over Labour policy before 1994, and that it was not until Blair's coming that the party endorsed the market economy, were both well wide of the mark.

Belief that Labour's character has altered dramatically since 1994 should be further qualified once the heterogeneous nature of the party is taken into account. As has been pointed out many times, no major political party is a perfectly unitary actor: each is composed of ideological factions whose interpretations of their organizations' purpose often conflict (Bale, 1999a, 6). Labour members in particular have long disputed their party's ultimate purpose: some thought it was to reform capitalism while others imagined it was to transcend it (Fielding, 1997c, 4–13). As a result, even if Blair meant what he said in asserting the existence of 'New' Labour, many others in the party resisted what they took to be its implications. Thus one needs to be clear who is referred to when mention is made of the 'Labour Party': is it the leader and his closest advisers; the Parliamentary Labour Party including venerable back-bench rebels; trade union leaders; councillors elected in the party's heartlands; activists in marginal middle-class constituencies; or those who sit at home, pay their dues by direct debit and never knowingly engage with another member? We might mean all of these groups or perhaps only one, yet each has their own distinctive perspective and set of interests. Indeed, the supposed law of 'curvilinear disparity' suggests that these differences are structural to all parties. According to this dictum Parliamentary leaders are inherently less radical than their keenest active members, although closer to the opinions of the majority of their members and voters (Webb, 2000, 210–13).

While at various moments taking the entire party into account, this study will concentrate on the party's Parliamentary leadership because it is only in relation to the assumptions that motivated the actions of previous post-war Labour leaders that a proper comparison between past and present can be made. For instance, to contrast Blair's present views with those of left-wing party activists during the late 1970s would not be to compare like with like: it would give an exaggerated impression of change. It is instead more profitable to contrast the present leadership with those who might be most reasonably seen as their predecessors: the party's post-war revisionists, most notably Hugh Gaitskell and Anthony Crosland, and followers such as Roy Jenkins and David Owen (Desai, 1994). As we shall see, such figures, just like Blair and his closest adherents today, often found themselves assailed by active members and union leaders. In particular, the revisionists' attempt to reconcile the party's working-class support with its electoral need to appeal to those from other social groups, along with their effort to make the market work while still improving the material conditions of the majority, was widely considered a betrayal of Labour's supposed traditions.

As a consequence of the above considerations, in this work ' "New" Labour' is the favoured means of denoting the party under Blair. This is meant to imply a rejection of the notion that Labour has changed utterly since 1994 alongside a recognition that Blair promoted some important developments, albeit ones which moved the party in an historically well-established direction. Overall, however, the chosen form represents a healthy scepticism with regard to the very utility of the term. However it is transcribed, 'New Labour' seriously distorts our proper understanding of the party's development. Indeed, given its pragmatic and rhetorical genesis, the term has probably been taken far too seriously by those analysing the contemporary party. We are nonetheless, for the time being at least, stuck with it.

'New' Labour and Thatcherism

While some 'New' Labour zealots treat 1994 as 'year zero', even those academic commentators who think the coming of Blair marked a decisive break with the party's past see it as the culmination of a decade-long process (Richards, 1998, 37). Although some consider the 1992 reverse as key, most suggest 'New' Labour's roots are located in the aftermath of the earlier 1987 defeat and the wide-ranging Policy Review that followed. A few have suggested the point is better traced to 1985 and Mandelson's appointment as Labour's Director of Communications. Others consider 1983, the year of Kinnock's election as leader, more influential. At least one has posited the Labour left's loss of control of the party's National Executive Committee in the autumn of 1981 as the moment when the party's reinvention truly began. While all such moments undoubtedly contributed something to the party's transformation, as Adam Lent has suggested, none can be seen as 'New' Labour's definitive 'point of origin'. Instead, he argues they should each be seen as 'transition points in the complex and unending process of development and flux' (Lent, 1997, 15). Yet, despite disagreement as to when the process precisely started, the majority of analysts concur that the engine of change was the leadership's desire to 'catch up' with Thatcherism. As Richard Heffernan has put it, 'New' Labour was merely the climax of a 'gradual and incremental' 'accommodation' with the Conservatives' neo-liberal agenda (Heffernan, 1998, 103–5). It was this 'accommodation' that caused the party to alter its electoral strategy, organization, policy and ideology.

It would be foolhardy to deny that the eighteen years of Conservative rule which began in 1979 did not have a significant influence on Labour. During this period Thatcher steered her party to three General Election victories, while its fourth success under Major in 1992 was based on a continuation of her outlook. In office the Conservatives curtailed the size of government and reshaped both its structure and purpose; they also fostered economic changes that altered the nature of the electorate. Most directly, Thatcher and Major cut income tax and encouraged widespread fatalism about collective action (Hall and Jacques, 1983; Kavanagh, 1987; Gamble, 1988; Evans, 1997).

As a result, Britain in 1997 was a very different place from the country that had last elected a Labour government. It is worth noting some of these changes, the most significant of which was the deregulation of the economy through the privatization of many state-owned industries and the lifting of most restrictions on market activity. These changes helped reduce the number of those who had once supplied Labour with its most loyal support. Thus, in 1979 around 32 per cent of workers were employed in manufacturing, but by 1997 this figure was only 18 per cent; in contrast service employment had risen from 58 per cent to 75 per cent. There was moreover an especially precipitate decline in manual, low-skilled occupations that had once provided many working-class men with a chance of full-time employment. Partly as a result of this shift, the number of trade unionists fell, from rather more than 12 million to just under 7 million, barely one-third of the total number employed. Conservative legislation played its part here, as did the increase in insecure part-time work and the number of small employers who refused to recognize the authority of unions to represent their workforce.

According to various measurements, as a result of these changes Britain became a richer society under the Conservatives. Economic growth meant that household incomes rose on average by 40 per cent, so the majority benefited from the Thatcher–Major years. However, at the same time Britain also became a much more unequal society: the period 1979–97 saw a doubling in the number of those living on less than half average earnings, the conventional definition of poverty. With 22 per cent of its population designated as living in poverty in 1997 Britain had the largest proportion of poor citizens within the European Union (EU) apart from Greece and Portugal. The main cause of this change in income distribution was unemployment. Official figures suggested that 1.5 million were jobless by 1997 but its true extent was obscured as Conservative ministers manipulated the statistics. In fact, 4.5 million of those of working age lived in households where no one worked; of these about 1 million had never been in paid employment. As a result, by 1997 one in six Britons was on social assistance, the highest proportion in the EU and three times the rate found in Germany. Consequently the social security budget had increased fivefold since 1979 even though Britain spent much less than equivalent nations on social security, health and education as a proportion of its Gross Domestic Product. While never especially generous, government spending on pensions had also declined, at least relative to comparable countries. The basic state pension fell in relation to average male earnings, from being worth 21 per cent in 1979 to just 14 per cent by 1997. This meant that over 4 million pensioners required means-tested benefits to cover the shortfall.

If the British economy expanded, its rate of growth was, however, only in line with the disappointing established post-war trend. There had been a modest rise in productivity but this was not sustained as it was mainly the result of more goods being produced by fewer workers rather than increased capital investment. Moreover, in 1997 output per head still lagged far behind most other major economies. Despite this, by the early 1990s enough individuals had done well out of the Thatcher–Major years to give the Conservatives an unprecedented grip on power and to associate many of the measures they employed in government, such as privatization and low income tax, with the glow of success. Labour's established methods, in contrast, were associated with a mythologized version of the 1970s, part of the same false popular memory that gave rise to 'Old' Labour. As a result, the party was linked to massive industrial discontent and unprecedented economic failure. Significantly, when the Conservatives lost support after 1992 it was more because voters had become alienated from the party's leading figures than the policies they advanced.

Under the Conservatives, therefore, the electoral terrain had altered significantly. Government policy contributed to this change, although in many ways it merely accelerated established trends: since the late 1950s Labour's revisionists had warned that the unskilled manual working class was in decline and would eventually be supplanted by skilled and white-collar workers. The unique contribution of the Conservative years, however, was the deliberate following of policies designed to increase inequality. Thus between 1979 and 1997 not only did the number of Labour's most enthusiastic supporters fall precipitately, but the divide between such voters and the rest of society also increased markedly. Both factors conspired to make Labour's attempt to construct an election-winning coalition, one that united society's winners and losers, much more difficult; indeed, by the early 1990s some considered it an impossible task. Even worse, it was thought that the Conservatives had undermined most voters' faith in the efficacy of what was seen to have been Labour's policy hallmark: higher taxes and state intervention.

Thatcherism Mark 2?

Given the undoubted scale of change during the 1980s it would be surprising if Labour under Blair had not been influenced by Conservative success. As is well known, the British electoral system promotes emulation between the two main parties; to win a Commons majority they usually have to compete for the same small number of electors in the same handful of marginal constituencies. This tends to encourage the promotion of policies designed to appeal to very similar voter types (Webb, 2000, 110–39). The success of one party in this regard causes the other to investigate the reasons and then incorporate any lessons into its strategy. Nonetheless, such lessons are typically applied in terms compatible with the party's established ideology.

Thus, after the party's crushing 1945 defeat the Conservatives amended their policy to echo aspects of Labour's winning manifesto

(Jones, H., 1999). This led to a 'consensus' between the parties which embraced the most significant areas of policy: in particular the Conservatives accepted much of Labour's nationalization programme (something they had vigorously attacked during the 1945 campaign). If the level of agreement was never as great as some later thought, a few leading Conservatives genuinely believed limited state ownership was the only means of saving capitalism in the immediate post-war period. This was an enforced 'consensus' that other Conservatives felt had to be accepted for the sake of their party's electoral survival. Thus, after winning back power in 1951, the party watered down the consequences of many of Labour's reforms and returned a few concerns to the private sector. Moreover, as soon as economic and electoral conditions allowed (that is, from the later 1960s), the party argued more overtly for a free market. With their main rival in disarray, after 1979 Thatcher's Conservatives reversed most of the major changes introduced by the first post-war Labour government (Fielding, 2000a, 13–19).

In contrast to the Conservatives' earlier pragmatic adaptation to Labour success, the general view is that tentatively under Kinnock and enthusiastically under Blair the Labour leadership believed the road to electoral recovery lay in unquestioningly embracing Conservative ideology. Thus by 1997 analysts of all colours were united in their belief that 'New' Labour merely offered a 'kinder Thatcherism'; it was 'neo-Thatcherite' or simply 'Thatcherite' (*The Observer*, 22 June 1997; Marqusee, 1997, 130). As the historian Brian Harrison judged, Thatcher 'more than anyone else, created New Labour' (*The Guardian*, 9 October 1997). Free market ideologists, such as the director of the Adam Smith Institute, were even led to suggest that the newly elected Labour Chancellor, Gordon Brown, was 'definitely to the right' of his Conservative predecessor (*The Guardian*, 31 July 1997). On the left, Martin Jacques and Stuart Hall described Blair's vision of the future as almost indistinguishable from Thatcher's (*The Observer*, 13 April 1997). Labour's adaptation was seen to be anything but pragmatic. As the journalist, Nick Cohen, put it, Labour ministers were 'the blind, doltish, doddering and wildly imprudent relics of Thatcherism' who genuinely believed that in all circumstances the market was superior to the state (*New Statesman*, 9 July 2001). If some commentators expressed their thoughts in rather colourful language, much academic analysis endorsed their basic proposition. Thus, as Colin Hay in particular argued, so as to catch up electorally with the Conservatives 'New' Labour had scrupulously 'neo-liberalized' party policy (Hay, 1999; Heffernan, 2000, 172).

While convinced of the decisive importance of Thatcherism to 'New' Labour, Stephen Driver and Luke Martell have advanced a more nuanced analysis which has led them to describe Blair's party as 'post-Thatcherite'. By this they mean that while Labour adopted some key Conservative policies it also retained a number of those commonly associated with 'Old' Labour. More importantly they consider that 'New' Labour assumed a critical attitude to both sets of policies and, as such, embodied a new ideological configuration that cannot be reduced to either Thatcherism or 'Old' Labour (Driver and Martell, 1998; Driver and Martell, 2001).

A Modernized Social Democratic Party?

However the process is conceptualized, most analysts consider that Labour's electoral recovery under Blair was accompanied by a massive infusion of ideas, policies and attributes once exclusively associated with its Conservative rival. Some observers nonetheless keenly dispute the importance of Thatcherism to 'New' Labour; indeed, a few go so far as to suggest that 'New' Labour is not so different from the historical party (Bale, 1999b, 198–201; Rubinstein, 2000).

David Coates in particular has questioned the novelty of what followed 1994 by stressing 'New' Labour's 'underlying continuities' with the party's past (Coates, 1996, 62–77). The contemporary party, he suggests, is different only in so far as it distanced itself from the programme promoted during Labour's uniquely leftist phase of the late 1970s and early 1980s. In most other respects 'New' Labour represents a return to a way of thinking that predated the late 1970s and one that formed the basis for all Labour governments since 1945. Thus Blair – like Labour's post-war prime ministers, Clement Attlee, Harold Wilson and James Callaghan – seeks to 'work with the grain of market forces, in a collaborative relationship with senior managers in major companies, to trigger privately-generated economic growth'. To Coates' mind, 'New' Labour's originality mainly derives from the context in which it operates. Most importantly, compared to the period before 1979 the trade unions are weaker and so less able to resist the Labour leadership's long-standing desire to pander to capitalism. Thus Coates believes that, whereas previous Labour leaders reluctantly went through the motions of proposing to reform the economy through state intervention with the notional intention of benefiting the majority, Blair was under no obligation to do even that.

Coates considers that 'New' Labour is, as was 'Old' Labour, a social democratic party and that Blair is much like other centre-left 'modernizers' evident elsewhere in Europe. That being the case, to illuminate this perspective further it is necessary to widen our perspective to include continental Europe, for Labour is but one of a number of social democratic parties that emerged towards the end of the nineteenth century throughout the industrializing West. Since then, Labour's progress has echoed that of its sister parties and so it is especially instructive to take this broad experience into account when assessing the impact of Thatcherism on 'New' Labour.

Mainly based in the manual working class, social democrats initially sought to improve their constituents' lot by contesting elections, winning office and using power to extend the state ownership and regulation of capitalism. Their object was to make the economy operate more efficiently and in the interests of the majority: by using the opportunities offered by political democracy to influence economic activity they hoped to make society more equal. Yet, by the post-war period, left-wing critics such as Coates consider that social democracy had become 'structurally dependent' on capitalism. This is because such parties supposed that the lot of the majority could only be improved once capitalism's need for a sufficient level of profit had been satisfied. Thus a political creed aspiring to social equality had become tied to an economic system in which inequality was apparently inherent. As Donald Sassoon has asserted, the fortunes of all social democratic parties – notwithstanding their individual national circumstances – therefore came to depend on developments within capitalism. At any one point in time, it was capitalism that created the parameters of what social democrats took to be possible (Sassoon, 1996, 772–6).

According to some, this historically ironic dependence of social democrats on the system they hoped to reform was such that by the post-war period they had embraced economic policies explicitly designed to bolster the rate of profit. This was partly because, as Eric Hobsbawm has suggested, 'for practical purposes' social democrats 'had no economic policies of their own' (Hobsbawm, 1995, 272). Adam Przeworski has shown that while social democrats were initially committed to transcending capitalism, they had always been unsure how to achieve that end. Thus, it took the British Liberal, John Maynard Keynes, to furnish the European centre-left with its post-war economic policies (Przeworski, 1985, 31–43). During the interwar period Keynes developed what were considered radical ideas about how government could manipulate the market by varying taxes and interest rates so as to maintain demand for goods. Keynes drafted such measures to save capitalism from the consequences of free market anarchy, but they went against the *laissez-faire* nostrums that dominated most national treasuries. Social democrats saw his demand management techniques as an invaluable means of reducing mass unemployment, something free market advocates considered an inevitable consequence of market freedom. Thus when across Europe the likes of Labour took office after the defeat of Hitler and implemented Keynesian policies while increasing the direct state ownership of industry, some capitalists at least saw them as dangerous innovators. Yet by the early 1950s these methods seemed to be working: economic expansion was unprecedented, profits increased, living standards rose, poverty was reduced and unemployment almost abolished. As a result, during the 1950s and 1960s social democrats found themselves championing policies many capitalists had come to see as a rational alternative to the purely free market, while at the same time satisfying the material demands of their constituents.

Struck by the performance of what they took to be a permanently reformed capitalism, most social democrats ceased to seek its replacement. Some revisionists even argued that capitalism, in the sense understood by turn-of-the-century social democrats, no longer existed: even amongst entrepreneurs the power of the profit motive had been weakened and was now complemented by wider social considerations. As they now believed it possible to advance the interests of the majority without altering the basic nature of the economy, leading social democrats no longer sought to replace capitalism but wanted to make it work. Yet what historians now refer to as this 'golden age' of post-war expansion turned out to be simply a phase in capitalist development. By the 1970s, what was to be described as 'globalization' made individual governments weaker; technological change and competition outside Europe created unemployment; increasingly sluggish growth placed pressure on tax-payers; and as a result welfare budgets were more closely scrutinized. In this context Keynesianism now seemed to hinder economic activity: capitalists began to see it as an impediment to profit making, while many workers lost faith in its ability to improve their standards of living.

All European social democratic parties eventually responded – after considerable internal upheavals – to the demise of Keynesianism in the form of 'neo-revisionism'. This embraced a greater stress on the market and a reduction of the state's economic role, both of which were designed to bolster profit, increase economic activity and so reduce unemployment as well as poverty (Sassoon, 1996, 730–54). In Britain it was Callaghan's Labour government that abandoned Keynesianism (Artis and Cobham, 1991; Dell, 1991; Tiratsoo, 1997). Thus, as Steve Ludlam has pointed out, it was leading members of the last 'Old' Labour Cabinet who set in train those policies that would later be exclusively associated with Thatcherism (Ludlam, 2001b, 13–14, 27–9). This was not exactly done with a singing heart, but many in the leadership, including Denis Healey (Callaghan's Chancellor), saw no alternative: economic 'reality' appeared to dictate a change of course just as a generation before it had called for Keynesianism. This policy shift was, however, vigorously opposed by many of Labour's affiliated trade unions as well as numerous active members. After 1979 these elements briefly took control of the party to ensure it became a stronger, not weaker, advocate of state intervention. The party's performance at the 1983 and 1987 General Elections meant Labour's *démarche* was resumed under Kinnock, a process – it should be noted – encouraged but not initiated by the success of Thatcherism.

Such were the changes to policy that by the time Blair won the 1997 election even some of those schooled in the assumptions of post-war revisionism considered Labour had abandoned social democratic principles (Marquand, 1999, 225–46). Yet it could be argued that the pan-European neo-revisionism, of which 'New' Labour formed part, merely marked the closure of one phase in the history of social democracy and the opening-up of another. This development had been made necessary by the conclusion of a particular episode – the 'golden age' – within capitalism. If policies drafted during this earlier period had been replaced by others designed to meet the needs of the new era, the basic purpose of social democracy – the promotion of greater equality through some form of collective action that compensated for market failure – had not altered, but neither had its essential dependence on capitalism.

Structure and Agency

Part of a broader pattern of change, 'New' Labour is generally seen to have gone much further than most – although by no means all – European social democratic parties in its embrace of the market (Callaghan, 2000). If Labour's distinctiveness can be overplayed, it still needs to be asked why, if such parties were structurally dependent on capitalism, should there be this variation? Possible answers to this question are often taken to lie in the nature of the Labour Party itself, specifically in the disposition of its leaders. Yet, as Karl Marx pointed out in 1845, if human beings make their own history they do not do so in conditions of their own choosing (Marx, 1975, 421–3). Subsequent social scientists have debated, whether in the form of individuals or organizations such as political parties, how far human agency can alter or simply reinforce those conditions. Most would now agree that the truth lies in the interaction of what are normally referred to as 'structure and agency', meaning that in relation to the context in which they exist, humans are both product and producer. Thus, it would be prudent to consider that both the party and the context in which it worked enjoyed a significant influence over the character of 'New' Labour (Kenny and Smith, 2001).

Given the impressive number of biographies of 'New' Labour's leading lights, many observers nonetheless appear persuaded that the actions of a few individuals were crucial in dictating the party's course. Indeed, in some accounts it seems 'New' Labour would not have happened at all had it not been for the actions of Blair and Brown (Naughtie, 2001). This stress on the agency of a few individuals encompasses many of 'New' Labour's internal critics: they have long thought the party's transformation to be the result of a conspiracy perpetrated by a cabal based in London (*Tribune*, 21 July 1995). It is a view supported by those drawn from across the party, including figures such as the MP, Peter Kilfoyle (who was once a keen Blair supporter) and others like Liz Davies who left the party to join the far-left Socialist Alliance (Kilfoyle, 2000, 305–10; Davies, 2001, 70). Just after the 2001 election, Roy Hattersley, Kinnock's deputy and follower of the revisionist Anthony Crosland, went so far as to state that Labour had been the victim of a *'coup d'état'*, the leaders of which had committed 'apostasy' against its traditions (*The Observer*, 24 June 2001; *The Guardian*, 27 June 2001). Even those once closely associated with 'New' Labour appear to believe it was never more than a 'tiny coterie within the party, a revolutionary cell' of but three people: Blair and his advisers, Peter Mandelson and Philip Gould (*The Sunday Telegraph*, 11 March 2001).

While all forms of political change require individuals to enact them it is wise to see such actions as the culmination of a process in which they are but one influence, albeit the most immediately obvious. Thus, for example, neither Blair nor Brown caused the ending of the 'golden age'; they were obscure party members when Callaghan abandoned Keynesianism, and junior MPs when Kinnock moved the party back to the centre ground. Very much in accord with Marx's dictum, the conditions in which Blair's and Brown's actions were undertaken had been the result of forces outside their control. This is not to say, however, that 'New' Labour was the inevitable outcome of such events. The decision to revise clause four in 1994 was, for instance, the decision of a small group around Blair, and was made in the face of considerable opposition: another leader might not have taken this initiative. Yet without prior events there would have been little perceived need for such a deed and even less chance of it succeeding. More intriguingly, Blair's belief in the need to change the clause formed part of a well-established response to the party's electoral decline, one first mooted in the later 1950s by the Labour leader Hugh Gaitskell. In deciding to change the clause, Blair showed how much he relied on the Labour revisionist tradition to map out his direction as leader (Jones, 1996).

There are in any case considerable grounds for stressing the importance of the context in which Labour operated. In particular, analysts have long considered British capitalism to be historically distinct from the form evident on continental Europe, and much closer to that of the United States. It is generally considered that this 'Anglo-Saxon', as opposed to 'European' economic model, is based more on market freedom and less on state intervention (Coates, 1999). For reasons going back at least as far as the Industrial Revolution, British capitalists and trade unionists have also been less tolerant of government intervention than their counterparts on the continent. Thus, even when Labour sought to establish support for its collectivist measures in the immediate aftermath of the Second World War, the likes of Attlee found the ground less fertile than elsewhere in Europe. Moreover, the British economy was for much of the post-war period less competitive than its German, French or Italian rivals and more dependent on international trade. Therefore the end of the 'golden age' hit Labour harder than other social democratic parties: measured in terms of collectivism, it fell further and from a lower base (Scharpf, 1991; Callaghan, 2000, 26–53). While improving competitiveness slightly, the Thatcher–Major years further accentuated Britain's economic distinctiveness. Thus by 1997, manufacturing was much weakened compared to finance, while employment as a whole was based more than most on low-wage occupations dependent on foreign and so less steadfast investors. While there is some disagreement on this front, some observers now consider that the period 1979–97 made it virtually impossible for any incoming Labour government to reform capitalism to the significant advantage of the majority, even had the party's leaders wanted to (Coates, 2001a).

It would nonetheless be dangerous to overstress the influence of the economy on political change in general and the creation of 'New' Labour in particular. For, while Marx's colleague, Friedrich Engels, famously stated that 'in the last instance' the nature of the economy must be seen as a significant influence on political activity, it is by no means the only one (Althusser, 1977, 87–128). Politics can exert its own autonomous influence on events. Thus the importance of certain institutional factors has recently been highlighted. In particular, Geoffrey Garrett has suggested that the lack of an 'encompassing' labour movement was an important reason for 'New' Labour's more enthusiastic embrace of the market. It is certainly true that the existence of powerful, centrally-directed labour organizations has been widely credited with helping to establish and buttress post-war continental social democracy. It is also true that in Britain before 1979 the unions had many members but these were poorly coordinated by the Trades Union Congress while, during the 1980s, the number of trade unionists declined. Thus 'New' Labour could be seen as a response to a weak and fractured labour movement: turning to the market in the manner it did was due to the fact that, unlike its many counterparts in Europe, the party had no viable institutional alternative to managing capitalism (Garrett, 1998; Wickham-Jones, 2000).

Conclusion

Tony Blair's description of his party as 'New' was not entirely disingenuous. If it had not been transformed simply as a result of Blair becoming leader, since the 1980s Labour changed in a number of important respects. Indeed, it will be argued in later chapters, 'New' Labour's origins go back much further than 1994, or even 1979. Many of these roots can be discerned in the writings and actions of the party's revisionists during the post-war 'golden age'. Figures such as Crosland and Gaitskell encouraged Labour to take account of those social and economic developments which they considered would forever change the electoral landscape. It was, however, only in the 1980s that the consequences of these changes became most starkly apparent. 'New' Labour's roots can also be found in the response of the 1974–9 Labour governments to the end of that 'golden age' when capitalism took what was for revisionists an unexpected and unwelcome turn. What some have taken to be 'New' Labour's 'control freakery' also derives from this period, in particular Callaghan's inability to take his activists and affiliated unions with him as the Cabinet sought to adapt policy to this economic sea-change. The resulting split in the party's ranks is something that clearly dominated Blair's horizons for much of his first term as Prime Minister. For the result of this internal dissension was that Labour followed an unprecedented left-wing route and so paved the way for the prolonged Conservative period in power. It was to help Labour better challenge this Conservative dominance that Kinnock redirected the party down a less unfamiliar path, a process that culminated in Blair's assertion of 'New' Labour. Yet, despite the appearance of profound novelty, the period after 1994 was merely a further – if conspicuously successful – instalment in Labour's protracted effort to adapt to its ever-changing electoral and economic environment.

1
Historicizing 'New' Labour

This chapter moves on from current debates about 'New' Labour to the wider historical context, starting with a brief overview and chronology of the key landmarks in Labour's hundred-year history. It will then consider how the study of the party's past can illuminate an understanding of its present. An acquaintance with historical 'facts' can however only be a start, albeit an essential one, towards getting to grips with 'New' Labour. This is primarily because there is no single universally accepted version of the party's history with which to compare its contemporary development; indeed there are as many arguments about Labour's earlier trajectory as there are about its present course. The final section of this chapter contrasts the three major competing frameworks that dominate the study of Labour Party history. As will become clear, these different interpretations of Labour's past in many ways mirror those analyses of 'New' Labour discussed in the Introduction.

A Trade Union Party, 1900–18

Labour's organizational origin lies in a resolution passed by the Trades Union Congress (TUC) in 1899 to establish an independent political body whose purpose was to represent the unions in Parliament. To this end, a meeting was held in February 1900, attended by delegates from various socialist societies, including the Independent Labour Party (ILP) and the Fabians, as well as interested unions. Those present agreed to form the Labour Representation Committee (LRC), resolving to create a group of MPs whose object was to promote legislation 'in the direct interest of labour'. On the face of it, therefore, the LRC sought little more than the election of MPs willing to defend the unions from adverse changes to the law. Largely on that basis it contested the 1906 General Election and won 5.9 per cent of votes cast on a franchise that at the time was only open to men with access to private property. Thirty LRC candidates, many of whom were union officials standing in industrial

Table 1.1   Chronology of events, 1900–37

Year	Event
A trade union party	
1900	LRC established
1903	Lib–Lab electoral pact signed
1906	Liberal government elected, supported by Labour MPs
1910	Liberals returned to power with continued Labour support
Consolidating second party status	
1918	Clause four endorsed as part of Labour's new constitution
1923	First Labour government formed with Liberal support
1926	TUC calls General Strike with lukewarm support from MacDonald
1929	Second Labour government formed with Liberal support
1931	MacDonald forms National Government and is expelled from party
1937	*Immediate Programme* commits party to widespread state control

Source: Hamer (1999).

constituencies, were returned to the Commons as part of an electoral pact with the Liberals. They formed what was subsequently known as the Labour Party.

If the LRC was only committed to improving the legal position of the unions within capitalism, the likes of the ILP hoped eventually to transcend this position. Appreciating that without union money, votes and organization they could achieve little, such socialists advocated more ambitious policies, sought to break with the Liberals and appealed to those beyond the union diaspora. Yet they made little progress and, in the last election prior to the outbreak of the First World War (held in December 1910), Labour won 6.4 per cent of votes cast.

Consolidating Second Party Status, 1918–40

The war gave those who wanted to extend Labour's role an invaluable opportunity. Not only did the conflict split the Liberal Party but it also saw the extension of the franchise to all men and most women, thereby increasing the number and proportion of working-class voters. These developments encouraged Labour's leaders to declare their independence from the Liberals and appeal more overtly to non-union members. An important expression of this desire for independence was the party's commitment to common ownership, contained in clause four of its founding 1918 constitution. This constitution marked Labour's transformation into a national organization with branches across the country.

Yet, if Labour was no longer simply the political expression of the unions, they nonetheless retained a privileged position in the party.

Despite the advantages granted by war, Labour remained some way from being a serious contender for national office. By the end of the 1920s, however, it had established a secure niche in the industrial working class and proved it could sometimes appeal to certain middle-class voters. During this decade Labour twice held office under Ramsay MacDonald (1923–4 and 1929–31: see Tables 1.1 and 1.2), although both governments were only based on a minority of Commons seats and relied on the support of Liberal MPs. Largely for that reason these administrations achieved few changes of note as at this stage the Labour leader disavowed radical policies as part of his attempt to reassure middle-class voters. MacDonald's pursuit of 'respectability' also meant he refused to do the bidding of the unions. Indeed, when the TUC called a General Strike in 1926 his support was lukewarm at best. Most union leaders accepted this state of affairs as under MacDonald Labour appeared to be making steady progress: in 1929 the party won 37.1 per cent of votes cast.

MacDonald's strategy came to a disastrous end in 1931. Labour ministers had been unable to reduce unemployment, which rose to 3 million due to the international slump. However, they were also unwilling to cut unemployment benefits and so curtail spending as dictated by those bankers whose financial assistance the government required. Convinced that national disaster would follow if the bankers were not satisfied, MacDonald formed a so-called National Government with the Conservatives and some Liberals. He led this coalition against his old party in

Table 1.2   Labour governments, 1923–2001

Duration	Prime Minister	Commons majority on election
1923–24	Ramsay MacDonald	No majority
1929–31	Ramsay MacDonald	No majority
1945–50	Clement Attlee	146
1950–51	Clement Attlee	5
1964–66	Harold Wilson	5
1966–70	Harold Wilson	97
1974 (Feb.–Oct.)	Harold Wilson	No majority
1974–79	Harold Wilson (1974–76)	3
	James Callaghan (1976–79)	
1997–2001	Tony Blair	179
2001–	Tony Blair	167

Source: Hamer (1999).

Table 1.3   Leaders of the Labour Party

1906–8	Keir Hardie
1908–10	Arthur Henderson
1910–11	George Barnes
1911–14	Ramsay MacDonald
1914–17	Arthur Henderson
1917–21	William Anderson
1921–22	J.R. Clynes
1922–31	Ramsay MacDonald
1931–32	Arthur Henderson
1932–35	George Lansbury
1935–55	Clement Attlee
1955–63	Hugh Gaitskell
1963–76	Harold Wilson
1976–80	James Callaghan
1980–83	Michael Foot
1983–92	Neil Kinnock
1992–94	John Smith
1994–	Tony Blair

Source: Hamer (1999), 5.

the 1931 General Election and reduced Labour to a rump of 52 MPs, although it still won 30.9 per cent of votes cast.

Later in the decade Labour formulated a programme encapsulated in its 1937 *Immediate Programme*, designed to tackle the country's economic problems. The party's main focus was the reduction of mass unemployment and its solution included direct state intervention in the form of planning and the nationalization of key industries. Whatever the merits of these policies the National Government, from which MacDonald retired in 1935, remained securely in power.

A National Party, 1940–70

Only the outbreak of another world conflict in 1939 gave Labour the chance to implement its programme. Military reverses during 1940 weakened the National Government so much that the new Prime Minister, Winston Churchill, was forced to offer the Labour leader, Clement Attlee, participation in office on equal terms.

The sacrifices of the war years, and the spirit of collective endeavour in the face of a shared enemy, gave rise to a popular sentiment that post-war Britain should be free of the evils associated with the interwar years, most especially unemployment. As the war progressed, concrete

Table 1.4   Chronology of events, 1940–69

Year	Event
1940	Labour enters Churchill's wartime coalition government
1945	First majority Labour government elected
1946	Bank of England and coal industry nationalized
1947	Electricity and rail industries nationalized
1948	National Health Service established; gas industry nationalized
1951	Iron and steel industry nationalized; Labour loses General Election
1955	Labour loses General Election
1957	*Industry and Society* limits party's commitment to nationalization
1959	Labour loses General Election
1959–60	Gaitskell tries but fails to revise clause four
1964	Wilson ends 13 years of Conservative rule
1965	Liberals' offer of a Lib–Lab pact rejected
1966	Election of only the second Labour government with working majority
1969	Wilson tries to qualify the unions' right to strike with *In Place of Strife*

Source: Hamer (1999).

proposals were drafted (usually at Labour's behest) for the creation of a National Health Service (NHS) (see Table 1.4) and the state-sponsored pursuit of full employment. Unprecedented numbers even supported nationalization and government direction of economic activity. At this point, Labour appeared in tune with the new mood, while leading Conservatives stood against the tide. The General Election of July 1945 demonstrated the extent to which the war had mobilized support in Labour's favour: the party won 47.8 per cent of all votes cast and formed its first government to enjoy a Commons majority.

In office, Labour implemented a far-reaching reform programme that sought to increase economic efficiency and bring about a more equal society through state intervention. Members hoped this would lead to the creation of what the party's manifesto described as a 'Socialist Commonwealth'. To that end, Labour nationalized 20 per cent of the economy and created a welfare state, in which the NHS held pride of place: this granted the poorest members of society unprecedented security. These measures required a level of taxation that effectively redistributed wealth, for the richest members of society largely subsidized benefits granted to the poorest.

While Labour's measures reduced inequality, Britain remained an unequal society and some distance from the 'Socialist Commonwealth'. Towards the end of its time in power, the party was increasingly divided over what direction it should take next. Some on the left thought further state control was needed and supported moves to nationalize more industries. Others, close to the leadership, called for a consolidation of the 1945 programme and a cautious approach to the extension of state control. Furthermore, by the government's mid-term, the Conservatives had won back much of the middle-class support lost during the war, sufficient to return to power in 1951. Despite this, Labour won 48.8 per cent of votes cast and its official membership peaked in 1952 at just over one million: the party was never again to be so popular (see Figure 1.1).

During the 1950s, Labour lost a total of three general elections, and each time its vote declined in size so that by 1959 it stood at 43.8 per cent. Some believed the party was losing touch with the concerns of younger and better-off working- and middle-class voters who saw nationalization as old-fashioned; others considered that the party's failure to fully embrace greater levels of state control was at the root of its electoral malaise. Those of the first persuasion – generally referred to as revisionists – won out and tried to make Labour less class-conscious and not so dependent on state control, which was achieved in the 1957 policy document *Industry and Society*. With that in mind the leader, Hugh Gaitskell, attempted to revise clause four after the party's 1959 defeat, but was prevented through lack of trade union support. Electorally, however, this approach seemed to work and in 1964 under Harold Wilson Labour narrowly won office, in 1966 winning re-election on the basis of 48 per cent of votes cast (see Table 1.5).

Despite great hopes, Labour in power proved a disappointment to many voters, especially those in the working class. The economy suffered numerous problems which saw promised government spending

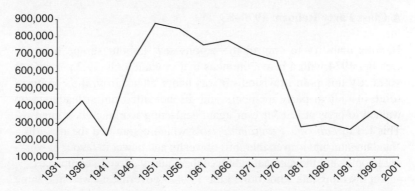

Figure 1.1   Labour's individual membership, 1931–2001 (selected years)
Source: Tanner, Thane and Tiratsoo (2000), 394–7; and *The Daily Telegraph*, 28 January 2002.

Table 1.5   The Labour vote, 1945–2001

Election	Vote	% votes cast	Commons seats
1945	11,632,191	48.3	393
1950	13,266,592	46.1	315
1951	13,948,605	48.8	295
1955	12,404,970	46.4	277
1959	12,215,538	43.8	258
1964	12,205,814	44.1	317
1966	13,064,951	47.9	363
1970	12,178,295	43.0	288
1974 Feb.	11,646,391	37.1	301
1974 Oct.	11,457,079	39.2	319
1979	11,532,218	37.0	269
1983	8,456,934	27.6	209
1987	10,029,778	30.8	229
1992	11,559,735	34.4	271
1997	13,518,167	43.2	418
2001	10,724,895	40.7	412

Source: Butler and Kavanagh (2002), 260–1.

curtailed. Ministers managed to limit wage rises but union leaders bitterly complained that Wilson was too preoccupied with middle-class concerns. In 1969 he introduced proposals under the title of *In Place of Strife* to limit the number of wildcat strikes, but was forced to withdraw in the face of union outrage. Possibly as a result of their alienation from Wilson's strategy, many manual workers stayed at home for the 1970 election, which Labour lost to Edward Heath's Conservatives.

A Class Party Reborn, 1970–83

Heath's inability to control the unions saw Labour scrape home in October 1974 with a bare Commons majority and only 39.2 per cent of votes. By this point, revisionism was under attack from the combined force of radical party members and disenchanted union leaders who wanted to prevent Labour ever again neglecting working-class interests. This led to *Labour's Programme 1973* which committed the party to a 'fundamental and irreversible shift of wealth and power in favour of working people' and the nationalization of the country's top 25 companies.

Yet the ministers who formed the 1974–9 government were the same ones who held office in the 1960s; moreover, the worldwide slump meant that retrenchment rather than expansion appeared the only course. *Labour's Programme 1973* was never implemented: indeed, under the

Table 1.6   Chronology of events, 1970–94

Year	Event
A class party reborn	
1970	Wilson loses General Election, partly due to working-class disaffection
1973	*Labour's Programme* commits party to nationalize 25 top companies
1974	Labour returned in two elections held in February and October
1976	Callaghan informs Labour conference of death of Keynesianism
1977	Lib–Lab pact formed in Commons to keep Labour in power
1979	'Winter of discontent' helps Thatcher win General Election
1981	Labour leader to be elected by all party; SDP established
Slow road to recovery	
1983	Kinnock becomes leader after Labour loses General Election
1984–85	Miners' strike held with qualified support from Kinnock
1987	Policy Review inaugurated after defeat in General Election
1992	Labour loses General Election, partly due to 'tax bombshell'
1994	Blair elected leader: asserts reality of 'New' Labour

Source: Hamer (1999).

pressure of recession, leading revisionists began to question some of the policies associated with the Attlee government, in particular the notion of demand management first articulated by John Maynard Keynes. The Prime Minister, James Callaghan, also provoked the 1979 'winter of discontent' because he refused to give poorly-paid public-sector workers the wage increases they demanded (see Table 1.6). In the wake of the ensuing strike wave, Margaret Thatcher won the May 1979 General Election.

In Opposition, the party turned on its leaders and insisted they remain true to the 1973 programme, adding, for good measure, support for unilateral disarmament and definite withdrawal from the European Economic Community. Power in the party had now shifted to its active members who enjoyed unprecedented trade union support: this disparate coalition introduced various constitutional reforms, hoping these would entrench its dominance over MPs. The most noteworthy innovation was the creation of an electoral college that gave activists and unions a decisive say in the election of the party leader. Such changes were achieved in the face of resistance from the party's revisionists, some of whom left Labour in 1981 to form the Social Democratic Party (SDP). Led by Michael Foot and advocating a manifesto widely thought to have been the most left-wing in the party's history, the 1983 General Election saw Labour reduced to 27.6 per cent of votes cast. At this point the party was losing votes from all classes and was on the verge of being relegated into third place behind the Liberal–SDP Alliance.

Slow Road to Recovery, 1983–94

Under Neil Kinnock, who took over after the 1983 defeat, the leadership sought to recover ground lost since 1970; there was, however, much territory to make up. While Kinnock had been a man of the left – and for the early part of his leadership remained a committed unilateralist – he nonetheless began to reassert the revisionist strategy employed by Gaitskell and Wilson, while taking into account the changed conditions of Thatcher's Britain. In particular, he tried to enhance Labour's appeal to voters outside the industrial working class. This meant distancing the party from the unions – an aim not helped by the abortive but prolonged 1984–5 miners' strike which associated Labour with the ultra-leftist union leader Arthur Scargill – and making policies more acceptable to affluent voters. Kinnock was unable to employ this strategy fully until after the party had lost the 1987 election; thereafter, his Policy Review shifted Labour away from the preoccupations of the party's left. Yet this policy overhaul failed to impress a sufficient number of voters; the public appeared fixated by the party's modest tax and spending plans. Thus, in the midst of a Conservative-induced recession, Labour still failed to come close to winning office in the 1992 General Election.

In the aftermath of this fourth defeat in a row, some commentators declared the working class dead, the unions finished, state intervention discredited and the Conservatives the only party capable of winning power. It was in this inauspicious context that in June 1994 Tony Blair was elected Labour leader following the death of Kinnock's successor, John Smith.

Comparing the Past with the Present

As has already been made clear, this book is firmly focused on analysing patterns of continuity and change in the party's past to illuminate the present. Politics specialists have been periodically reminded of the virtues of using the findings of historians to inform their work (Kavanagh, 1991). If such calls are usually ignored, when students of politics adopt a clear theoretical approach allied with a suitable appreciation of the past, their work can illuminate both disciplines (Marsh *et al.*, 1999). While some political historians do employ the insights of students of contemporary politics to good effect (Garrard, 2002), for many historians the essence of their craft lies in the fine points of the historical moment and the 'facts' uncovered by their research. This, in turn, can lead to a reluctance to generalize from the particular for fear of distorting each moment's unique truth. While it is necessary to respect the 'facts', as E.H. Carr famously stated, 'facts' say nothing by themselves. In order to have any significance they need to be placed within generalizing interpretive frameworks, many of which originate in social sciences such as politics (Carr, 1964).

While much historical writing is over-conservative in resisting generalization and theory, historians are nonetheless right to fear that bringing together the study of the present and past can promote error if we forget the novelist L.P. Hartley's suggestion in *The Go-Between* that 'The past is a foreign country' where people do things 'differently'. For example, at various points during the twentieth century, particular ideas have appeared more plausible than at others. Most relevant to this study, changing circumstances mean that the merits of state economic intervention have waxed and waned, being more widely accepted during the twentieth century's middle decades than at either its start or conclusion. It was, therefore, sometimes easier for Labour to promote common ownership than at other times. Party leaders, immediately after 1945, addressed a public amongst whom most saw some merit in nationalization: this was not the case in the 1920s or 1990s. Thus, we should be wary of deducing that Attlee and his cohorts were more 'left wing' than MacDonald and Blair without careful consideration of the contrasting contexts in which they operated. Indeed, the very category 'left wing' has shifted its meaning over time, such that to be on the 'left' at the start of the twentieth century meant something different from being on the 'left' at the beginning of the twenty-first. Over the century the question of ethnic and gender equality, along with issues such as the environment, have increased in salience while the centrality of the manual working class and the state have declined (Bobbio, 1996). Yet, taking account of such changes should not lead one to conclude that the 'left' of 1900 cannot be compared with that of 2000; or that, if they can, the earlier version must be considered the best. As any visitor to France will confirm, if the French enjoy better roads than in Britain they exhibit a less than laudable attitude to roundabouts, but they still drive cars. In other words, if the past is undoubtedly a 'foreign country', foreign countries combine the familiar with the alien as well as what we might subjectively judge to be 'the good' with 'the bad'.

It is consequently confusing to state baldly, as many have done, that Blair is probably the most 'right wing' of Labour's leaders. If one compares Blair's attitude to nationalization with that of his predecessor, Hugh Gaitskell, it may well be that on the basis of Gaitskell's 1950s

endorsement of a large state sector, Blair stands to the 'right' of his predecessor even though at the time Gaitskell was viewed as conservative on
this issue (Brivati, 1996, 441–5). The implication sometimes drawn from
this supposed insight is that Blair has assumed his position because he
wants to, and that he is a wholly free agent unaffected by historical context. There is, therefore, no reason why he could not simply adopt the
policies once advocated by Gaitskell. It also gives force to the view that
'New' Labour marks a decisive break with Labour's past.

In spite of that, as will be argued in more detail in later chapters, revisionists such as Gaitskell share a common general outlook with Blair in
regard to electoral strategy, party management, the economy and equality.
As those most responsible for the making of 'New' Labour concede, the
revisionists anticipated many of their themes (Gould, 1998, 31–3). Yet,
if the means by which Gaitskell sought to achieve his ends were different from those of 'New' Labour, the ends themselves were markedly
similar. To the extent that both men exhibited differences of approach,
this was because they were embedded in the times in which they lived
and so were in thrall to their conflicting realities and assumptions.
Gaitskell lived in a period when the Soviet command economy was
believed to be on the verge of seriously challenging American capitalism,
when Keynesian demand management was generally seen as the key to
economic growth and the manual working class formed a majority of the
electorate. In contrast, Blair became party leader after the gross inefficiencies of the Soviet Union had been exposed (the United States having won the Cold War), when demand management had fallen into
widespread disrepute and the manual working class constituted a social
minority. One of the jobs of the historian is to take account of such
difference while still promoting an understanding of what links contemporaries to their past. If this task is not easy, it is not yet impossible: if
we are to have a better sense of where we have come from and where we
might be going, it is absolutely necessary.

Contrasting Impressions of Labour's Past

We are fortunate that a small band of academics has explicitly tried to
reconcile an informed historical understanding with a close appreciation
of the present: we are doubly lucky that a disproportionate number of
this minority study the Labour Party. Despite this, as one of the group,
Eric Shaw, has complained, too many students of the contemporary

party investigate short periods of time, and on that slim basis make dubious claims about long-term trends (Shaw, 2001a, 172). Moreover, according to Tim Bale, the lack of engagement between historians of the party and those interested in its present-day character is especially debilitating in the era of 'New' Labour. For Bale, the extent to which Blair and his followers have based their case for change on a very particular view of the past, makes it especially important that the *bona fides* of their claims are investigated (Bale, 1999b). Without a doubt, the need for a properly informed analysis of 'New' Labour's historical context is more pressing than even Bale believes. This is because it is not just 'New' Labour partisans who adhere to a contestable version of the party's past: so do their detractors (Fielding, 2000b).

Critics of 'New' Labour tend to cohere around a common view of the party's past in which two dates enjoy particular prominence: 1918 and 1945. As noted earlier, in 1918 Labour committed itself to the extension of public ownership through clause four of its constitution. In 1945, Labour achieved its first working Commons majority, armed with which Attlee applied a massive nationalization programme and pursued full employment through state planning and Keynesian demand management. The two dates are linked due to the belief that Labour won in 1945 precisely because it had advanced the vision established in 1918. Consequently, these two moments have come to be seen as encapsulating Labour's essential identity. Thus the historian Royden Harrison went so far as to claim that the 'best' of the party's tradition was the 'settlement which followed victory in the Second World War: it was and it will always be the Party of full employment; comprehensive social services and extended common ownership' (Harrison, 1996, 26–7). This perspective suggests that any weakening of the party's commitment to public ownership represents a betrayal of its history: on this basis 'New' Labour stands condemned.

'New' Labour advocates, none more so than Blair himself, dispute this view by distinguishing between means and ends (Blair, 1996, 4–21). They argue that the commitment to extend common ownership embraced in 1918 and manifested in 1945 had, by the end of the twentieth century, ceased to be practical or necessary. However, the cause the party once thought could only be advanced through more public ownership – greater equality – remained relevant. Thus, the party had to change its attitude to nationalization in order to remain true to its basic purpose. According to this perspective, to consider that Labour's distinctiveness relied upon a particular form of influencing economic activity distorted the importance of the party's allegedly timeless and more profound ethical motives.

Due to Blair's 'Old'/'New' dichotomy, the bearing on current party debates enjoyed by interpretations of Labour's past is exceptionally weighty; the lack of a consensus about 'New' Labour's historical context is, in contrast, not so unusual. Labour politicians, just like all their contemporaries, often exhibit a less than scrupulous attitude to the past.

As already noted, Blair's 'Old'/'New' Labour distinction is based on a questionable version of party history which was employed for immediate political advantage. Yet if some versions of the past are deliberately self-serving they may also be self-deceiving: just because it is in the interests of a person to believe erroneously that certain things happened in a particular way does not mean they actually know such historical 'facts' to be untrue. Moreover, like everybody else, Labour members are prone to look back to a period when things were supposedly better and, on that basis, criticize the times in which they live. Such nostalgia can have its own political effects. For example, during the 1950s many Labour activists considered the 1930s to have been a better time to be in the party, yet the latter decade was a time of high unemployment and poverty; Labour was a marginal force whose ideas were widely derided. All indicators suggest the party's position had drastically improved by the 1950s. Nonetheless, this belief encouraged activists to reject the emerging new post-war world in favour of what was for them a comforting version of recent history (Fielding, 2001a). Similarly, by the early 1980s, it was the period 1945–51 that had assumed the character of a 'magical moment' to whose supposed certainties all wings of the party yearned to return (Stedman Jones, 1983, 239). Once again, this vision was flawed. If Labour did well in terms of votes, some historians have suggested that during this 'magical moment' Labour's popular support was less firm and more pragmatic than was assumed by those who looked at the period with misty eyes (Fielding, Thompson and Tiratsoo, 1995).

In short, a more complete integration of politics with history is a vital first step towards a fuller understanding of the meaning of 'New' Labour. However, it would be naive to believe that this will produce insights with which all will readily agree: both disciplines are too dominated by major differences of interpretation to allow this to happen. Indeed, as one perceptive reviewer of the literature has noted, even academic accounts of the party under Blair are 'riddled' with 'normative assumptions and partisan bias' (Ludlam, 2000, 266). The next section will suggest that the position is little different with regard to the work of Labour historians.

Historical Interpretations

To help us better situate the contemporary debate about 'New' Labour's historical significance, the following outline of the party's historiography has been divided into three essential schools of thought. What is here termed the 'socialist' school is the product of those wanting to demonstrate Labour's shortcomings as an anti-capitalist party. In contrast, the 'social democratic' viewpoint considers that Labour too closely reflected the trade union interest to be a successful party of reform. While deriving from differing political positions both perspectives emphasize the significance – and limitations – of the party's organizational and ideological character. This stress on agency stands out against the final 'constraints' school, whose adherents consider that the context in which the party operated played a decisive role in determining its actions.

Before looking at these schools in more detail, it should be stressed that many of those who have studied the party's past consider Labour's character and trajectory to have been largely determined by its initial role as the political expression of the unions. There are solid theoretical grounds for considering that the manner in which any party is established can structure its later development (Panebianco, 1988). It is, moreover, true that for much of the twentieth century most of Labour's income came from the unions and many of its members and voters were trade unionists, while the unions enjoyed a formally decisive say in party policy-making. Thus, as late as 1991, Henry Drucker could state that Labour was 'unthinkable without the unions', in as much as he considered it was the union experience that forged the party's 'ethos': that is, its 'traditions, beliefs, characteristic procedures and feelings' (Drucker, 1979 and 1991). The unions certainly enjoyed considerable influence within the party and were vital to the creation of the LRC. Yet, as Henry Pelling made clear in an early study of the subject, even at its point of origin, Labour was a 'curious mixture' of political idealists and hard-headed trade unionists (Pelling, 1965, 216–28). Thus, while some in the party wanted it to reflect the unions' interests directly, this did not mean it always did; as we shall see, Labour's 'curious mixture' was to be the cause of much tension within the party over the years.

The Socialist School

The most influential work produced by the socialist school is Ralph Miliband's *Parliamentary Socialism*, first published in 1961. In this study, Miliband wanted to establish that Labour's history showed it had never been committed to the radical transformation of the economy because it was a party of 'modest social reform' 'irrevocably rooted' in capitalism (Miliband, 1972, 376). Early exponents sought to explain this moderation by referring to the nature of the British trade union movement. By the end of the nineteenth century, most unions were thought to have become preoccupied with 'labourism', that is improving their position in capitalism and uninterested in changing the system itself. Thus, given the unions' predominance within the LRC and the reasons for their support, it was almost inevitable that Labour MPs elected in 1906 reflected their priorities (Rothstein, 1983).

By 1945, Labour's leaders were thought to have assumed a more active role in the promotion of labourism. If Attlee's ministers improved living conditions through the introduction of a welfare state and the regulation of the market, they are also thought to have preserved the status quo, as these reforms reduced the pressure for more radical change while leaving the fundamental basis of capitalism intact (Saville, 1967 and 1973). Indeed, from the outset, the party's leaders were thought to have merely aimed to make capitalism more rational and efficient through state intervention. If this promised to attenuate inequality – as it did for a time after 1945 – it could not abolish those class differences generated by the pursuit of private profit (Anderson, 1965 and 1987; Nairn, 1965).

For much of the post-war period, Labour's social democratic priorities proved compatible with the unions' labourism: as the latter's policies seemed to generate full employment, the former supported the leadership against their more uncompromising activists. As Pelling noted, this relationship was never without its tensions. Moreover, during economic downturns the leadership's commitment to maintain capitalism came into conflict with the unions' ambition for better pay and conditions. Moreover, due to their keen belief in Parliamentary democracy, the leadership vigorously opposed any work-based militancy, and strikes in particular (Miliband, 1972, 13–14). Certainly, numerous studies written by prominent exponents of the socialist school considered that the Labour governments of 1964–70 and 1974–9 exposed the extent to which the leadership sacrificed working-class interests when this was deemed necessary to save capitalism (Coates, 1975 and 1980; Panitch, 1976). As Miliband put it, if Wilson's ministers 'carried out

Conservative policies in a Labour way', the end result was nonetheless fundamentally the same (Miliband, 1972, 364).

The Social Democratic School

If adherents of the socialist school believed Labour's post-war trajectory was defined by its abandonment of working-class interests, those belonging to the social democratic school considered the party was too closely associated with the manual working class (Fielding and McHugh, 2001). This is the central element in David Marquand's influential notion of the 'progressive dilemma' (Marquand, 1999, 19–25). Marquand's contention is that Labour's historically poor electoral performance was due to the party's inability to make a sustained appeal to those beyond the working class. Labour was, he believed, far too successful in articulating the unions' labourist outlook as this resulted in its 'structure and beliefs' (as codified in the party's 1918 constitution) paying scant attention to those not part of the manual working class. Thus, the party's 'saturation' by a strongly proletarian ethos was at the heart of its failure to construct a successful anti-Conservative coalition.

According to Marquand, Labour should have emulated the model established by the Liberal-led Edwardian 'progressive alliance'. Indeed, he argues that it would have been better all round had Labour not sought independence in 1918 but remained within an alliance reconfigured to take more account of the labour interest. As some suggest, had it not been for the First World War the 'progressive alliance' might indeed have survived (Clarke, 1971). The so-called New Liberals in particular charted a course that could have incorporated the unions within a reformed capitalism which would have looked similar to the one produced by Attlee in 1951. The ability to mobilize a broad-based, cross-class coalition in which the working class were a 'crucial, but not dominating, part' would, Marquand thinks, have meant Labour could have extended the post-war settlement during the 1950s and beyond. Instead, however, the party prioritized the interests of its union backers, lost middle-class support and allowed the Conservatives to hold office for most of the post-war period.

The Constraints School

Both socialist and social democratic schools largely base their analysis of Labour's history on a critique of its internal character. They also proceed from related counter-factual assumptions. The former considers that it would have been possible to build a more socialist Britain had Labour's leaders sought to encourage rather than subdue working-class militancy. The latter assumes that had Labour been able to restrict the influence of its union cohorts Britain would have developed a more vigorous social democratic culture. Members of the constraints school disavow such devices, focus on the party in its own terms and assess Labour's history in that light. Their main emphasis is on the importance of matters outside the control of the party's leaders. As a result, they take issue with some of the propositions advanced by adherents of the other two schools.

One of the most influential voices within this school belongs to Ross McKibbin, who assessed Labour's progress with direct reference to the social and political order in which the party operated. In particular, McKibbin has underlined the extent to which the working class accepted the legitimacy of established political institutions, based as they were on a highly stratified social order. In addition, he has emphasized the implacable opposition of the middle and upper classes to collectivism even when advanced by New Liberals (McKibbin, 1991 and 1998). Such a context gave Labour little room for manoeuvre and bred an understandable caution amongst its leaders when it came to policy innovation and electoral strategy.

This standpoint has been developed in numerous detailed studies of particular moments in Labour's post-war history, in most of which Nick Tiratsoo has taken a leading part (Tiratsoo, 1990 and 1991; Coopey, Fielding and Tiratsoo, 1993; Fielding, Thompson and Tiratsoo, 1995). Such work has highlighted not just the limited aspirations of proletarian voters but also exposed the severe economic problems faced by the party in power. It has also indicated the extent to which the leadership sought to extend support from its working-class bastions and evolved policies designed to appeal to the middle class. In addition, this work has suggested that if the party was concerned to improve capitalism rather than replace the system in its entirety, Labour at least adhered to policies that put the interests of the working class higher up the agenda than their Conservative opponents.

Structure and Agency (Again)

Some deprecate explaining Labour's past through this emphasis on constraints – or structure, as it might also be described – rather than agency for being too one-sided (Bale, 1999b). If the constraints school has sometimes been guilty of under-playing the importance of agency this was largely to offset the practice of many adherents of the socialist school who exaggerated it. As suggested in the introduction, both structure and agency have to be properly integrated into any account of political change. Nonetheless, arriving at the right balance is undoubtedly problematic, if not at times apparently impossible, which can be illustrated by taking the example of the lack of enthusiasm of most British workers for socialist politics. This is an important starting point for the constraints school as the paucity of working-class political ambition is taken to be one of the most important explanations of Labour's own moderation. Even leading adherents of the socialist school have accepted the non-revolutionary temper of British workers, but they see this to be largely the product of Labour's chosen course (Miliband, 1972, 90, 119, 228; Coates, 1975, vii–ix). Thus, on the one hand working-class conservatism is seen to have produced Labour moderation; on the other, Labour's caution is considered to have resulted in workers antipathetic to socialism. Given such seemingly irreconcilable differences of interpretation, Labour's past remains a deeply controversial subject.

If divided on many issues, leading members of each of the three schools nonetheless believe that (compared to other social democratic parties) Labour was profoundly different. Explanations of how and why the party was distinct can vary: some think it due to the leadership's greater reverence for the parliamentary system (Miliband, 1972, 13); the extent to which the party was dominated by the working class (Marquand, 1999, 16–17); or the existence of native political and cultural forces preventing Marxism from enjoying much influence in Britain (McKibbin, 1991, 1–41).

Those who currently adhere to the view that Labour was and remains the black sheep of European social democracy can point to the greater levels of government spending on welfare services and higher rates of income tax evident in most other comparable continental countries to support their case. The extent to which Labour's leaders or the party's institutional culture were responsible for this relative lack of achievement is, however, debatable. It might well be argued that comparable European parties operated in more favourable contexts and that the reputedly egalitarian societies which now exist in Western Europe are the result of more than the militancy of indigenous social democrats. It is hard to avoid the suspicion that belief in Labour's inferiority derives from an assumption prevalent amongst the British left (and cruelly parodied by Edward Thompson) that the experience of 'other countries' has been in each and every respect more radicalizing than that evident in

Britain (Thompson, 1978). In fact, one of the few comparative historical studies of the Labour party convincingly challenges the ingrained view that the German *Sozialdemokratische Partei Deutschlands* was a more developed example of social democracy than Labour: if anything, the similarities were more striking than any differences (Berger, 1994).

Conclusion

By the time Tony Blair led Labour to victory in 1997, key areas of policy – indeed its very ideology – appeared to have been transformed, such that many contemporaries believed 'New' Labour was an appropriate description of the party. This chapter has suggested that a proper appreciation of the party's past can help us better understand the significance of this particularly dynamic period in Labour's history. The rest of the work will substantiate that case in more detail, but it would be useful to recapitulate what has been said here and in the preceding chapter so as to put what follows into relief.

Without some knowledge of the past it is likely that one will misinterpret the present. Unfortunately, despite thinking themselves objective, most contemporaries hold to comforting or convenient but largely mythical versions of the past, a tendency that is no less true of those connected to the present-day Labour Party. Indeed, it was suggested in the Introduction that the very dichotomy upon which Blair hoped to revive his party's fortunes – which divided Labour history into the 'Old' and 'New' – seriously distorts understanding of the party's development. Nevertheless, even the most serious students of the past, those who spend their time unearthing historical 'facts', often produce contrasting versions of how things were. As the nature of the three schools discussed above indicates, Labour's historiography comprises areas of profound disagreement between those who are equally committed to producing an accurate picture of the party's development.

If it does not give us privileged access to the 'truth', an awareness of such differences of interpretation and the evidential basis for historical dispute can only help us better understand 'New' Labour. If nothing else it should make us appreciate how far the means by which contemporaries understand the significance of 'New' Labour existed long before Blair became leader. For example, critics of the party today often argue that it has changed due to the leadership's desire to 'catch up' with Thatcherism. This led Blair and his colleagues to embrace capitalism fully and cease defending working-class interests. Whatever the merits of that argument, many of the characteristics it ascribes to 'New' Labour are similar to those certain academics and activists believed defined the party when led by Wilson in the late 1960s (Williams, 1968). From this we could draw one of a number of possible conclusions. It could be that 'New' Labour had somehow emerged unnoticed over a decade prior to Thatcher's first General Election triumph, although this seems unlikely. Alternatively, it is possible that what contemporaries take to define 'New' Labour has actually characterized the party for some time: indeed, possibly since its foundation. On that basis, the role played by Thatcherism in the making of 'New' Labour should be questioned. This would certainly be a line of argument favoured by many adherents of the socialist school. In contrast, like one of the leading advocates of the constraints school, we might consider that the case made in the 1960s was simply inaccurate (Tiratsoo, 1993). An implication here is that present-day critics who think 'New' Labour has abandoned the established concerns of social democracy are the victims of a venerable, influential but wrong-headed view of the party.

It was not the purpose of this chapter to identify the one true way of understanding the party's past, for it is unlikely that such means exist. Instead the chapter has made an uncontroversial case that those wishing to understand Labour's present should become better aware of its past, for if it is doubtful that this will give us access to the unalloyed 'truth' it can at least promote a more judicious appreciation of how 'New' Labour is presently understood.

2
The Liberal Connection

The feature many commentators initially considered most novel about 'New' Labour was Tony Blair's desire to build a new relationship between his party and the Liberal Democrats (LibDems). Blair certainly went out of his way to highlight the Liberals' contribution to Labour history and claimed that even the Attlee government – so beloved by adherents of 'Old' Labour – owed much to the work of Liberals such as John Maynard Keynes and William Beveridge. With that in mind, Blair suggested his members should in future 'welcome the radical left-of-centre tradition outside our own party'. He went so far as to express regret that Labour's Edwardian association with the Liberal Party had given way to full independence after the First World War as it had obscured an 'intellectual bridgehead' that linked these two 'progressive' forces. The split was not only politically unnecessary but, Blair believed, had also allowed the Conservatives to hold on to national office for too long. The Labour leader consequently claimed he wanted to re-establish this lost 'radical centre' and so lay the electoral foundations for a 'progressive century' (Blair, 1996, 7–12).

Some LibDem and Labour members saw Blair's desire to promote cooperation between the parties as consistent with their own pursuit of what they termed a 'pluralist' politics based on 'inclusion, autonomy and empowerment' (Lawson and Sherlock, 2001). Many others in Labour's ranks, however, feared the consequences of Blair's attempt to build a closer relationship with Paddy Ashdown, the then LibDem leader. If before 1997 most saw merit in a tactical anti-Conservative arrangement, few saw the need to take matters further after the General Election. Those of this persuasion were disturbed by talk of electoral reform, something which Ashdown stated was the price for a more permanent and closer relationship, as they believed Labour could only lose from such change. A number even viewed Blair's courtship of the LibDems as evidence of his desire to totally and finally transform Labour through a merger of the two parties. It was not for nothing that some Cabinet colleagues referred to their Prime Minister as 'the Liberal'.

This chapter will put into context Blair's pursuit of the LibDems as a means of exploring the substantive meaning of 'New' Labour. It will suggest that many of the Labour leader's comments and actions were comparatively not unusual: all European social democratic parties have been influenced by liberalism, while most have cooperated with their native Liberal parties. The chapter will also argue that the Blair–Ashdown relationship formed part of a historically well-established process as, for much of the twentieth century, Labour and the Liberals fitfully tried to establish a mutually rewarding bond that often involved talk of electoral reform. Even after their relationship had ended by 1918, both engaged in an on-off, love-hate affair that sometimes looked as if it would end in remarriage, or at least cohabitation. Finally, if fostering reconciliation between the two parties was genuinely important to Blair, the lack of dynamism evident since 1999 requires some explanation. In many ways, therefore, while initially appearing to support the reality of 'New' Labour, Blair's apparent pursuit of a closer relationship with the LibDems was in truth one more episode in a long-running political soap opera.

Social Democracy and Liberalism

Blair was right to suggest that his party owed much to the thoughts and actions of earlier Liberals. Moreover, Labour was not alone in enjoying such a link: all European social democrats were intellectually indebted to liberalism, particularly its stress on the need for democracy and individual freedom (Breuilly, 1992). In 1899 the influential revisionist German social democrat, Eduard Bernstein, went so far as to announce that socialism was 'spiritually' liberalism's 'legitimate heir'. Bernstein claimed socialism shared with liberalism the desire to increase individual autonomy, the difference being that the former considered it necessary to reduce certain economic freedoms in order to increase the sum total of liberty. In that sense, he wrote, socialism was 'organising liberalism'. Bernstein even went on to claim that the principle of 'economic responsibility', conventionally seen as the central motive force of *laissez-faire* economics, was also necessary to socialism. 'Without responsibility', he asserted, 'there is no freedom', and in modern economies 'a healthy social life' was 'impossible if the economic personal responsibility of all those capable of work is not assumed' (Bernstein, 1961, 148–54).

Not all social democrats endorsed the philosophical implications of Bernstein's outlook although in Britain Ramsay MacDonald wrote in

1905 that socialism retained 'everything of value in Liberalism' (Marquand, 1997, 92). Yet even continental social democrats during their earliest days cooperated with their Liberal counterparts, even if this was sometimes due more to necessity than choice. In Belgium, for example, a shared hostility to the Catholic Church united the parties, while in Sweden social democrats owed their first appearance in Parliament to Liberal help. Moreover, after 1945 many noted an increasing ideological convergence between Liberals and Social Democrats. In West Germany, so extensive was the common ground that the *Sozialdemokratische Partei Deutschlands* shared power with its Liberal rival the *Freie Demokratische Partei* between 1969 and 1983 (Boggs, 1995, 18–19; Sassoon, 1997, 11–19, 317–18).

Despite their partisan desire to prove otherwise, politicians can only respond to the same problems with a limited range of intellectual tools: as a result, there has been considerable doctrinal cross-fertilization between parties over the years. Such intersections of ideas and concerns can often make a mockery of formal party labels. This is no less true in the case of liberalism and social democracy, even in those countries where the latter assumed an overtly Marxist form. In Britain, however, this rapport was especially pronounced. In an almost literal sense, Labour grew out of late nineteenth-century liberalism; Labour then helped stimulate the development of an Edwardian New Liberalism, some of whose ideas and personnel were grafted back on to the party after 1918. As historians of the pre-1914 period have confirmed, there was a considerable overlap of concerns between 'progressive' exponents of the two creeds which allowed them to debate the different ways in which individualism and collectivism could be combined to promote their common end: the reduction of poverty (Clarke, 1978; Freeden, 1978; Blaazer, 1992).

One reason for the more extensive ideological intermingling between social democracy and liberalism in Britain was that the latter, in the shape of the British Liberal Party, was much more popular with the working class than elsewhere in Europe. Indeed, as late as 1881, Friedrich Engels despairingly described the British working class as simply forming the 'tail of the great Liberal Party' (Pelling, 1965, 7). Liberal success was partly due to the fact that, unlike in the rest of industrial Europe, workers did not live under an authoritarian state. By the end of the nineteenth-century, generally speaking, British trade unionists were not spied on or shot by representatives of the ruling class. This encouraged them to advance their interests within the existing political system: it seemed plausible to believe such efforts would eventually bear fruit

(McKibbin, 1991, 27–32; Berger, 1995, 250). Liberal success was, however, not simply the reflection of structural forces: the party had its own merits. While led by aristocrats and supported by factory owners adhering to free markets, the party also mobilized a coalition of the excluded, including religious Nonconformists, those seeking Home Rule for Ireland, Scotland and Wales and skilled workers. Thus, as late as the 1890s, most leading trade unionists were content to support Liberalism and left unmoved by the claims of groups such as the Independent Labour Party and Social Democratic Federation. Consistent with their 'labourism', the unions used their influence with Liberal politicians to achieve modest but tangible improvements to their position within capitalism. It was only after the Liberals no longer appeared willing to defend the unions' interests that some leaders altered their tactics and supported the Labour Representation Committee (LRC). Yet most of those elected Labour MPs in 1906 remained at heart Liberals, owed their votes to working-class men of a similar persuasion and sat in the Commons as a result of an electoral alliance with the Liberal Party.

The 'Progressive' Dilemma

Due to Britain's majoritarian electoral system, since the creation of the LRC, Labour and the Liberals have been forced to periodically reflect on relations with each other. For, if both their candidates stood in certain types of constituencies, the parties risked allowing the Conservatives to win seats which a Labour or Liberal candidate might have taken had they been allowed a free run by the other. If the terms of trade altered over time, with first the Liberals, then Labour, being the major force, the dilemma remained the same. Would it be best to unite against the Conservatives for mutual benefit, or operate separately in the hope that the other party would eventually be cast to the margins? At times, such considerations were more important to one party – invariably the Liberals – rather than the other; on a few occasions, such as the 1990s, it preoccupied both almost equally.

As noted above, by 1900 a sufficient number of unions had been persuaded they could enhance their interests by seeking independent representation in the Commons. The LRC planned to stand candidates in constituencies in which the Liberals hoped to win in a straight fight with the Conservatives. If the LRC's intervention might harm the chances of the Liberal candidate then the latter could also only hurt the former's ability to defeat the Conservative. Recognizing their mutual interest in avoiding conflict, in 1903 the LRC's Secretary, Ramsay MacDonald, and the Liberal Chief Whip, Herbert Gladstone, agreed to allow the other to stand alone in a set number of constituencies (Bealey and Pelling, 1958). Partly as a result, the Liberals achieved a landslide victory in 1906 and formed a government that introduced measures of benefit to many of Labour's constituents, such as the reform of trade union legislation, the implementation of a minimum wage for some low-paid workers and the introduction of a limited state pension. At the two subsequent elections held in 1910, Labour and the Liberals, some tensions notwithstanding, remained in harness.

The motives behind this 'progressive alliance' were many and varied. Some Liberals saw cooperation as a short-term tactic designed to allow their party to win back union voters from Labour. Others – mostly those referred to as New Liberals – believed Labour was an established force that would not go away; both sides could, however, benefit from a permanent alliance based on a redrafting of liberalism that legitimized limited forms of government intervention. Within Labour's ranks there was hostility to supporting the Liberals, a party many saw as little different to the Conservatives. On the other hand, MacDonald believed that while Labour would eventually supplant the Liberals, the time was not yet right for independence. In the meantime, Labour could work with the New Liberals to achieve important reforms, and possibly win them over to more radical change.

It was during this period of cooperation that electoral reform was raised as a major issue. A 1908 Royal Commission and a Speaker's Conference held during 1916–17 debated the matter: both gestured towards a new system that mixed proportional representation (PR) with the alternative vote (AV). The subject was again raised during the passage of the 1918 Representation of the People Act that gave the vote to all adult men and women over thirty years of age (Joyce, 1999, 68–9). Labour also considered the issue and, while rejected by the party's conference, some activists saw PR as the means of giving Labour independence from the Liberals since there would then be no need for pacts (Barrow and Bullock, 1996, 274–81; Taylor, 2000, 154–5).

Historians have debated the reasons why the 'progressive alliance' ended during the First World War and have come to a variety of conclusions (Thorpe, 2001, 27–35). Some believe the Liberal Party as a whole was incapable of meeting working-class demands as too many of its members adhered to strictly *laissez-faire* economics. They consequently saw the unions in negative terms and disliked even the limited examples of state-sponsored social policy introduced after 1906. Labour was also coming under increasing pressure to strike out on its own as the unions gained in power and influence. Others consider the New Liberal-inspired reforms had done the trick by 1914: the Liberals were now able to appeal to a sufficient number of working- and middle-class voters to hold on to power. While Labour was set to increase its influence within the 'progressive alliance', cooperation could have been sustained and developed. Unfortunately, for those of the latter persuasion, the First World War tore such possibilities asunder by, amongst other things, dividing the Liberal leadership, giving the unions a massive boost and forcing the hand of those Labour leaders who had doubted the time was ripe for independence.

To mark its break with the Liberals, in 1918 Labour created a new constitution that entrenched formal union influence within the party and underlined its commitment to 'socialism' through clause four (McHugh, 2001, 47–76). Some 'New' Labour advocates have come to see this as an unfortunate development as they believe it encouraged Labour to become overly reliant on the working-class and focus too much on state intervention (Gould, 1998, 23–9). Yet, while Labour assumed the outward appearance of a union party committed to the ineluctable extension of common ownership, the likes of MacDonald still sought to attract the votes of Liberals and the membership of prominent New Liberals. If some of the latter remained outside, many others joined, seeing through the party's superficial appearance to what lay beneath. Indeed, Charles Trevelyan stated that 'I have not been required to shed anything of my Liberalism' as a result of joining the party, and he became a Cabinet minister under MacDonald (Freeden, 1986, 210). Even those who stayed with the Liberals, such as Keynes, knew the score: he famously once declared that Labour's leaders were the 'heirs of eternal Liberalism' (Clarke, 1983, 39). Increasingly, it seemed to 'progressives', Labour was the only practical vehicle for change. This was partly because under MacDonald Labour aspired to establish a political 'respectability' whose aim was to maximize the party's support across society. If MacDonald wanted to replace the Liberals as the dominant anti-Conservative force, that did not prevent Labour leaning on Liberal ideas and relying on the votes of Liberal MPs if it helped the party win and hold on to office.

At elections held between 1918 and 1929, Labour established a position of superiority over the Liberals, one measured more surely in terms of constituencies than votes. As would remain the case for the rest of the century, Labour's vote was more socially and geographically concentrated than the Liberals': this gave the former the upper hand in terms of winning Commons seats. With half-hearted Liberal support MacDonald was even able to form a minority government for a few months during 1923–4. He repeated the trick in 1929: although Labour's position was much stronger than on the first occasion, MacDonald still required Liberal support. There was talk of coalition but, given the hostility of the Liberal leadership to the unions, this was always unlikely (Joyce, 1999, 67). Moreover, not all Labour members looked on cooperation with MacDonald's equanimity. Despite this, the government established a committee to investigate electoral reform in order to help promote an atmosphere conducive to cooperation. Anticipating positions that would become familiar after 1994, the Liberals wanted full PR but the Cabinet would go no further than AV. A Bill was eventually drafted which proposed AV but it found progress difficult: Labour MPs refused to swallow this measure and it eventually fell as a result of MacDonald's defection to form a National Government in 1931 (Joyce, 1999, 70–2; Riddell, 1999, 137–9).

Labour entered the electoral wilderness after MacDonald's 'betrayal', while several leading Liberals participated in his new administration which was returned with massive majorities in both 1931 and 1935. As a result, Liberal–Labour cooperation became largely irrelevant until the outbreak of the Second World War. Partly due to their culpability in nearly losing Britain the war by not making adequate preparations for the conflict, the Conservatives haemorrhaged support after 1940. As a result of their association with many of the interventionist measures introduced by government to rescue the situation, Labour's position improved. The party's promise of full employment and a welfare state free at the point of delivery helped it win the 1945 election by a landslide. As Blair noted in 1995, such notions were largely the product of the 'progressive' Liberals: Keynes and Beveridge.

At this moment of triumph Labour sought to tempt remaining 'progressive' Liberals into the party by stressing how much liberalism had contributed to its programme. As Harold Laski, a leading party intellectual and prominent left winger, happily conceded, liberalism constituted part of Labour's 'great tradition' and was in some sense its 'parent' (Fielding, 2000b, 377). While Labour nationalized much of the economy and introduced planning to an unprecedented degree, it claimed that the advance of the state posed no threat to individual freedom. Such measures, party leaders stated, were actually necessary to promote individuality and liberty (Fielding, Thompson and Tiratsoo, 1995, 91–2). This approach paid dividends. The future Labour leader, Harold Wilson, was a Liberal until late in the war but became a Labour MP in 1945. Beveridge, briefly a wartime Liberal MP, stated that, had he been younger, he would have joined Labour, albeit with the aim of 'liberalising it from within' (Joyce, 1999, 109). The extent to which the party had successfully appealed to those from Liberal backgrounds was demonstrated by a 1962 survey of Labour MPs. When asked which figure had most influenced them in their early political life, they placed their party's founder, Keir Hardie, at the top, and the Liberal Prime Minister, David Lloyd George, a very close second (Alexander and Hobbs, 1967, 114–15).

The Road to the SDP

By the early 1960s, the terms of trade between the parties appeared to have altered once more, this time in favour of the Liberals. While the party won only six seats in the 1959 election, Labour had failed to win office for the third time in a row. Some believed clause four 'socialism' had become irrelevant and that social change was undermining the salience of class: 'affluence' seemed to be creating a 'new middle class' out of the working class. One of those persuaded Labour was in trouble was the Liberal leader, Jo Grimond, who had dispensed with many of his predecessors' *laissez-faire* prejudices. Very much as Paddy Ashdown would in the 1990s, Grimond envisaged creating a radical, non-socialist party based around the Liberals and incorporating elements from both major parties. In particular, Grimond sought to appeal to Labour's revisionists, or 'liberally-minded socialists' as he called them (Joyce, 1999, 129–31).

Grimond's social analysis was strikingly similar to that of the Labour leader, Hugh Gaitskell, and his supporters. Like Grimond they also believed in the common interests of all classes and accepted the continued existence of a reformed market. This outlook already influenced Labour's official policies, although it was opposed by many activists and some union leaders. Thus, while a few revisionists called for a tactical alliance with the Liberals, Gaitskell and his successor, Harold Wilson, decided it would be better to make Labour more attractive to the 'new middle class' and so prevent Grimond reviving his party's fortunes (Fielding, 1993, 33–4). Despite this, the Liberals doubled their vote in the 1964 election although that still meant they had only nine MPs. Nonetheless, as Wilson could only form a government with a bare majority Grimond offered Labour the chance of a pact. Although rebuffed, informal cooperation ensued and caused Wilson's Chief Whip to hold out the prospect of electoral reform (Joyce, 1999, 139–40). Labour attitudes changed, however, when the 1966 election gave it a majority of 97: now Wilson could govern alone.

Despite failing to promote realignment, Grimond's perspective is thought to have held a longer-term significance: Samuel Beer, for one, considers he anticipated many of the themes associated with 'New' Labour (Beer, 2001, 25–8). Thus, if Grimond reasserted the classic liberal belief that the state posed a danger to individual freedom and the market encouraged liberty, he also reiterated the need for social reform. Nevertheless, Grimond thought such reform should not rely on the agency of government, at least as it was expressed by the welfare state at mid-century. Indeed, he criticized Labour's revisionists for relying too much on the state to achieve their ends. This was because Grimond thought the dispensation of benefits denied those who came to depend on them ultimate responsibility for their own lives. The passivity fostered by welfare meant recipients became unable to eventually free themselves. In order to become truly free, Grimond believed, people needed responsibility for their own lives but that could only come about once power, wealth and ownership had been more evenly spread. Grimond's critique of welfare dependence was not, then, the same as Thatcherism's but a left-leaning variant, stressing, as it did, cooperation and community as alternative means of help. Grimond believed in collectivism, but one that complemented rather than threatened individualism (Joyce, 1999, 153–5, 188–9).

Even though Labour formed a government in October 1974 this soon fell into a minority position in the Commons. In order to avoid an election neither wanted, James Callaghan and the Liberal leader, David Steel, formed a pact during 1977–8 to ensure the government's survival. In return for their support, Liberal MPs attended consultative meetings with ministers but exerted no formal influence. Nonetheless, the Liberals still persuaded Callaghan to introduce a Bill proposing the introduction of PR to European Parliamentary elections. As an insufficient number of Labour MPs supported it, this failed to see the light of day until 1999.

The formation of the Social Democratic Party (SDP) in 1981 indicated that a number of revisionists considered Labour's lurch to the left meant they could no longer achieve their ends within the party. Even before this, many began to echo earlier Liberal criticism that Labour was too closely tied to the unions and obsessed with nationalization to be electorally viable (Marquand, 1979). Increasingly, their concerns, such as the devolution of economic and political power, seemed compatible with long-standing Liberal themes and at odds with Labour's own perceived trajectory. Moreover, as Labour moved left and the Conservatives under Margaret Thatcher went right, the 'centre ground' appeared vacant. If the Liberals stood on that territory, by themselves, they seemed unlikely to take full advantage. Roy Jenkins (the former Labour Cabinet minister who would be the SDP's first leader) and Steel believed that a new centre-left party, acting in alliance with the Liberals, would be better able to exploit the situation (Crewe and King, 1995; Joyce, 1999, 208–11).

The ultimate objective of the SDP–Liberal Alliance was to introduce PR in the expectation that this would prevent Labour or the Conservatives ever again forming a government on their own: cooperation would be enforced by the electoral system (Bogdanor, 1983, 180–1). In the first instance, however, the Alliance had to overtake Labour as the main anti-Conservative force and in 1983 they nearly did by polling 25.4 per cent of votes to Labour's 27.6. Had these votes been cast under a directly proportional system, the three parties could theoretically have formed a coalition that would have denied Thatcher office. The 1983 result was, however, the Alliance's high-water mark, partly because Neil Kinnock moderated Labour policy while the SDP and Liberals became preoccupied by the matter of whether they should merge. Once again, in 1987 the Alliance and Labour outpolled the Conservatives but fell foul of the electoral system. Following the election, Liberals and Social Democrats decided to combine, but the fractious nature of this process lost them much support.

What eventually became known as the Liberal Democratic Party was an amalgam of social democratic and liberal concerns and, in many respects, was the organizational expression of 'progressive' thought. It remained formally committed, as Ashdown confirmed on becoming leader in 1988, to replacing Labour as the main anti-Conservative party as the precursor to introducing electoral reform. Labour, however, also had a strong claim to be considered a 'progressive' force. The party had retained most of its social democratic personnel and, by the late 1980s, had moved back to many of the positions sketched out by those who left in 1981. As the 1992 election campaign also revealed, anticipating a 'hung' parliament in which LibDem MPs would hold the balance of power, Kinnock countenanced supporting electoral reform as the price of gaining office (Westlake, 2001, 521–3).

Despite this, 1992 saw the return of the Conservatives. Whatever comfort Labour took from the fact that the campaign entrenched its position as the leading 'progressive' party was undercut by its continued inability to take power on its own. Once again, the centre-left parties had out-polled the Conservatives but were forced to sit on the Opposition benches. After this fourth defeat in a row, some in Labour's ranks believed the time was ripe for some serious thinking about the party's relationship with the LibDems; John Smith, Kinnock's successor, was not among that number.

The Impact of 'New' Labour

During Smith's leadership Blair met privately with Ashdown to discuss fostering cooperation; at these meetings he talked of the 'desperate need to reformulate the politics of the left' (Ashdown, 2000, 242–4). Ashdown was keen to build on these thoughts as he had come to recognize that the LibDems could not displace Labour (Leaman, 1998). Thus, after Smith's death, Ashdown sought a relationship with Blair that would allow the LibDems to express support for 'New' Labour while still giving disillusioned Conservatives wary of Labour a reason to support his party. He hoped this would foster a realignment of British politics along lines outlined by Grimond some 30 years before. To enable Ashdown to facilitate his short- and long-term objectives, he also wanted Blair to commit Labour to electoral reform.

If Ashdown initiated talk of realignment, the novel aspect of the situation after 1994 was that Labour – or at least Blair – appeared willing to take him seriously. Blair's election as Labour leader undoubtedly pushed relations between the parties into a new but not exactly unprecedented phase. It had long been Labour orthodoxy to accept that the party owed much to historical liberalism in part to encourage Liberal supporters to join with Labour. Yet, as Labour presented itself as having evolved out of liberalism, the party implicitly claimed superiority over contemporary Liberals. Blair's attitude was different, although it could be argued this said less about him and more about how far the LibDems had travelled from pure liberalism. In his 1995 speech, Blair followed convention by describing Labour as 'the political heir of the radical Liberal tradition'. However, within the same sentence, he portrayed democratic socialism and progressive liberalism as 'cousins'. This description implied neither was further up the evolutionary chain than the other. If he believed the parties' creeds were equal, that was because Blair not unreasonably considered they had become very similar. As he declared when Prime Minister, 'a large part' of the LibDems were, like himself, 'modern social democrats' and shared the 'same value systems' (Blair, 1996, 12; *The Guardian*, 3 October 1998 and 3 April 2000).

Even so, whereas Ashdown's motives for increasing cooperation were obvious, the reasons for Blair's interest were less clear-cut. Early on in his many confidential discussions with the LibDem leader, Blair bluntly stated that he looked to 'create a climate for co-operation, which sent messages to the British electorate without us actually putting anything specific on paper' (Ashdown, 2000, 311, 416). Such an anti-Conservative arrangement would have more than suited 'New' Labour, for an implicit

LibDem endorsement promised to: reassure sceptical voters that Labour had truly changed; encourage tactical anti-Conservative voting; and, in the case of a minority Labour government, pave the way for coalition. Finally, such an informal arrangement would give the impression Blair was pursuing what he liked to refer as a 'new politics' and so invest Labour's campaign with a principled tone. On their own, such considerations would have made Blair's position purely pragmatic. However, he was keen to reassure the LibDem leader that he saw cooperation as more than a manoeuvre to win one election. Thus Blair held out the prospect of 'rearranging the centre-left of British politics' so that Liberal and Labour 'could come back together again' (Ashdown, 2000, 276, 452, 456).

A small handful of Labour members were genuinely enthusiastic for cooperation as they hoped this would create a 'new political culture' based on 'constructive dialogue' that would not only result in a Labour government but also a 'lasting progressive consensus' (Labour Initiative on Co-operation, or LINC, leaflet; no date). Those of this persuasion cohered around the LINC, many of whose leading lights had argued during the 1980s that Labour's only hope of regaining power lay in cooperating with the centre parties. By the mid-1990s, LINC could point to numerous jointly run Labour–LibDem local authorities and a substantial policy overlap between the national parties (MacDonald and Arnold-Foster, 1995; Ruhemann, 1995). Yet, despite this, one of LINC's concerns was that cooperation was too much of a top-down enterprise: it enthused a few party intellectuals and tacticians but antagonized most activists, whereas LINC hoped to encourage cooperation at the grassroots. It is doubtful the organization enjoyed much success, especially in those parts of the industrial north where Labour's main municipal enemy was Ashdown's party. Yet even LINC's enthusiasm for cooperation did not preclude its recognition that the two parties also had to continue to compete: merger was never mentioned.

How far Blair's private comments were made to obscure the fact that he really did only seek short-term advantage is moot. It is, however, plausible that Blair thought it possible to finally resolve the troubled Liberal–Labour relationship in a manner beneficial to both sides. Blair was, in any case, sympathetic to those who had felt the need to leave Labour in 1981: he confided to Ashdown that as he watched Roy Jenkins on television at that time, he wondered: 'Why aren't I in that party?' (*The New Statesman*, 9 July 2001). Some of his key advisers – such as Peter Mandelson – also considered joining the SDP; a few – such as Roger Liddle – had done. Thus Blair did not necessarily see realignment as a threat to his particular point of view. Yet, while considering realignment a theoretically desirable, if distant, possibility, Blair's primary objective remained that of winning a Commons majority for Labour. Prior to 1997, however, both objectives could be served by promoting cooperation.

There were numerous obstacles to a closer relationship, the main one being the question of electoral reform. Blair conceded that a 'huge advantage' of PR was that it would encourage a 'reshaping of politics along more rational lines'; he seemed happy that one consequence might be that the Labour left would establish their own party (Ashdown, 2000, 353, 357, 380). If willing to hold a referendum on the subject to please Ashdown, Blair was nonetheless sceptical about the wider merits of reform. When he appeared to change his mind in private, Ashdown wanted Blair to announce his conversion in public; this he refused to do, claiming it would cause major difficulties in his party (Ashdown, 2000, 276, 336). Reform was moreover not just a matter of replacing first-past-the-post with an agreed alternative, for no such alternative existed. LibDems favoured the single transferable vote as this meant that votes cast were directly reflected in seats gained. As in the 1920s, however, even Labour's advocates of change generally favoured AV under which voters list candidates within a constituency in order of preference; their preferences are then allocated until one candidate has over 50 per cent of support. If not proportional, AV promised to be fairer to the LibDems than first-past-the-post, while still enabling Labour to form a government without automatic recourse to coalition.

Despite refusing to inform the public of his apparent change of heart, Blair wanted to give the parties' new relationship a concrete expression, and consequently in October 1996 they formed a joint committee on the reform of the electoral system. This reported in February 1997 and agreed that a future government would establish an independent commission to investigate the subject and work towards holding a referendum in which 'an appropriate proportional alternative' to the existing system would be put to the people. Labour's 1997 manifesto echoed this commitment. Significantly, no mention was made of when any referendum would be held.

In Government

Before the 1997 campaign Blair privately stated that his 'preferred option' was to include LibDems in any future Labour administration even if his party enjoyed a Commons majority (Ashdown, 2000, 429). The resulting landslide nonetheless temporarily weakened the new

Prime Minister's resolve. What one analyst described as a 'revolutionary moment, probably the best opportunity of all to break the mould of three-party politics' saw Blair baulk at taking the decisive step (*The Independent*, 10 August 2000). Even so, on the day of the election, Blair reassured Ashdown that he remained 'absolutely determined to mend the schism' between the parties. 'It is', he stated, 'just a question of finding a workable framework'. While that 'framework' was for the moment not to involve coalition, Blair offered Ashdown membership of an unprecedented Joint Cabinet Committee (JCC) with a remit to discuss constitutional change. Enjoying the status of a Cabinet sub-committee, this would meet once every two months, be chaired by the Prime Minister and have as members an equal number of Labour and LibDem representatives. Blair described the JCC as 'a means of transition' that might still include a coalition (something which he considered was possibly but months away). 'Who knows what the ultimate destination might be?' he asked, unsure of the answer himself. 'It could be merger some way down the track', he speculated, but then added, '[o]r maybe not' (Ashdown, 2000, 555, 560; *The Guardian*, 3 April 2000).

Labour's massive majority only added to the confusing variety of possible tactics that underpinned any move towards realignment, such that even those favouring a closer relationship could not agree how to proceed. For example, prior to joining the Number 10 Policy Unit, Andrew Adonis considered Blair's interests were best served by having the LibDems remain outside government until Labour had won a second term. By staying independent, he believed, the LibDems would retain their electoral strength: if they moved too close to Labour too soon, some of their supporters might move back to the Conservatives (*The Observer*, 11 January 1998). LibDems close to Ashdown seemed to agree and considered the parties should remain independent, even under a reformed electoral system, as to unite would probably only reduce their respective appeals (Leaman, 1998, 168–9).

Electoral reform, however, remained central to any deepening of cooperation, let alone to realignment. Confounding LibDem cynics, in December 1997 the government established an independent commission chaired by the LibDem peer, Roy Jenkins, whose object was to recommend an alternative to first-past-the-post. Jenkins reported in October 1998 and proposed a system that was the most Labour could accept and the least LibDems would tolerate: 'AV plus'. Under this system, the majority of MPs would be elected under AV and be linked to a particular constituency, as with the existing regime. However, electors would have two votes, the second being cast for a minority of 'top-up' representatives, elected on a bigger, county basis in a directly proportional way. So as to address some of the concerns of Labour sceptics, this hybrid would allow a party with less than half the votes to win a Commons majority while, to please LibDems, the result would be more proportional than under first-past-the-post. If Blair appeared to favour an exclusively AV system he also claimed to find merit in such a hybrid, although with how much enthusiasm was not clear (Ashdown, 2000, 381, 421, 482).

A Waning of Enthusiasm

Blair had long before promised Ashdown that on publication of the Jenkins report he would immediately announce his support for the commission's findings and set in train the process for holding a referendum to change the electoral system before the next election (Ashdown, 2000, 507–8; Ashdown, 2001, 266–74). Although the Prime Minister 'warmly' welcomed the report he did not amend his publicly sceptical view and left the question of a referendum open. While formally neutral on the issue, Blair nonetheless implied that a referendum could still be held before the election and even told MPs in favour of reform he was 'on their side' (*The Guardian*, 2, 10 and 21 November 1998). The reality, however, was that without the Labour leader's unqualified and public support reform could not happen.

Labour's official position, as submitted by the National Executive Committee to the Jenkins commission, had reflected the Prime Minister's public view: while doubtful, it did not oppose the principle of reform and AV remained an option (*The Guardian*, 10 August 1998). There were, however, powerful elements in the party opposing change of any sort. The Amalgamated Engineering and Electricians' Union – normally loyal to Blair – financed an organization intent on defending the status quo (*The Observer*, 23 August 1998). Some members also undoubtedly shared Roy Hattersley's belief that any proportional system would forever 'extinguish all hope of a democratic socialist government ever being elected' (*The Guardian*, 10 January 2000). While a majority of Labour MPs were said to favour changing the system in favour of AV, those publicly supporting the campaigns to promote or oppose reform were evenly split (*The Observer*, 3 May 1998; *The Guardian*, 31 October 1998). The signals from ordinary members were similarly inconclusive: research indicated that only a small majority favoured reform (*The Guardian*, 5, 6 and 11 January 2000). Blair also found that those associated with 'New' Labour were unenthusiastic: Gordon Brown was concerned it would promote unstable government, while Jack Straw and John Prescott were hostile in principle. Blair claimed that an 'overwhelming majority' of his Cabinet colleagues opposed change. Ironically, his strongest support came from Robin Cook, who hoped reform would strengthen the Labour left. The Prime Minister therefore calculated that he had insufficient support to proceed to a referendum (*The Observer*, 4 October 1998; Ashdown, 2000, 488; Ashdown, 2001, 322). In truth, Blair could live without reform: if he privately considered it ultimately desirable it was not of immediate importance. Blair would push for change only when it was absolutely necessary to sustain his party in power.

Ashdown was deeply disappointed. To maintain the sense that cooperation retained momentum, Blair proposed extending the remit of the JCC to include consideration of health, education, welfare and Europe. In so doing he hoped to further incorporate the LibDems into the government's decision-making and encourage them to continue their 'constructive' opposition (Ashdown, 2001, 318–20, 332–3). This move only provoked resentment amongst both sides: neither party was comfortable about being forced together by their leaders (*The Guardian*, 12 and 15 November 1998). Nonetheless, in January 1999 the JCC's responsibility was increased further to embrace foreign affairs and defence (*The Guardian*, 22 January 1999).

Cooperation Assessed

When the JCC was first established, Tony Benn and others on the Labour left thought it marked 'the beginning of the end of the Labour Party' (Rentoul, 2001, 492). Many LibDems saw it differently, fearing it would be the means by which the government could associate their party with its policies without ceding them real influence. It was certainly unclear how much authority the JCC exerted over the direction of policy, and even Ashdown considered that by 1998 its meetings had become 'more ceremonial than functional' (Ashdown, 2001, 302–3). On the central issue of constitutional change the government had introduced PR to elections for the European Parliament, as well as a mixed system in contests for the Scottish, Welsh and London devolved bodies. It is likely that this was largely due to LibDem pressure. However, the party's criticism of the limited nature of Labour's Lords reforms came to nothing, as did its support for the introduction of PR to council elections. At the very least, the JCC was window dressing for Blair's 'new politics'; at most, it was an unproven quantity.

Recognizing that his wider ambitions for realignment were now frustrated, in January 1999 Ashdown announced his resignation as LibDem leader. While the rhetoric of his successor Charles Kennedy was less friendly to 'New' Labour, he barely altered Ashdown's policy of encouraging the Prime Minister to hold a referendum on electoral reform. Some optimists argued Blair was playing a waiting game, allowing the changes he had introduced to charm disbelieving colleagues. Thus the JCC would persuade the Cabinet that cooperation had its benefits: but it rarely met after Ashdown's departure. Moreover, the Liberal–Labour coalitions that followed elections in Scotland and Wales would show that both parties could work together; however, there was only resentment when the LibDems forced Labour to retreat over student tuition fees in Scotland. Finally, the 1999 European elections fought under PR largely at the LibDems' behest were very bad for Labour, although that was more the fault of the party's desultory campaign. It was doubtful that sceptical Labour members would be persuaded of the merits of reform after such experiences. Indeed, rather than advancing cooperation, Blair had to fight just to keep open the option of holding a referendum on electoral reform. At one point, Labour's July 2000 National Policy Forum looked as if it would throw out any commitment to change. However, as a result of assiduous lobbying, while the gathering rejected 'AV plus' it merely urged the government to 'proceed slowly' on the issue (*The Independent*, 10 July 2000).

Hoping to force something out of Blair, prior to the 2001 campaign Kennedy threatened to end his participation in the JCC unless Labour committed itself to a referendum during the next Parliament. This proved impossible and Labour's manifesto merely proposed a 'review' to be held in light of the 'experience' of the Scottish, Welsh, London and European contests to see if change should be considered for Westminster (Labour Party, 2001, 35). On that basis, some suggested that a referendum was still possible half-way through the next Parliament: yet as the appraisal would not be conducted before 2003–4, and did not in itself guarantee a thing, this view was based more on hope than experience.

After the 2001 election, Kennedy and Blair agreed to work together, at least on Europe and constitutional reform, where their parties' positions were most obviously different from those of the Conservatives. The precise form such cooperation would take was left vague but, in September 2001, they announced the suspension of the JCC. This had followed Blair's refusal to accept Kennedy's attempt to put on the committee's agenda consideration of a number of constitutional changes that inevitably included reforming the electoral system for Westminster elections

(*The Financial Times*, 27 June 2001; *The Times*, 12 September 2001). This did not mean, the two leaders stated, that the JCC had been abandoned for all time: it remained 'available to resume its work if further constitutional items become ready for discussion' (BBC website, 20 September 2001). In reality cooperation, let alone anything more ambitious, had been placed in very cold storage.

Conclusion

Political scientists have generated an impressive literature on the making of coalitions, much of its based on the reasonable assumption that parties seek to maximize their own position (Schofield, 1993; Laver, 1997, 135–52). Such work is based on the experience of multi-party systems in which PR plays some part and coalition-building is an unremarkable feature. In Britain's majoritarian system peacetime coalitions are exceptionally rare: perhaps this explains why academics have little to say about the kind of arrangement entered into by 'New' Labour and the LibDems.

Blair's approach was, however, not exactly unprecedented. At the same time as he was talking to Ashdown, French Socialists sought to recover from their massive 1993 election defeat by constructing what was referred to as the 'plural left'. As with 'New' Labour, they ceded limited short-term advantage to certain rivals within the left – in particular the Communists and Greens – so they could win the greater prize, namely national office (Hanley, forthcoming). Even so, French Socialists operated in a system where coalitions were required, whereas this was not the case in Britain. Indeed, from the perspective of rational choice theory, Blair's approach appears wholly illogical. After all, by 1997 Labour appeared well able to win a majority on its own: in that context the LibDems were technically a 'surplus' party as their seats added nothing to Labour's ability to govern. This is, however, to look at the matter too narrowly. There were sound reasons for Blair to pursue cooperation before 1997; moreover, given the shallow nature of Labour's support, it remained plausible to believe the arrangement might be necessary to secure a second term. It was therefore prudent to maintain LibDem support after 1997 and that meant Blair had to keep electoral reform on the agenda and give Ashdown grounds to believe he would eventually deliver. It was not, however, in Blair's interest to enact the measure any time soon. Not only would that have divided his own party but, as he feared, it would also have freed the LibDems from their dependent position (Ashdown, 2001, 27–32).

Such practical considerations were a long way from Blair's rhetoric about the historical necessity of reuniting the centre-left and even further from talk of the Prime Minister fostering a new type of 'pluralist' politics. The extent to which Blair meant what he said about these matters is uncertain: his most authoritative biographer is certainly sceptical (Rentoul, 2001, 493–5, 497–9). In any case, while the likes of Philip Gould shared their leader's apparent desire to rebuild the 'progressive alliance', as he noted there was more ways than one to do this: either the two parties could merge, or Labour by itself could embrace the 'the broad progressive church' (Gould, 1998, 397–8). According Ashdown at least, by 2001 Blair had adopted the latter course (*The New Statesman*, 9 July 2001). As Blair had bluntly told the dying philosopher, Isaiah Berlin, before 1997, he wanted to find a way of 'appropriating the great aspects of the liberal tradition' so Labour could occupy the centre ground (*The Times Higher Education Supplement*, 6 November 1998). This does not sound like a politician keen to embrace the politics of pluralism, except perhaps 'pluralism in one party'.

Despite such suspicions, it is perhaps going too far to describe, as Vernon Bogdanor has done, the present situation as 'the politics of the Gladstone–MacDonald pact adapted to changed conditions' (Bogdanor, 2001, 140). Yet it would also be wrong to discount the essential pragmatism of 'New' Labour's leading lights towards their party's abiding, problematic relationship with the organizational expression of Liberalism. It is certainly salutary to compare how much Blair promised the LibDems when he thought he needed their support with how little he gave them once he realized he did not. If nothing else, therefore this subject should provide a warning to those who, in seeking to interpret 'New' Labour's character, rely too much on what Blair says and neglect what he actually does.

3

From Clause Four to Third Way: Labour's Ideological Journey

Despite the scepticism of the previous chapter's concluding remarks, those wishing to understand 'New' Labour should still carefully attend to the words of its leading exponents. Indeed, according to those who believe Tony Blair's leadership marks a decisive break with Labour's past, its defining moment occurred in 1995, when members voted to revise clause four of the party's constitution. Since 1918 this had committed Labour to advancing the 'common ownership' of the 'means of production, distribution and exchange'. In so far as these words demonstrated a principled desire to reduce the scope of the free market, many viewed them as denoting the party's commitment to socialism. By modifying the clause, 'New' Labour was seen, by enthusiast and detractor alike, as announcing the party's full acceptance of capitalism. This supposed change of direction was entrenched by Blair's elaboration of what he termed the Third Way. There is, however, another view that needs to be considered: namely that, despite changes in emphasis, the principled basis of Labour ideology has remained remarkably constant. From that perspective, 1995 was not a break with the past but the conclusion of some unfinished business.

To help us understand this matter properly the present chapter will review the party's ideological relationship with capitalism over the last century. This will be facilitated, first, by highlighting how European social democrats initially addressed the phenomenon and, second, by investigating the reasons for the drafting of clause four. Analysis of Labour's debate about how to build on the 1945–51 Attlee government's achievements will then follow and this will focus on the disagreement over how much common ownership and market freedom were necessary to advance equality. This historical context having been established, the chapter will assess the importance of the 1994–5 campaign to repeal clause four. It concludes by using Blair's articulation of the Third Way as a means of questioning how far the party can still be viewed as social democratic.

The Nature of Ideology

To have any hope of appreciating the dynamics of Labour's ideological journey, we should take account of Donald Sassoon's statement that when 'capitalism changes so must socialism', although it might be more accurate if it read: when 'capitalism is generally thought to have changed so must socialism'. This qualification is required to make it clear that while at certain times some ideas appear more plausible than others, this does not necessarily mean they are correct. The crucial point, however, is that from the start European social democrats have endured a largely dependent relationship with capitalism, in which the development of the latter has required the former to reconsider their programmatic basis (Sassoon, 1997, 745, 754–77). Thus, changing clause four forms part of a process of permanent reflection that can be traced back to social democrats such as Anthony Crosland in the 1950s and Eduard Bernstein in the 1890s. Of course, the impact of change means 'New' Labour's leading thinkers view capitalism in a different light from the British Cabinet minister and the German philosopher. Yet, if they embraced distinct manifestations of state intervention, accepted contrasting forms of market freedom and conceptualized the pursuit of equality in different ways, the basic framework in which these subjects were located would have been recognizable to all.

To consolidate this claim we need to consider the nature of ideology, if only because some of Blair's interventions have made this matter especially opaque. The Labour leader has claimed that he is not motivated by 'ideology' but is a pragmatic politician for whom 'what matters is what works' (Blair, 1998b, 4). This statement should be read as his rejection of 'ideology' as popularly defined: that is, something thought to be a closed intellectual system with aspirations to explain all aspects of human behaviour which, in so doing, squeezes reality to fit its precepts. Such a view is common among politicians who wish to appear in touch with modern developments. That Blair accepts this definition does not, however, mean he has no intellectual moorings since, on other occasions, the Prime Minister has stated that his government's actions have been articulated by 'a very clear political philosophy' and he adheres to a set of 'timeless' social democratic 'values' although, as Blair has put it, 'we should be infinitely adaptable and imaginative in the means of applying' them (Blair, 1993, 11; Blair, 1998a; Blair, 1998b, 1–4; *The Observer*, 9 April 2000). On this latter reading, and despite earlier claims, 'New' Labour does possess an 'ideology' especially if we accept another way of defining that term (Plant, 2001, 555–7).

Taking their lead from Blair's apparent rejection of ideology, many critics consider 'New' Labour embodies a pragmatism that permits it to say and do virtually anything, so long as it is in the party's electoral interest. Even the relatively friendly Paddy Ashdown has described the Labour leader as the 'least ideological politician I know' (*The Guardian*, 15 June 1999). Others think 'New' Labour does adhere to ideology, but one deriving from another political tradition: Thatcherism. Such analysis appears to assume that ideologies cannot change, but consist of everlasting concepts whose configuration and meaning cannot vary over time. Thus, it seems, even to question or reinterpret one thought within an existing system of ideas is to betray it. This popular perspective has been challenged by Michael Freeden, who sees ideologies as 'systems of political thinking, loose or rigid, deliberate or unintended [but] ... distinctive configurations of political concepts' which 'create specific conceptual patterns from a pool of indeterminate and unlimited combinations' that can change over time (Freeden, 1996, 4).

Freeden's is a useful means of understanding 'New' Labour's relationship with the party's past thought given the extent to which analysis is frequently distorted by an exaggerated emphasis on the 'New'/'Old' dichotomy. As will be argued further, Labour in the past was never the party of state ownership many would have us believe, while Labour now is hardly the party of market freedom some appear to think. It is, however, true that the relationship between the state and market has been reconfigured while the means of achieving greater equality has been recast. Nonetheless, to see this reconstitution as marking a break with Labour's established ideological tradition belies a misunderstanding not only of the party's political thought but also – as Freeden makes plain – the true nature of ideology.

It should, finally, be borne in mind that ideological change is rarely undertaken within the disinterested calm of the philosopher's study. Ideologies do not just exist on paper but in real contexts in which interests collide and are articulated by politicians who have to satisfy a variety of constituencies. Consequently, meanings have to be nuanced to allow for a number of possible interpretations; robust concepts have to be finessed to facilitate their acceptance. Thus, at different times and to different audiences, change can be presented as marking a fundamental continuity, whereas actual continuity may be depicted as radical change. This means that while words are important, in trying to fully understand any party's ideology, intention – and thus context – need to be attended to.

Social Democracy and Capitalism

Unlike most of its European peers the Labour Representation Committee (LRC) was not originally pledged to transform capitalism into socialism. If many of Labour's earliest partisans described themselves as socialists, unlike most of their continental counterparts they were motivated less by Marxism and more by ethical concerns commensurate with radical liberalism. As the LRC also granted trade unions a greater influence over policy-making it was further distinguished by the unions' pressure to focus on more limited issues. For these reasons many have stressed Labour's ideological exceptionalism (Foote, 1997). Nonetheless, national peculiarities notwithstanding, Labour was simply a more temperate exponent of the social democratic creed. If the party interpreted its purpose without the same theoretical rigour, and conceptualized it within a distinct idiom, members addressed the same problems and came to a similar answers as their European cousins (Tanner, 1991).

If national differences imbued social democracy with diverse emphases, even members of the same party bitterly argued over strategy. However, all social democrats sought to transform free market capitalism into a more regulated system they described as socialism. Unfettered capitalism was considered unfair and inefficient as it allowed the minority owning most of the means of production to profit from the labour of the majority. Socialism would end this situation by bringing the economy under a form of collective control that would allow government to manage it in everybody's interests. It was taken to be a matter of fact that common ownership was a superior form of running the economy. If social democrats differed as to how best such ownership should be arranged – and how much was required at any one point in time – they all agreed that an economy based solely on private ownership could never satisfy the needs of all the people.

As the development of capitalism was crucial to the prospects of socialism many on the left studied the system they hoped to replace: Karl Marx's *Capital* (1867) was but the most famous work of interpretation. As a result of such investigations, by the end of the nineteenth-century all social democrats believed capitalism would inevitably be succeeded by socialism, and the only questions that divided them were when and how? A particular reading of Marx initially provided the answer. This envisaged that capitalism would enter a final crisis in which the overwhelming majority would, as Marx and Friedrich Engels' *Communist Manifesto* (1847) put it, have 'nothing to lose but their chains'. Moreover, having concentrated ownership into fewer and fewer hands, social democratic governments would merely assume control of cartels and monopolies already produced by capitalism. This view bred what Sassoon describes as a 'passive' political strategy because many social democrats believed they just had to wait for capitalism to develop into socialism (Sassoon, 1996, 26).

Eduard Bernstein revised significant aspects of this orthodoxy in *Evolutionary Socialism* (1899) by arguing that the evidence suggested capitalism was not going to end any time soon. In particular, the number of capitalists was increasing while the conditions of the working class were improving. Moreover, workers formed only a minority in society and were divided amongst themselves: the proletariat was unlikely ever to become a unified majoritarian force. Thus, Bernstein suggested, the notion of an inevitable final crisis was flawed: social democrats had to take account of reality. As a result, he declared that the 'ultimate aim of socialism is nothing, but the movement is everything': social democrats should cease to be concerned with the final transformation of capitalism and instead focus their energies on achieving more 'proximate aims' (Bernstein, 1961, 200–24).

Bernstein underlined the view that social democrats had to operate within capitalism as it actually existed and should work for what the system currently allowed. Those opposing Bernstein argued that his evidence was unsound: capitalism, they argued, was still taking the path outlined by Marx. As with the 1990s debate over globalization, differences over theory were justified by contrasting views of capitalist development. Bernstein and his critics could each point to certain 'facts' that supported their general positions. Nonetheless, it was Bernstein's revisionism that shaped twentieth century social democratic thought.

Bernstein's significance is emphasized here for another reason: his British connection. As a London resident during the 1890s he met leading socialists of the day, and Bernstein's views were at least reinforced by the opinions of Sidney Webb who helped draft clause four. The German's perspective also influenced the course of Labour thinking through his friendship with Ramsay MacDonald; indeed, the former has been described as the latter's 'philosophical mentor' (Gay, 1952, 67–8; Marquand, 1997, 164). Thus Bernstein's revisionism, through his influence on MacDonald and thence MacDonald's role in shaping Labour thinking, helped set the party's ideological compass. Yet one reason for MacDonald's intellectual prominence was his talent for harmonizing existing party thinking (MacIntyre, 1980), and therefore the emphasis on 'proximate aims' that MacDonald took from Bernstein was readily embraced by union leaders not famous for their interest in the details of ideological debate.

The Significance of Clause Four

The First World War strengthened the hand of those wanting to extend state control as the conflict forced government to intervene in areas considered sacrosanct by *laissez-faire* theory. As a result, workers' conditions improved while trade union authority at the workplace increased. If they remained undogmatic on the subject of state control, many unionists hoped to maintain this position after the war's end. Such a shift in opinion weakened opposition to drafting a statement of Labour's ultimate aims, something that appeared increasingly vital as party leaders sought to make a clean break with the Liberals. Clause four was produced with that objective in mind and worded so as to appeal to a disparate constituency that included sceptical trade unionists, workers who might be drawn to the new Communist Party and middle-class 'progressives' (Harrison, 1971; Barker, 1972; Winter, 1972; McKibbin, 1974; McHugh, 2001).

As a consequence, Labour committed itself to securing, in the words of the clause,

> for the workers by hand or brain the full fruits of their industry and the most equitable distribution thereof that may be possible upon the basis of the common ownership of the means of production, distribution and exchange, and the best obtainable system of popular administration and control of each industry or service.

According to many on the party's left this meant Labour was subsequently bound to extend state control. Reference to workers securing the 'most equitable distribution' of the 'full fruits of their industry' also appeared to require a considerable redistribution of income. Yet, as Webb (the man most responsible for drafting the clause) stated, it was in truth 'no more specific than a definite repudiation of the individualism that characterized all political parties ... that still dominate the House of Commons' (McHugh, 2001, 61–2).

The limited impact of the clause was demonstrated during MacDonald's leadership. Like many others, MacDonald considered common ownership one of the best means of establishing a socialist society, although it was just a means. Yet his belief in the evolution of socialism meant he was unwilling to make any significant intervention in the economy for fear of distorting capitalism's 'natural' development. This meant his governments effectively accepted the *laissez-faire* orthodoxy of the day and at no time looked for inspiration to the newly minted clause. In the case of his 1929–31 administration this meant considering cutting benefits to the unemployed so as to balance government expenditure during a period of severe recession. The Labour Prime Minister and a few like-minded colleagues proposed this measure, believing capitalism could only be stabilized on the basis of terms dictated by capitalists. Once spending had been curtailed, they assumed the slump would make way for recovery and so capitalism would renew its progress towards socialism.

Other European social democrats confronted similar dilemmas as the world entered recession: in response they rethought their attitude to capitalist development (Thompson, 1996, 87–104). Many began to think capitalism had reached a new stage: having evolved out of its free market phase it was now subject to numerous controls, albeit ones directed by private hands. The slump was evidence that this system could not generate sufficient demand for the goods it produced: only government could do this. Thus, in order to save capitalism and so encourage its final development towards socialism, social democrats believed government should assume a greater level of direction. While Labour thinkers formed part of this process, debate raged over the extent to which common ownership was necessary in comparison with indirect forms of manipulation favoured by John Maynard Keynes. For, if considered flawed, the future Cabinet minister Douglas Jay could still assert that in 'an imperfect world', the market remained 'the only, or perhaps least undesirable system which is in fact available' (Thompson, 1996, 118).

Confidence in government intervention found vindication during the Second World War when Winston Churchill's coalition government applied many of the measures Labour had called for during the 1930s. The party won the 1945 General Election by proposing to nationalize industries that had 'failed the nation' on the basis that state intervention was more equitable and efficient than private control. Significantly, however, the party made its case without reference to clause four but instead to the belief that such policies were the only 'practical' ones available (Donoughue and Jones, 1973, 332).

Debating Capitalism

The ultimate purpose of Labour's nationalization programme was never made clear. Some in the party saw it as a means of enabling the private sector to achieve higher levels of efficiency, whereas others imagined it to be the first instalment of a cumulative extension of common ownership designed to replace capitalism. Most Labour ministers saw merit only in the former argument (Tomlinson, 1997, 94–123). In fact, the experience of managing the economy exposed what Harold Wilson described as 'almost a vacuum in Socialist thought': the party's attitude to the private sector (Mercer, Rollings and Tomlinson, 1992, 4). Clause four implied the party was hostile to the market, and many members assumed private ownership would evaporate as a result of natural development and government action. However, Attlee's ministers were confronted with the problem of increasing output in an economy, 80 per cent of which remained in private hands. In such circumstances government saw the private sector as, in David Howell's phrase, 'an appropriate and necessary partner': this led them to embrace profitability and competition (Howell, 1980, 159–62).

After the government had applied most of its programme Labour members debated what direction they should now take. Certain thinkers argued that as a result of the changes engineered by Attlee, capitalism had been transformed so that the party's commitment to extend common ownership was irrelevant. Others believed capitalism had not changed, so the state sector should expand until it became dominant. These stances were echoed in most other west European social democratic parties. Faced by a resurgent post-war capitalism that confounded expectations of decline, social democrats felt it necessary to reconsider their ideological foundations. If in the 1890s Bernstein asserted that change meant the transition to socialism would be a very long time coming, second wave revisionists believed it would possibly never come (Sassoon, 1996, 241–73). Yet, if the means employed by social democrats had to be modified to take account of capitalist development, the ends could remain the same.

Able to point to an impressive stack of evidence, Labour's revisionists considered that the transformation of capitalism had created a society of unprecedented affluence in which poverty had been virtually abolished and class differences much reduced. Moreover, Attlee's successor as leader, Hugh Gaitskell, believed clause four had become an electoral albatross as it gave the impression that public control was 'the be all and end all, the ultimate first principle and aim of socialism'. This, he claimed, arose 'from a complete confusion about the fundamental meaning of socialism and, in particular, a misunderstanding about ends and means'

(Labour Party, 1959, 107–9). If revisionists believed capitalism in the 1950s made further nationalization irrelevant, even before 1939 many had questioned how much state control was necessary to achieve economic efficiency and social equality. While conceding that some nationalization was required, they saw greater merit in the fiscal and monetary controls advocated by Keynes. There was, therefore, no need to remain wedded to a general assertion of the superiority of common ownership. Indeed, Gaitskell tentatively suggested that common ownership was sometimes less effective than the market (Gaitskell, 1956, 17).

This case was most fully developed by Anthony Crosland in *The Future of Socialism* (1956). Crosland started from the proposition that capitalism had been 'reformed almost out of existence' and entered an era of ineluctable growth, while Attlee had shifted power from those who owned private industry towards government, the unions and managers. Crosland believed full employment gave unions equality with employers; he accepted that those who owned industry had ceased to control it, having been replaced by salaried managers seeking harmonious relations with employees. Thus the worst excesses of the market had been eliminated and it had become a 'reasonably satisfactory method' for distributing the 'great bulk of goods'. In addition, consumers were the 'best judge' of how to spend their money; and even if not, the 'principle of individual liberty' would still require that they be 'left free to spend it' (Crosland, 1956, 89, 504–5, 517). As one revisionist-influenced policy document of the time stated, a new and distinctive form of business had emerged in the most dynamic sectors of the private sector, and this was one in which the profit motive was less and less significant (Gaitskell, 1956, 17; Labour Party, 1957, 11–18, 23, 25). As would Tony Blair in the 1990s, revisionists thought capitalism in the United States was at the cutting edge of change and hoped Britain would emulate aspects of the American model (Fielding, 2001b).

Others defended what they took to be Labour's basic rationale: their most important voice was that of Aneurin Bevan, a leading member of Attlee's Cabinet. In 1952, Bevan published *In Place of Fear* in which he bluntly asserted that socialism required more nationalization. If he thought Keynesian policies had merit, Bevan believed that on their own they could never ensure equality: only more common ownership would do that. Thus, Bevan thought Labour should make the public sector predominant. Unlike Crosland, Bevan was not convinced capitalism had been fundamentally transformed: the market to him was at best an ugly necessity, and he attacked the 'amoral climate' and 'vulgarity' of commerce (Bevan, 1952, 48–50).

It was to entrench his perspective that Gaitskell attempted to change clause four. In private he had long considered the clause of no practical importance: like most of his predecessors, he ignored it. Increasingly, however, Gaitskell thought he would have to demonstrate publicly that it did not reflect Labour's purpose, and his mind was made up after it appeared the clause had hampered efforts to win the 1959 General Election. Inaugurating a debate remarkably similar to the one conducted 35 years later – except for its outcome – Gaitskell told the subsequent party conference of his wish. In so doing the Labour leader comforted members that revision would not change the party's 'eternal' and 'basic principles' but would simply amend how they were expressed. Echoing Crosland, Gaitskell declared he merely wished to clarify the meaning of the clause, as it appeared to suggest that common ownership was an end whereas it was but a means to an end – equality – and merely one means among many (Williams, 1982, 318–24).

Gaitskell's assurances did not persuade the likes of Bevan who stated that, if the clause was revised, Labour 'would not differ in any important respect from the Tory Party'. To Bevan, common ownership was both means and end, and the party's most distinctive means at that. The revisionist outlook, he declared, touching on concerns aroused by Blair's later change, 'would take us back to the situation as it existed when the Liberal Party was in its heyday'. Supporters of change, Bevan believed, considered 'private enterprise should still remain supreme but that its worst characteristics should be modified by liberal ideas of justice and equality'. If they succeeded, he announced, Labour might as well merge with the Liberals (*Tribune*, 11 December 1959; Miliband, 1972, 344–6).

Gaitskell was unable to revise the clause, the main reason being that the unions upon whom he normally relied to deliver conference and National Executive Committee votes were divided. In fact, many union leaders opposed to change had no intention of demanding the clause be ever applied: their affiliation was due less to the words themselves and more to their symbolism (Jones, 1996, 1–24). Thus Gaitskell's defeat did not indicate massive support within the party for the principle of an ever-expanding public sector. If many active members endorsed Bevan's opposition, the same cannot be said of their more inactive counterparts. When asked their opinion on the matter, only one-quarter of members in the safe Labour seat of Newcastle-under-Lyme championed the clause, and just over half claimed to have never heard of it (Bealey, Blondel and McCann, 1965, 283–4).

Many revisionists had opposed their leader's attempt to revise the clause, considering it of no consequence: after all, during the 1950s party policy had been taken in a more market-friendly direction unhindered by its existence. The Labour governments of the 1960s and 1970s also ignored the party's commitment to common ownership, yet they still nationalized industries when considered necessary; indeed, even the 1970–4 Conservative government employed state ownership when conditions seemed to call for it. This was, however, not due to a principled commitment to public control but conceived as a pragmatic response to events: during this period most economists considered state intervention an acceptable tool. However much their leaders nationalized, it was never enough for those on the Labour left who referred to the clause to bolster their demand for the common ownership of industries working efficiently in private hands. Indeed, Gaitskell's attempt to change the clause had given common ownership a prominence it had previously lacked: it was only in 1959 that the clause first appeared on membership cards. Thus the left came to enjoy a spurious degree of ideological legitimacy that became especially useful during the bitter disputes that afflicted the party during the 1970s and early 1980s.

Equality

Many in the party opposed revising clause four because they considered public ownership to be a crucial means of reducing inequality; yet even in 1945 few of those leading the party believed nationalization was decisive in that respect and, by the 1950s, Crosland made the case that there was no link between more common ownership and greater equality. Instead, revisionists suggested, society could be made fairer through the extension of the welfare state.

The establishment of the welfare state undoubtedly improved most Britons' quality of life and it was appropriate that it became one of Labour's proudest achievements. Yet the 1942 Beveridge Report, which gave a powerful impetus to its development, was not (strictly speaking) a social democratic document as its proposals were heavily influenced by the New Liberals' 'progressive spirit'. Beveridge's intention was to promote mutual respect rather than a redistribution of wealth between the classes. Nonetheless, he still described 'want' as 'a needless scandal' that could be overcome by taxing the rich, while his National Insurance (NI) system promised to redistribute income. Philosophers, most prominently T.H. Marshall, saw the resulting welfare state as a guarantor of the citizens' social rights that complemented their political rights. Just as they shared a common entitlement to vote at the ballot box, so all people enjoyed the same birthright to sit in a doctor's waiting room. Such rights, however, had to be paid for: NI relied on a large element of compulsory self-insurance, albeit subsidized by employers and government. Moreover, as Beveridge recognized that any welfare system might promote 'idleness', these would be modest rights. He also believed government should ensure that the provision of benefits was offset by an 'enforcement of the citizen's obligation to seek and accept all reasonable opportunities to work' (Addison, 1975, 211–28; Freeden, 1986, 368–9; Marquand, 1988, 28–31).

Labour embraced much of Beveridge's approach: as one 1956 policy document announced, no one benefiting from the welfare state could 'contract out of the social obligations which must support these reforms'. Indeed, it went on, the 'citizen's sense of responsibility must keep pace with the increase in his rights and powers if society is to renew itself spiritually and materially' (Labour Party, 1956a, 14–15). Herbert Morrison, Attlee's deputy, had early on acknowledged that Beveridge's proposals required full employment as that would keep the demand for benefits low and create enough tax-payers to ensure the system was properly financed. 'Real social security', he stated, 'means work' (Fielding, 1997b, 43–7). If responsibilities, in particular the expectation that the unemployed would seek work, were not vigorously enforced during the welfare state's first 30 years it was because full employment meant there was little political or economic imperative to do so.

Crosland assumed the Attlee government had corrected the 'worst economic abuses and inefficiencies of modern society'; in particular, he considered welfare and full employment had largely abolished poverty and reduced inequality (Crosland, 1956, 113–14). Sociologists would later challenge that view but, even in the 1950s, revisionists still considered tackling poverty a priority. As they conceived it, the furtherance of freedom and equality were the party's two main aims, the latter being a precondition of the former. Indeed, the pursuit of greater equality was, according to Crosland, 'the strongest ethical inspiration of virtually every socialist doctrine' (Jones, 1996, 25–40). Moreover, if greater equality was an end in itself, Labour thinkers at this time considered it would also enhance economic efficiency (Labour Party, 1956b, 4; Jenkins, 1970, 71).

Establishing what the revisionists meant by equality has become crucial to determining how far 'New' Labour can claim continuity with the past. This is because many appear to think the likes of Crosland disavowed equality of opportunity and embraced something close to equality of outcome. In contrast, Blair is considered to promote opportunity at the expense of outcome. It is true that Crosland believed the 'distribution of rewards and privileges' in society was 'highly inequitable, being poorly correlated with the distribution of merit, virtue, ability, or brains'. Yet, like Gaitskell, he did not support equality of outcome because he feared it would reduce the incentive to work hard. Gaitskell in particular stressed the need to eradicate 'feelings or attitudes of superiority or inferiority between groups' rather than the abolition of the groups themselves. Nevertheless, even Gaitskell conceded that equality of opportunity would be impossible if private wealth was not 'fairly evenly distributed' (Gaitskell, 1955, 165–7; Gaitskell, 1956, 3). As Michael Young's satire on the subject made plain, while they wanted merit rewarded, revisionists also opposed the creation of a pure 'meritocracy' because it would establish just another form of social division (Young, 1961).

If a more equitable distribution of income was necessary to foster greater equality, revisionists did not think raising income tax the best means of achieving that end. In the early 1950s Roy Jenkins considered income tax had reached its effective limit: any more might undermine individual liberty to no general benefit (Jenkins, 1970, 75–6). As one 1956 policy document conceded, contemporary rates were forcing some abroad (Labour Party, 1956b, 13–14). Instead, taking the post-war boom as permanent, Crosland thought growth would generate most of the necessary income tax revenues that would finance those welfare schemes designed to reduce inequality. Expansion meant funding welfare would be relatively painless for income tax-payers: even if the proportion of income taken remained constant, in absolute terms government revenues would increase (Crosland, 1956, 89). When revisionists discussed raising tax they looked to inherited wealth rather than earned income. Even then, as they had no wish to undermine 'effort and thrift', this would only be levied on the largest of inherited fortunes. Indeed, Crosland predicted state income would rise so high as a result of tapping this source that government could reduce income tax. This, he believed, would restore some reward to that 'individual effort and enterprise' lost under the existing tax regime – an interesting admission to say the least (Crosland, 1956, 331–2).

Apart from devoting more resources to welfare, revisionists believed the main duty of government was to ensure that, as Gaitskell put it, 'a person's income, way of living, education, status and opportunities in life' should not depend on the class into which he or she had been born (Gaitskell, 1956, 3). The most significant means of preventing this, revisionists believed, was educational reform: in particular, Crosland wanted to abolish socially divisive private and grammar schools. As with the provision of a universal health service used by all citizens, Crosland considered an education system used in common would produce 'a greater equality in manners and the texture of social life'. This is why he supported comprehensive education: it would give each child the same start in life, irrespective of their parents' circumstances (Crosland, 1956, 143, 258–77).

As a result of these considerations, revisionists should be placed somewhere between those who advocated equality of outcome and supporters of equality of opportunity. As Crosland wrote in the early 1970s:

> By equality we meant more than a meritocratic society of equal opportunities in which the greatest rewards would go to those with the most fortunate genetic endowment and family background; we adopted the 'strong' definition of equality – what Rawls has subsequently called 'democratic' as opposed to the 'liberal' conception.

Unfortunately, how distant 'democratic' equality was from those of outcome and opportunity cannot be measured with any precision. It was sufficiently far, however, to be criticized both from the left for being too cautious and from the right for being too demanding (Crosland, 1974, 15; Plant, 1981, 137–44). The suspicion is that revisionists were much nearer equality of opportunity than that of outcome. As Crosland warned, 'justice must be tempered with efficiency': in other words, the pursuit of equality should never endanger economic growth (Crosland, 1962, 28–9).

The Emergence of Neo-Revisionism

During James Callaghan's 1976–9 government it became clear that revisionist expectations of ineluctable growth had been confounded. By the mid-1970s profitability was in decline, which meant welfare spending could only be financed by increasing relative levels of income tax on white-collar and manual workers whose votes Labour desperately required. This economic shift therefore provoked a political crisis that gave rise to what has been termed 'neo-revisionism'.

Increasing unemployment quickly led some in the leadership to question the efficacy of demand management: it was a Labour Chancellor, Denis Healey, who abandoned Keynesianism. To make them aware of the new economic 'realities', in 1976 Callaghan informed party conference delegates that inflation, not lack of demand, had become the main cause of unemployment. Declaring the public demise of Keynesianism, the Labour Prime Minister stated that unemployment could no longer be reduced through further indirect or direct intervention: low inflation was the only solution (Labour Party, 1976, 188–9). While the transitional nature of this period needs to be borne in mind, as Martin Holmes has put it, whether he intended to or not, Callaghan's speech 'effectively broke the mould of post-war economic policy-making', marking as it did a 'watershed in attitudes to the expectations and effectiveness of government stimulus to the economy'. It was, he concludes, the Callaghan government that facilitated a 'change of intellectual direction', one preceding Thatcher's assumption of office (Holmes, 1985, 163, 179–82).

If Callaghan stumbled rather than strode through the 1970s, some revisionists cautiously but deliberately remapped their attitude to the market, state and unions, if not redistribution. The main impetus here was that by the 1970s some of Labour's own working-class supporters opposed those tax increases deemed necessary by ministers to promote equality. In the early days of the welfare state many employees stood outside the income tax system: as late as 1955, married manual workers on average wages paid nothing. However, as wages rose and governments required a broader tax base, the overwhelming majority was drawn in. By the late 1960s, the redistribution of wealth had in practice become a matter of taking money from well-paid workers and giving it to public sector, unskilled, unemployed or retired workers. This situation was exacerbated when unemployment rose, meaning government was forced to put more pressure on those in work. Thus, by the start of the 1970s raising taxes to tackle poverty had become more politically perilous than ever assumed by Crosland, while social democrats began to appreciate that poverty was itself a more intractable problem than they had thought.

Initially, MPs such as David Marquand and David Owen hoped affluent workers could be persuaded by Labour politicians of their need to pay more income tax: to that end they wrote a series of speeches for the Deputy Leader, Roy Jenkins (Jenkins, 1972). The case when made, however, did not persuade. Thus, by the mid-1970s the journey to a more equal society had reached an impasse: it was politically unwise to raise taxes but, if progress was to be made, government needed more money. Moreover, if the pursuit of equality had always involved the restriction of certain personal freedoms, some social democrats now believed this trade-off had become especially problematic. According to the MP, John Mackintosh, equality 'may have gone far enough' and it was probably time to 'reassert' the 'freedom of the individual' (Marquand, 1982, 182–9). Indeed, he went on to argue that the solution to the country's problems was a reform of the state itself, while the private sector needed liberation from a tax burden which had grown too heavy (Mackintosh, 1978, 266–7). Thus, while generally continuing to believe their aim should remain the reduction of poverty, such neo-revisionists stressed that this could only come about with a greater role for the market and the decentralization, if not contraction, of government.

Even those who left Labour in 1981 to form the Social Democratic Party (SDP) endorsed the pursuit of greater equality. Just after helping to establish the SDP, Owen remained convinced of the need for a major anti-poverty programme even though he realized it would require unpopular higher taxes (Owen, 1981, xviii, 4–6, 69–72, 247–8). Significantly, when in the middle 1980s he presented his vision of the 'social market', Owen decided it would be politic to accommodate public hostility. To that end he abandoned the general pursuit of income equality through the provision of universal benefits, and instead sought to target the worst off. In particular he proposed concentrating on low-paid families with children through creating an integrated tax and benefit system. Owen was obviously attempting to reconcile voter opinion and the perceived need to increase economic competitiveness with the established social democratic stress on equality. In his advocacy of an 'enabling government' it is obvious how far Owen anticipated many key 'New' Labour themes (Owen, 1984, 28–9, 104–31; Owen, 1986, 186–97).

The Policy Review

The loss of figures such as Owen was a severe blow to the development of Labour's neo-revisionism. It was not until the 1987 Policy Review that the party, having been rescued from the dominance of the left, started fundamentally to rethink the relationship between market and state (Hughes and Wintour, 1990). The context had, however, dramatically altered since the late 1970s, largely due to successive Conservative governments whose actions – the Labour leader Neil Kinnock was forced to concede – were both popular and irreversible in the short-run.

Those who have studied the Review differ markedly as to its ideological significance. A common view is that it saw Labour embrace a watered-down version of Thatcherism (Hay, 1994). Many of this persuasion would agree with Eric Shaw's characterization that, as a result, the party became 'post-revisionist' (Shaw, 1994, 103–7). Others, most prominently Martin Smith, suggest the Review should instead be seen as a return to, not a rejection of, Croslandite revisionism (Smith, 1992 and 1994). Whatever the merits of these perspectives, each overlooks the extent to which Labour's neo-revisionists had begun to anticipate the Review over a decade earlier. Thus, if the Policy Review marked a return, it was to an interrupted neo-revisionism, something that was itself a critical response to post-war revisionism.

The basic object of the Review was to make the party more electable as the leadership believed Labour had to develop policies that appealed to those individualist values apparently embraced by many voters and distance itself from remedies that were overly reliant on the state (Gamble, 1992). The Conservatives had privatized many state-owned industries, ensuring popular support by selling shares at a discount rate to small investors. Labour's first response was to promise it would return these industries to state hands. However, as time went on, more industries were privatized, meaning that a future Labour government would have to spend billions of pounds just to alter ownership. Thus, instead of renationalization, the Review proposed controlling any privatized concerns indirectly by granting more powers to bodies already charged with their regulation so as to better ensure they represented the interests of consumers and the economy as a whole. The Review therefore confirmed Labour's earlier move away from direct state intervention and put a large question mark against Keynesianism. Party policy in fact accepted the market was 'essential' to efficiency, a view consistent with the earlier Croslandite approach; it went on to note that, while the state retained an economic role, this was 'not to replace the market but to ensure that markets work properly' (Labour Party, 1992, 1).

The Kinnock leadership therefore accepted the neo-revisionist belief that nationalization and demand management had failed to promote sufficient growth and efficiency. John Smith, Kinnock's shadow chancellor, argued that the power of global capitalism was such that a Labour government attempting to spend its way out of a recession would provoke the international markets to cause the currency to collapse. Consequently, Labour had to embrace the new macro-economic orthodoxy, one associated with Thatcherism but increasingly adopted across the world. This stipulated that the pursuit of low inflation was government's primary goal, something Callaghan had made clear in 1976. Generally speaking, Labour's economic policy after the Review was based on encouraging private sector production and investment rather than having the state do these things itself.

In terms of welfare policy some see the Review as cautious, in as much as it reaffirmed the party's faith in the revisionist strategy of relying on the fruits of growth to fund extra spending. Thus the basic function of a Labour government remained that of financing those established institutions and practices that constituted the post-war welfare state (Alcock, 1992). Shaw has, however, stressed the Review's distinctive character and considers it marked a retreat from the Croslandite aim of reducing inequality through redistribution, in favour of promoting opportunities and only ameliorating the extremes of social distress (Shaw, 1994, 101–7).

Kinnock and his deputy, Roy Hattersley, set the Review within an over-arching ideological framework by producing a statement of Labour's aims and values in 1988. This restated the revisionist case for the late 1980s by stressing the importance of liberty, a matter neo-revisionists had taken especially seriously. Kinnock and Hattersley consequently stated that Labour's 'true aim' was the 'creation of a genuinely free society', in which government's 'fundamental objective' was the 'protection and extension of individual liberty'. If the rhetorical emphasis was now on 'freedom' rather than 'equality', they reiterated Crosland's belief that the pursuit of freedom and equality were complementary and not, as Thatcherites believed, contradictory. Freedoms, moreover, only had 'real meaning' if everybody could exercise them: without the 'power to choose, the right to choose has no value'. Thus, government had a crucial role to play in extending freedom by ensuring 'a more equal distribution' of wealth through levying 'fair taxes'. Even so, a future Labour government would only target the 'wealthy' – by which Hattersley meant the 'very rich' (Hattersley, 1987, 231–4; Labour Party, 1989, 30–3). It was not envisaged that the modest redistribution which would flow from this would by itself abolish poverty. To that end government had a responsibility to extend opportunity by ensuring the people could enjoy 'the fullest possible access to education, training, information [and] technology' (Labour Party, 1988, 3–5, 7). The aim was 'to enable people to be the independent' of welfare and create 'pathways out of poverty', by which the party meant it would reform the tax and benefits system to make low-paid work more attractive to the unemployed (Labour Party, 1989, 30; 1990, 36–8; 1992, 17–18). Just as had the revisionists in the 1950s, Labour in the 1980s considered it appropriate to mix equality of opportunity with that of outcome.

Revising Clause Four

Some commentators regarded the 1995 revision of clause four as 'New' Labour's 'defining moment' (Marquand and Wright, 1995, 123). Yet when Blair used his first conference speech as leader to call for change, he was not asking for anything new. Even those who supported Blair's initiative did not think the clause exerted much ideological authority: in fact, they regarded it as irrelevant (Straw, 1993, 4; *The Independent*, 29 April 1995). Indeed, Peter Mandelson and Roger Liddle thought the clause had only 'seemingly' made Labour appear hostile to the private sector (Mandelson and Liddle, 1996, 51–2). As a result, when Blair announced his intention, even some close supporters wondered what the point was.

As with its creation, the clause's revision was not a straightforward ideological act. Advocates hoped change would help Labour attract voters who had failed to support Kinnock at the 1992 General Election by demonstrating how far the party had changed (Radice, 1992, 18–19). If revision was not designed to initiate change, it would at least denote that it had already occurred in a manner that would grab the public's attention. Accordingly, what appealed to Blair's press spokesman, Alastair Campbell, was the 'sheer boldness' of revision itself and the extent to which this would show the new leader 'was someone who wasn't going to mess about' (Gould, 1998, 125). Significantly, had Kinnock's successor, John Smith, lived he would not have repealed the clause although he no more believed in it than Blair. Instead, Smith planned to issue a personal statement of values, hoping this would supersede the clause without provoking the fuss of actually changing it (Rentoul, 2001, 254). For Blair, however, the point of revision was to cause a fuss.

Despite the practical irrelevance of the clause, the party's left looked on change in apocalyptic terms. Ironically, such opposition was necessary to the drama the leadership hoped to choreograph: without it the sense of transformation would have been substantially diminished. For many on the left socialism remained impossible without substantial levels of common ownership, and to them the existence of the clause at least kept the issue alive. 'We are', Arthur Scargill, President of the National Union of Mineworkers, consequently told opponents of change, 'fighting for the very soul of our party' (*The Independent on Sunday*, 13 November 1994). Those of Scargill's persuasion gained heart two days after Blair had called for repeal when Labour's conference narrowly endorsed a motion reaffirming the party's commitment to the clause. It was, in the words of the delegate moving the resolution, a 'symbol of our commitment to the working class' and representative of Labour's core beliefs, specifically that the redistribution of wealth was a 'prime aim', and public ownership a crucial means of achieving it (*The Guardian*, 7 October, 1994). It was precisely due to its symbolic significance that Blair wanted the clause revised.

Others calculated that if the new leader wanted the clause changed then changed it would be, so they sought to influence his thinking. Thus, despite considering revision a 'navel-gazing exercise', *Tribune* and others hoped their participation in the process might mean the new clause would reaffirm the importance of public ownership (*Tribune* 14 October 1994; *New Statesman & Society/Tribune*, 1995). Prominent figures in the leadership also intervened for their own ends. John Prescott had initially opposed revision but used his acceptance to secure a promise that Blair would not introduce further changes to Labour's constitution before the next election (Brown, 1997, 285–94; Rentoul, 2001, 255). Similarly, Robin Cook had been appalled by Blair's initiative but, by becoming a 'critical friend', ensured the final draft did not contain an overly prescriptive statement about the family (Kampfner, 1998, 101–3). Showing disdain for the ideological implications of its revision, some union leaders were also apparently willing to support change if Blair agreed to some of their demands on issues such as the minimum wage (*The Guardian*, 9 February 1995; *The Independent*, 15 April 1995; Mandelson and Liddle, 1996, 54). In contrast to Gaitskell, however, Blair had ensured that the decision would be made through an electoral college in which ordinary trade unionists and individual party members had the decisive say. The Labour leader could therefore appeal over the heads of union bureaucracies and activists.

While 85 per cent of Labour's members participating in the exercise voted in favour of the new clause, this did not mean they had lost faith in public ownership. Indeed, a survey undertaken in 1992 revealed that nearly two-thirds favoured more nationalization of industry (*New Statesman & Society*, 9 December 1994). Possibly because of this, party leaders stressed how little the new clause would change matters. Prescott stated it would simply set out Labour's values 'afresh' and 'explain them in a language everyone can understand' (*The Guardian*, 8 October 1994). On a number of occasions Blair reassured members that common ownership would not be ignored, while Prescott claimed that 'we are certainly not running away from the concept of public ownership' (*The Guardian*, 11 and 16 January 1995). If they were not mollified by such assurances, members might have been influenced by their fear of the dire electoral consequences should they reject the new draft, which was something underlined by Blair and Prescott (*The Guardian*, 23 January 1995).

For an exercise designed, as the Labour leader put it in his 1994 conference speech, to stop the party 'saying what we don't mean and start saying what we do mean', the existence of such complex motives was paradoxical but inevitable. It would consequently be wrong to state categorically that the members' acceptance of the new clause meant they had embraced each and every letter. It would, however, be difficult to deny that the scale of support for the new clause indicated how far the original had fallen into disrepute. If nothing else, the process revealed the confusion of many leading members of the party about the merits of public ownership. The shadow cabinet minister, Clare Short, for example, had initially opposed revision while simultaneously considering the clause inadequate. She confessed to having once supported it through a 'youthful conviction' that public ownership promoted a 'desire to serve the public good rather than an individual greed' and furthered the creation of an egalitarian society. Yet, she claimed, experience convinced her neither was now necessarily true. Despite this, Short still believed common ownership was an obligatory means to an end, although on what basis it was unclear (*The Guardian*, 12 January 1995). No wonder opposition to change was ultimately ineffective.

For what it was worth, the clause passed by Labour's special conference held in April 1995 read:

> The Labour Party is a democratic socialist party. It believes that by the strength of our common endeavour, we will achieve more than we achieve alone; so as to create: for each of us the means to realise our true potential and for all of us a community in which power, wealth and opportunity are in the hands of the many not the few, where the rights we enjoy reflect the duties we owe, and where we live together, freely, in a spirit of solidarity, tolerance and respect.
>
> To these ends we work for: a dynamic economy, serving the public interest, in which the enterprise of the market and the rigour of competition are joined with the forces of partnership and co-operation to produce the wealth the nation needs and the opportunity for all to work and prosper, with a thriving private sector and high quality public services, where those undertakings essential to the common good are either owned by the public or accountable to them; a just society, which judges its strength by the condition of the weak as much as the strong, provides security against fear, and justice at work; which nurtures family life, promotes equality of opportunity and delivers people from the tyranny of poverty, prejudice and the abuse of power; an open democracy, in which Government is held to account by the people; decisions are taken as far as practicable by the communities they affect; and where fundamental human rights are guaranteed; a healthy environment, which we protect, enhance and hold in trust for future generations.

For some, the new clause was the end of the road. On May Day 1996 Scargill formed the Socialist Labour Party, believing Labour had 'abandoned any pretence of being a Socialist party' and 'openly embraced capitalism and the "free market"' (Socialist Labour Party, 2001, 31 July). So far as Blair was concerned, the phrase committing Labour to the 'rigour of competition' was certainly the one he most wanted to stress to voters and Philip Gould considered these few words a 'massive step forward' for the party (Gould, 1998, 230). Indeed, the meaning Labour's leaders wanted voters to draw from the new clause was best summed up in a headline that followed the April conference: 'Blair buries socialism' (*The Sunday Telegraph*, 30 April 1995).

Scargill and Gould were nonetheless both wrong: the new clause changed little of substance. Labour had long before effectively embraced capitalism and accepted the merits of competition. Moreover, as Raymond Plant argued, the new clause placed Labour's endorsement of the market into a moral context that stressed collective responsibility and cooperation, something advocates of *laissez-faire* refused to contemplate (*The Guardian*, 20 March 1995). To this could be added the observation that Labour was committed to the market in the same way it had previously been dedicated to state intervention: as a practical means to achieve the party's ends, the most important of which was now defined as realizing everybody's 'true potential'. Furthermore, as promised, the new clause still granted public ownership a continued role in the achievement of these aims.

There was therefore some understandable confusion regarding the precise meaning of revision. According to Mandelson and Liddle, the new clause merely eliminated any 'ambiguity' in popular perceptions of Labour's attitude to the market. In fact, they argued, the new clause better reflected the intentions of previous Labour governments than the one under which they had operated. Yet, on the other hand, they also claimed revising clause four was more than 'symbolic' and represented the 'essence' of 'New' Labour (Mandelson and Liddle, 1996, 19, 23–4, 51–2).

The Third Way

If the new clause confirmed Labour no longer wished to foster the ineluctable extension of common ownership, it did not give a strong sense of what the party now proposed. This was deliberate: in Opposition, Blair's electoral strategy was to obscure Labour's differences with Thatcherism and stress his willingness to maintain key Conservative reforms so as to appeal to wavering voters.

After power had been won, however, the new Prime Minister was keen to promote a popular understanding of what he liked to describe as the 'new politics' (Blair, 1998b). To that end, Blair tried to show how far Labour had moved on from what most believed was its time-honoured reliance on the state and hostility to the market, while illustrating how different the new position was to Thatcherism. He also wanted to indicate that, whilst pragmatic, his was not an unprincipled government but one rooted in social democratic ethics. To that end, Blair talked of a 'third way between unbridled individualism and laissez-faire on the one hand' and what he described as 'old style Government intervention, the corporatism of the 1960s social democracy, on the other'. This Third Way, Blair claimed, did not just 'split the difference' between right and left as it was based on values to which only the left adhered. However, this 'modernized social democracy' was defined by the reconciliation of 'individual liberty in the market economy', long advanced by liberalism, and the social democratic aim of 'social justice with the state as the main agent'. This settlement, according to Blair, had become necessary due to the way the world had changed; it was now possible because 'New' Labour had accepted that 'state power is one of the means to achieve our goals, but not the only one and emphatically not an end in itself'.

As earlier revisionists before him, Blair justified the need for change with reference to the transformation of economy and society, believing 'the rate of economic, political, industrial and social change is quicker than at any time in our history' (Blair, 1996, 15, 46–7, 55, 203–5, 213). In thinking this, the Labour leader echoed the opinions of others on the British left who argued that since the 1970s the economy had undergone significant structural shifts: most saliently, manufacturing and the 'traditional' manual working class had gone into steep decline (Finlayson, 1999). Thinkers who came to exert a profound influence over 'New' Labour's view of the world had a clear conception of the consequences of such change. The rise of the 'knowledge economy', for example, meant an increasing number of employees relied on their mental capacity rather than physical ability (Leadbeater, 1999). Britain was less hierarchical and more permissive than hitherto: people thought of themselves as individuals, and class feeling was in retreat (Giddens, 1994). Overall, their view was that diversity and fragmentation had superseded the homogeneity and the economies of scale that had once characterized post-war Britain (Hall and Jacques, 1990). As we shall see in Chapter 6, Blair supposed that the main agent of this process was globalization, which he considered both 'inevitable' and 'desirable'.

While arguing that change meant social democracy had to transform itself so it could exploit the possibilities inherent to the new context,

Blair's Third Way was consistent with earlier manifestations of revisionism. This did not mean the Third Way embraced similar policies to those advocated by Crosland, just as Crosland, did not advance measures endorsed by Bernstein. This is because, as Blair put it, 'the world of secure jobs, large firms, low unemployment, relatively closed national economies and strong communities underpinned by stable families' (which sustained Crosland's viewpoint) had disappeared. What he described as the 'highly statist brand of social democracy', once considered appropriate to the achievement of social democracy's goals, consequently had to be revised. If Blair under-played the Third Way's continuity with post-war revisionism, he was less shy of acknowledging the extent to which it incorporated some of the Thatcher governments' 'necessary acts of modernisation': in particular, their opening up of the state sector to 'reform and competition'. Yet, Blair also stated that Thatcher had gone too far in her hostility to public services such as health and education. Indeed, her dogmatism had prevented Conservative governments from taking collective action of any kind, thereby imperilling social cohesion and economic performance.

While Blair criticized the excesses of *laissez-faire*, the Third Way proceeded from the assumption that the market was essential to the advance of social democratic goals. Anthony Giddens, the most prominent academic exponent of the Third Way whose work reflected the Prime Minister's own approach, urged the left to 'get comfortable with markets'. Not only were markets more efficient than any other system of production but they could also promote desirable individual qualities such as responsibility (Giddens, 2000, 34–6). Blair made his own position clear in a 1999 statement, issued jointly with the leader of the German *Sozialdemokratische Partei Deutschlands* (SPD) and newly elected Chancellor, Gerhard Schroeder (Blair and Schroeder, 2000). Both men stated that the transition from industrial production to the 'knowledge-based service economy', implicit in globalization, 'offers millions of our people the chance to find new jobs, learn new skills, pursue new careers, set up and expand new businesses – in summary, to realise their hopes for a better future'. Such change was inevitable and the longer it was resisted, the more protracted and painful would be the period of transition. Blair and Schroeder furthermore asserted that the only way to ensure workers enjoyed the full benefits of reform was for governments to accept that 'competition and open trade' were 'essential to stimulate productivity and growth'. It was, consequently 'essential' that governments created a framework to allow market forces 'to work properly'. This primarily meant governments should reduce regulation and intervention while promoting more flexible markets: indeed, they described this latter task as a key 'modern social democratic aim'. Politicians needed to avoid using government as a substitute for 'enterprise'; instead, the 'essential function of markets must be complemented and improved by political action, not hampered by it'. As Blair and Schroeder put it, echoing a by-now well-worn metaphor, the state 'should not row, but steer'.

If some thought the Third Way sounded like a weak echo of *laissez-faire* ideology, Blair and Schroeder refuted the charge. As Giddens pointed out, while uniquely beneficial, markets also had some disadvantages that had to be tackled by some form of public action (Giddens, 2000, 36–7). Thus Blair and Schroeder claimed the distinctive attribute of the Third Way was its assertion that market-based flexibility had to be accompanied by a 'newly defined role for the active state', focused on investment in human and social capital. The primary purpose of this investment, largely in education and training, was to enable individuals to 'enhance their qualifications and fulfil their potential'. This in turn would make them and the businesses for which they worked 'fit for the knowledge-based economy of the future'. Government's second main responsibility was to ensure that the welfare system became 'a springboard to personal responsibility', rather than the means of paying out cash to passive recipients, something that would again benefit both the individual and wider economy. Finally, it was also the job of the state to establish minimum standards in the labour market.

If widely derided as vacuous, some at least saw the Third Way in a less negative light. According to Stuart White it was not so much an ideology as a 'rhetorically defined space', characterized by certain values and an openness to a variety of policies derived from numerous intellectual traditions, including (but not only) social democracy. Indeed, so generous was the space upon which the Third Way rested, it could include arguments both for and against income redistribution as a means of advancing equality (White, 2001, 3–4, 11–13). This was more than an accident for, as will be suggested in the next chapter, the Third Way was partly meant to serve as a 'catch-all' doctrine that would appeal to the diverse interests that formed Labour's 1997 electoral coalition. Such openness irritated those who wanted 'New' Labour to define its ideological position in a strongly social democratic direction (Jacobs, 2001).

As the 2001 election approached the Prime Minister tried to give his notion greater clarity (Blair, 2001b). The result was, however, only slightly less obscure than the original, but in this reiteration Blair was rather clearer about the parameters that bounded the Third Way. It was much more certainly 'social democracy renewed'. This meant it proceeded from the desire to advance the interests of all individuals, specifically to enable them to fulfil their potential through new forms of collective action. Moreover, while noting that '[e]ffective markets are a pre-condition for a successful modern economy', Blair was firm that only collective action could give individuals 'opportunities as well as safeguards within the market'.

A Social Democratic Party?

The extent to which the Third Way was coherent or novel was widely debated. Early seekers after clarification were not helped by Labour ministers and back-benchers who employed the term in an indiscriminate and ill-informed way, hoping to ingratiate themselves with their leader. The junior minister, Peter Hain, even claimed there was a 'Welsh Third Way', possibly to the surprise of the Welsh (Hain, 1999). Journalistic commentators took advantage of such confusion and ridiculed what they took to be the concept's meaninglessness.

More serious analysts traced the ideological origins of the Third Way and generally saw the heavy imprint of Thatcherism, much liberalism but – despite Blair's own comments – little social democracy (*The Observer*, 8 March 1998; *The Guardian*, 15 June 1999; McKibbin, 2000, 72–3). Such analysis took its lead from Blair's many pronouncements made in Opposition which stressed his criticism of social democratic thinking due to its supposed over-reliance on the state and hostility to the market (*European*, 19–25 January 1998). Given his outlook, many understandably questioned how far the Third Way could be social democratic. Most who posed this question did so imagining there was one particular model that defined European social democracy; yet, given the variety of ideological positions embraced at any one point in time by parties claiming to be social democratic and the numerous occasions such parties revised their positions, this belief was seriously flawed. It also discounted the extent to which differing national circumstances influenced the expression or even content of particular parties' ideologies (Lovecy, 2001).

Instead it is remarkable how far 'New' Labour still shared the same broad perspective with most of its European peers. All such parties had been forced to come to terms with adjustments in the world economy, and acknowledged that their purpose should be confined to encouraging market efficiency while ensuring it promoted greater equality. They also conceded that this could be pursued through indirect regulation more than direct ownership. 'New' Labour is generally thought to have moved furthest and fastest from the state to the market. This can be plausibly explained by reference to the impact of change on Britain, due to its more vulnerable position in the world economy and the alacrity with which Conservative governments forced policy in a *laissez-faire* direction. Moreover, closer comparison with attitudes evident in, for example, the Spanish and Dutch parties shows Labour was hardly unique (Sassoon, 1996, 730–54; Giddens, 2000, 14–19; Clift, 2001a). Indeed, as we already know, so strong was their sense of common purpose that Blair and the leader of the German SPD issued a joint manifesto.

The *Parti Socialiste Français* (PSF) is normally considered to be at the opposite pole to 'New' Labour in respect of the need to adapt. In particular, Lionel Jospin, when French Prime Minister and PSF leader, was widely thought to be critical of the Third Way (Clift, 2001b). Yet when Jospin summarized his party's philosophy for the benefit of a British audience, notwithstanding certain differences of emphasis and occasionally of content, he demonstrated how close the two parties actually were (Jospin, 1999). Thus he wrote of how French socialists accepted that the market economy was the 'most effective means ... of allocating resources, stimulating initiative and rewarding effort and work'. They had, he stated, similarly disavowed the idea that socialism could be defined by nationalization, accepted privatization when necessary, and also recognized the need for the French economy to be internationally competitive. Jospin in addition asserted the imperative for an 'equality of opportunity' that did not reduce 'differences arising from people's different abilities' but only tackled those that arose from birth or social background. French socialists, he claimed, also saw the necessity for welfare reform and recognized that redistribution 'will be better achieved if we give proper attention to production'. Finally, Jospin asserted the need to not just appeal to those for whom equality was the central purpose of politics, but also voters broadly satisfied with the status quo and reluctant to have their taxes increased to pay for welfare. All of these assertions would not have seemed alien had they been articulated by the British Prime Minister. Indeed, Jospin's characterization of his general position, that of supporting a market economy but opposing a 'market society', was subsequently appropriated by Blair and Schroeder's 1999 manifesto (Blair and Schroeder, 2000, 160).

Conclusion

This chapter has endeavoured to demonstrate that, ideologically speaking, 'New' Labour does not mark a decisive break with the party's past.

This general assertion will be elaborated further in chapters devoted to economic policy and equality. In particular, Labour's enthusiasm for common ownership, notwithstanding the 1918 version of clause four, was less than it seemed. Some in the party always considered that common ownership had a unique role to play in the making of socialism, as it both weakened capitalist power and redistributed income. Others, in particular but not exclusively the party's post-war revisionists, saw it as simply one way of improving economic efficiency and a flawed means of reducing inequality. As will be seen in Chapter 5, apart from a brief period in the 1970s and 1980s, those of the latter persuasion largely dictated party policy.

Thus, while the 1995 clause relegated public ownership to one of a number of means thought necessary to achieve the party's aims, this was where in practice it had always been. Moreover, although the new clause approvingly referred to the 'enterprise of the market and the rigour of competition', Labour's leaders had long accepted that the market had an important role to play. It is, however, true that Blair's elaboration of the Third Way indicated the extent to which Labour (along with other social democratic parties) now saw the market as much the most important means of achieving its ends. Those who measured socialism purely in terms of the size of the public sector saw this as a retreat. On the other hand, the Third Way could also be seen as simply a pragmatic shift in the focus of collective action so as to take account of change. The extent to which amending the means meant Labour could no longer achieve a more equal society, by far the most important of the party's ends, remains in dispute, and will be explored in more depth in Chapter 7.

4
Accommodating or Shaping? Labour's Electoral Dilemma

'New' Labour won the 1997 and 2001 General Elections by landslides, giving it Commons majorities of 179 and 167 seats respectively. This was a remarkable transformation: after losing its fourth election in a row in 1992, commentators speculated that Labour would remain in permanent Opposition (King, 1993, viii). Some analysts considered 'New' Labour regained power through following a 'preference-accommodating' strategy. By this they meant Blair had simply echoed the Thatcherite sensibilities of middle-class voters (those referred to as 'Middle England'). To achieve this, he had ditched policies favoured by the party's established manual working-class supporters (those designated 'heartlands' voters). Not everybody in the party saw merit in this alleged strategy. Some advocated a 'preference-shaping' approach, arguing that instead of pandering to Middle England's views Blair should have challenged them so they eventually accorded with the party's own beliefs. Labour would have won in 1997 on this basis and, such critics believe (given the dire state of the Conservatives), Prime Minister Blair could have been more radical in office and still gained re-election in 2001.

This chapter will argue that in many respects Blair's appeal to middle-class voters was consistent with an approach established in 1918 which proceeded from neither preference-accommodation nor preference-shaping but from what is here described as an 'accommodate-to-shape' strategy. This embraced the leadership's desire to appeal to voters from all classes, a need that became ever stronger as post-war social change caused the manual working class to decline. Others, however, saw this as betraying the party's purpose.

The chapter will also suggest that the party's position in 1994 was not as strong as some believe, and that its 1997 victory was largely based on highly contingent support. To win a second term, Blair needed to attend to Middle England while keeping the heartlands satisfied, a dilemma similar to that faced by the party earlier in the century. The governments elected in 1945 and 1966 both tried to maintain the cross-class coalitions that had brought them power. Nonetheless, Clement Attlee saw the middle class return to the Conservatives while Harold Wilson lost working-class support. What is more, Blair was faced with an additional burden: his government had been elected on a programme finessed to appeal to Middle England but whose substance was less Thatcherite than voters imagined. If many were impressed by Blair's promise not to raise income tax, they did not appreciate that Labour remained free to increase other taxes. As the Prime Minister would confirm, his first term was preoccupied with reassuring Middle England: but it was also concerned with moving them towards measures supposedly abandoned after 1994. This was undoubtedly a cautious strategy, but one based on a plausible reading of popular attitudes since, despite its sustained opinion poll lead, Labour's performance at the ballot box during 1998–2000 was unimpressive. Support for those protesting against petrol taxes in the autumn of 2000 vividly illustrated the voters' fickleness.

Nonetheless, 'New' Labour was at least credited with reversing what had once appeared to be the party's ineluctable post-war electoral decline. Thus, in order to assess Blair's impact, we need to first take account of how Labour's earlier performance at the polls has been explained.

The Impact of Social Change

Socialization has long been seen to be the most important influence on voting patterns (Butler and Stokes, 1969). Party loyalties during the immediate post-war period were generally believed to be the result of a cumulative process determined by contact with family, neighbours and work colleagues. The most decisive influence on such relationships was thought to have been class, given the extent to which the classes lived in distinct worlds. The resulting discrete cultures produced contrasting forms of allegiance so that, broadly speaking, manual workers supported Labour and the middle class voted Conservative. Once established, these loyalties were robust so long as circumstances remained constant. From this perspective, therefore, voting was less a reflection of support for a set of policies and more the expression of group loyalty. Another viewpoint challenged this analysis (while retaining its emphasis on social influences) and posited that voters consciously chose a party after making a 'rational' calculation as to which policies best represented their interests (Downs, 1957). Thus a party promising to increase welfare spending would be favourably viewed by poorer voters, while a party pledging to cut taxes would be met positively by those higher up the social scale.

Such general theories have coloured explanations of Labour's performance. They first focused attention on the decline of the manual working class as that reduced the number of those whose group loyalties drew them to Labour. Second, they stipulated that changes within the remaining manual working class caused the perceived interests of many such voters to be so transformed it became 'rational' for them to support other parties.

The decline in size of the manual working class is undoubted: during the 1950s this group accounted for two-thirds of the population but, by the 1990s, the proportion had fallen to near enough one-quarter. The waning of manufacturing and the use of capital-intensive machinery in the surviving manufacturing sector played their part. The rise of service-based employment produced a commensurate increase in lower-middle-class numbers. Some argued that, despite the numerical contraction of manual workers, the working class as a whole – those who laboured for modest incomes and had little control over their working environment – had not diminished; the proletariat had merely exchanged blue overalls for white collars. Matters, however, were not that simple and considerations such as status meant that at most only two-fifths of routine non-manual workers supported Labour at general elections prior to 1997 (see Tables 4.1 and 4.2).

The second social cause of Labour's electoral problems is believed to have been the fragmentation of the remaining working class. If class is thought to have demarcated relationships for much of the twentieth century, the 1950s saw these separate worlds based on class begin to break

Table 4.1   The Labour vote by social class, 1945–66

	1945	*1950*	*1951*	*1955*	*1959*	*1964*	*1966*
Upper-middle class	14	9	6	9	6	9	8
Middle class	24	17	22	21	16	22	24
Working class	57	53	52	57	54	53	61
Very poor	57	64	67	54	68	59	72
All figures are percentages							

Source: Gallup Poll (1976), 206.

Table 4.2   The Labour vote by social class, 1964–97

	1964	1966	1970	1974	1974	1979	1983	1987	1992	1997
1	18	19	22	17	17	24	8	11	16	34
2	20	29	32	26	30	19	16	19	21	42
3	26	41	40	29	32	32	20	26	30	49
4	15	20	20	18	13	13	12	16	17	40
5	48	61	56	39	52	45	28	37	45	62
6	70	73	63	59	62	58	47	48	50	67
7	66	70	61	61	65	53	49	48	60	69

All figures are percentages

1 = Higher service; 2 = Lower service; 3 = Routine non-manual; 4 = Petty bourgeoisie; 5 = Foreman and technicians; 6 = Skilled working class; 7 = Unskilled working class.

Source: Evans, Heath and Payne (1999), 90.

up (Hobsbawm, 1981). Full employment caused real wages to rise, allowing skilled and semi-skilled workers to purchase goods and services that were once the preserve of middle-class consumers, the most significant of which was a home. In the 1950s, less than one-third of the housing stock in England and Wales was owner-occupied; by the 1990s the proportion had more than doubled. Some of the barriers that had once distinguished manual from non-manual employees were being raised.

Early claims that 'affluent' workers would actually become middle class proved misplaced. No matter how well-off they became manual workers remained defined by how they earned their living, and this still separated them from those who relied on non-manual skills. Fragmentation nonetheless still had important political consequences as such workers became more 'instrumental' in their view of politics. If they had ever done so, better-off workers ceased to look on Labour as the 'natural' expression of their group loyalty. Instead, they supported the party only if it was thought to best represent their individual interests. This meant Labour could still win their support, but so could the Conservatives and Liberals (Goldthorpe *et al.*, 1968).

Uneven economic development increased distinctions within the working class after the 1950s. Newer industries based in England's Southeast and West Midlands expanded and employees saw their incomes rise; in contrast, older industries located in the English north, Scotland and South Wales contracted. Thatcherite policies exacerbated division during the 1980s by increasing unemployment. By this time, well-paid workers employed in the private sector saw their interests as conflicting with those working in the public sector. They became conscious that their taxes paid public employees' wages and, when the latter group went on strike, the former not only endured disrupted services but also footed the bill after a settlement had been reached.

Working-class fragmentation is seen to be one of the factors behind a more general 'dealignment' or weakening of political partisanship apparently evident since the 1960s (Crewe and Sarlvik, 1987). Thus, while at the 1951 General Election Labour and the Conservatives together captured 97 per cent of votes cast, by 1992 they could secure only 76 per cent. If this process hurt both parties, Labour nonetheless suffered the most.

The Party's Impact

According to the above schema, parties can do no more than tinker with the consequences of social change. Yet, while the nature of society plays an important role in determining the ground for party competition, the extent to which it is the first and final influence on political fortunes has been questioned (Dunleavy and Husbands, 1985; Heath *et al.*, 1991; Lawrence and Taylor, 1997). Thus, it has been claimed that government, business, the media and the parties themselves can structure political perceptions. According to this perspective, society generates a potential that parties can exploit or squander.

Therefore, if Labour was the victim of social change, it was also responsible for its own difficulties. This claim was substantiated by Herbert Kitschelt's analysis of how eleven European social democratic parties responded to change. Kitschelt established that working-class decline did not have to be followed by the left's demise, for if some parties prospered others did not. Significantly, of those studied Labour performed the worst. While circumstances varied between countries, Kitschelt identified party organization and discourse (or ideology) as the most important influences on electoral fortunes. In particular, he stressed how far political traditions identified 'acceptable arguments and ideas [which] shape the internal discourse in political parties and limit the range of strategic choices when parties are faced with new challenges'. Indeed, 'ideas are critical for explaining the direction in which parties diverge' from what he described as 'rational' vote-maximizing strategies. In fact, Kitschelt suggested that Labour provided the 'hardest evidence for the autonomous causal impact of ideas on party strategy'. As will be outlined in the next chapter, during the 1970s and early 1980s the Labour leadership's autonomy was challenged by the party's keenest exponents of socialist rhetoric who followed a strategy Kitschelt considered 'manifestly irrational' if winning elections was the object (Kitschelt, 1994, 181, 254–5, 271–2).

A Contested Strategy

Thus, while social and economic change altered the grounds for electoral competition, change by itself did not dictate the political consequences: Labour's response was critical. Yet party members reacted to its post-war predicament by cohering around one of two contrasting approaches, described by political scientists as 'accommodation' or 'strategy' (Dunleary with Ward, 1991).

The leadership had long favoured a 'catch-all' strategy that aimed to entrench support in the working class while extending it amongst the middle class. This implied what appeared to be a preference-accommodating approach, but it was based on the assumption that to alter voters' minds the party first had to take their concerns seriously. This was the rationale, for what is here described as an accommodate-to-shape strategy, that derived from a particular view of the party's ultimate purpose, for the leadership did not consider Labour to be an exclusively working-class party as they hoped to eventually promote class cooperation. In contrast, those who saw the party as the political expression of the working class favoured focusing on trade union concerns, which they considered required extending the state's economic role. As a result, they advocated a 'preference-shaping' approach to sceptical voters, believing Labour lacked support only when its leaders failed to advance a radical case.

As soon as the leadership decided Labour should become independent of the Liberals, they exhibited what has been described as 'a frank appreciation of psephology' (Tiratsoo, 2000, 295–6). They realized that Labour could not form a government on the basis of working-class support alone; thus, like their European peers, party strategists courted women, white-collar workers and professionals, as well as those living in the countryside. Subsequently, under Ramsay MacDonald, Labour sought the mantle of 'respectability' to win over not just the middle class but doubtful working-class voters (Thorpe, 2001, 49–57). This was also consistent with the Labour leader's belief that socialism was the means by which the classes would be reconciled: even at this stage Labour presented itself as the party of the whole nation (MacDonald, 1929, 305–7; McKibbin, 1990, 51–6).

After MacDonald's departure, Labour continued to assert that it stood for the interests of all classes (Jeffery, 1989). Vindicating this approach, the party won its first Commons majority in 1945 on the basis of a hitherto unprecedented proportion of working-class and middle-class votes, which helped secure numerous socially-mixed marginal constituencies. While most Labour support came from the manual working class, the party appealed to the 'people' as a whole. So far as its rhetoric was concerned, the main cleavage in society was not one dictated by class but by a mixture of individual virtue and utility: this pitched 'productive workers' against a 'non-productive' minority (Fielding, 1992, 143–5). Labour employed the same device when Wilson brought the party back to power in the mid-1960s. Wilson claimed the party would develop the capacities of those 'who earn money by useful service to the community' and displace others who controlled the economy on the basis of family connections rather than ability (Fielding, 1993, 39–40). Once again, class difference was not the main basis of the party's propaganda: it appealed to those from a variety of backgrounds whose hard work and talent were denied proper reward.

The party's post-war revisionists therefore only reformulated the leadership's dominant strategy when they stressed at the start of the 1950s that the party had to focus on middle-class 'floating voters'. According to the manifesto of their pressure group, the Campaign for Democratic Socialism, Labour 'should be a broadly-based national party of all the people' even if circumstances meant it must nonetheless 'be based predominantly on working people' (Fielding, 1997c, 61–2). Post-war social change made this strategy appear more relevant than ever as the number of floating voters increased. According to Anthony Crosland, however, appealing to middle-class voters did not mean Labour should merely ask them what they wanted and then deliver it 'regardless of principle'; the party instead should try to understand the deeper determinants of their views and assess how it 'might put itself into a better rapport with them'. Labour, Crosland argued, could be 'populist' without abandoning its established outlook (Crosland, 1962, 144; Crosland, 1974, 96–102).

Not all members endorsed this strategy. Socially conservative trade unions and politically radical – if often middle-class – activists were uncomfortable appealing to the suburbs. As early as 1923 officials warned members:

DON'T denounce as parasites all who do not happen to be manual workers. The idea that those who don the black coat and high collar are 'snobs' is a mistake. To be well dressed, is, to one class of the community, as essential as the bag of tools and the overall to another. (Tiratsoo, 2000, 296)

Yet many continued to dismiss the middle class as a whole as bulwarks of reaction (Wilkinson, 1935, 203–17). Moreover, while the national leadership appealed to the nation, in many industrial constituencies Labour assumed the identity of a party not of just of one class, but of one union. If they endorsed a catch-all strategy because it promised to win power, most union leaders disliked many of its implications.

From this viewpoint, the leadership's strategy appeared self-defeating. One prominent left-wing MP believed the Conservatives won in 1951 because they had secured the support of many working-class voters. This was due to such workers' 'confusion of mind' that was 'merely a reflection of the confusion into which we have allowed our own policy to fall'. He accused the leadership of advancing policies that were far too moderate: if the party was to regain power it needed to embrace a 'clear, simple Socialist policy' with common ownership at its heart (*Tribune*, 28 December 1951). As Ralph Miliband later warned, the more its leaders moderated Labour's programme to appeal to the 'middle ground', the more intolerant floating voters would become of party policy and so the further the leadership would have to amend it to win their support (Miliband, 1972, 348).

Defeat in 1970 gave advocates of this approach unprecedented influence, one that reached its zenith with the 1983 campaign. Labour was generally thought to have lost due to the defection of the working class, and activists blamed this on the Wilson government's attempt to placate suburban concerns and its neglect of union interests (Labour Party, 1970, 112–26). The party had to reset its course, reaffirm support for the unions and advocate more state control. The resulting strategy largely ignored public opinion: only after the National Executive Committee announced proposals to nationalize the most powerful 25 private companies did it commission a survey of attitudes and discover that even Labour supporters opposed the measures (Hatfield, 1978, 228–9). Yet those in charge of strategy believed that because they thought the policy right, compromise was unnecessary (Leonard, 1981, 47–53). As Tony Benn stated, the left was confident that 'if what we are saying gets through to the people at large it will win support'. They believed voters only thought Labour 'extreme' because it was described as such in the papers they read; once the leadership had advanced its policies with enthusiasm voters would soon change their minds (Benn, 1983, 6–7; *Tribune*, 10 June 1983; *The Guardian*, 20 June 1983).

Not all advocates of this preference-shaping strategy were so unwilling to take account of public opinion, but it is difficult to believe even they acted very prudently: it is also doubtful that this strategy shaped many preferences (Wickham-Jones, 1996, 189–92). Their strategy, designed to win back the party's lost working-class support by stressing its links with the unions and public ownership, actually helped to make the party's position even worse.

The Impact of Thatcherism

The 1983 election was but the most abject of four defeats suffered by Labour between 1979 and 1992. Many believed these were the result of a fundamental shift in popular values that saw voters move from collectivist to individualistic ways of thinking. Margaret Thatcher was widely regarded as the architect of this transformation.

What came to be described as Thatcherism promoted the belief that poverty was more the result of laziness than social circumstances, and that the comfortably off had achieved their position through hard work. Consequently, for government to tax the affluent to spend on the poor would not only fail to address the causes of poverty but also reduce the incentive to work. This would harm the economy because individual incentives were crucial to success. Thatcherism asserted that the country would only prosper under a free market system in which individuals were at liberty to pursue their self-interest. The aim of government should be to rid the country of impediments to this freedom, most especially public ownership, 'penal' rates of tax, high levels of public spending and strike-happy unions. The sense that individuals owed their first duty to themselves and their loved ones, and that they should expect little help from the state, was best summed up in Thatcher's claim that there was 'no such thing as society ... only individual men and women and ... families' (*Woman's Own*, 31 October 1987).

Observers were particularly impressed by Thatcher's apparent success in altering the views of many affluent working-class voters (Hall, 1983). It is indisputable that during the 1980s Labour's support amongst working-class voters in general and the skilled in particular slipped badly (see Table 4.2). Nonetheless, survey evidence suggests Thatcher failed to move opinion to the extent many thought. At the Conservatives' zenith in the late 1980s a majority of voters still believed, for example, that government should improve public services even if this meant tax increases (Crewe, 1988; Rentoul, 1989; Heath, Jowell and Curtice, 2001, 33–53).

This is not to say that the 1980s saw no change in attitudes, yet such a transformation was less striking and more uneven than supposed, while Thatcher's role was relatively unremarkable. It was obviously agreeable for the former Prime Minister to believe she had altered people's views. It was, however, also convenient for those critical of what they took to be the reassertion of preference-accommodation under Neil Kinnock to think this since, if the Conservatives had managed to shape preferences, there was no reason to believe Labour could not do the same. This view neglected the fact that many of the attributes associated with 1980s individualism had been evident well before Thatcher entered Downing Street. Popular hostility to nationalization had emerged in the late 1940s; the home-centred nature of affluent working-class life was obvious in the 1950s; and by the early 1970s skilled workers were already unwilling to pay more taxes to help the poor. Thatcher drew these strands together, but she did not create them. Still, if Thatcher acted merely as the conductor of public opinion, it did her party no harm. If support for the Conservatives during 1979–92 was never more than 44 per cent of votes cast, this was more than enough to win power four times.

It appears likely that Thatcher's electoral success was largely due to the fact that many voters believed her claim that there was 'no alternative' to her policies. Yet, this was as much Thatcher's responsibility as it was Labour's: the 'winter of discontent' reinforced perceptions that the party could not control the unions; Labour was divided on most of the crucial issues of the day; and, by demanding more public ownership, the left took the party in the direction least favoured by most voters (Heath, Jowell and Curtice, 2001, 54, 85–8). Moreover, when Labour tested opinion after 1983 the results indicated that those whose support the party needed most opposed party policy with the greatest vigour (Shaw, 1994, 185–6). More fundamentally, as Ivor Crewe pointed out, in contrast to Labour, the Conservatives were thought most 'fit to govern'. In accounting for their prolonged period in office the Conservatives' cohesion and purpose were more decisive than their ideology (Crewe, 1988, 44–9).

It is nonetheless likely that Thatcher's period in office had some impact on how voters thought about crucial issues. It is probable that a governing party asserting the superiority of individualistic values encouraged those holding similar opinions to become more confident and sway those of a less definite frame of mind. Moreover, by holding on to office for so long Thatcher pursued policies that might have been initially unpopular but over time gave every impression of working. If many voters did not approve of the privatization of certain industries in moral terms, they came to regard it as more efficacious than continued public ownership. In many ways, therefore, the success of Thatcherism was the product of voters' pragmatism: they were convinced it worked even if they doubted it was just. Labour, in contrast, may have been closer to the angels but its policies would have sent the country to the devil.

Responding to Thatcherism

Labour's response to Thatcherism has been criticized because many who pass judgement on party strategy after 1983 believe the Conservatives had aggressively reshaped voters' values and therefore they contend Labour should have responded in like manner; instead, they believe Kinnock followed a disciplined preference-accommodating strategy. For example, Labour did not try to persuade voters of the merits of the party's plans for increasing public ownership, but moved towards a qual-ified acceptance of privatization. This supposedly reduced the incentive of believers in public ownership to support Labour; it did not exploit uncertainties in voters' attitude to privatization; and it failed to impress those who considered the Conservatives more competent managers of the economy (Heffernan and Marqusee, 1992; Shaw, 1994, 167–99; Hay, 1999, 58–71, 92–103).

Labour's attitude towards Conservative policies was, however, not entirely determined by electoral considerations: few in the leadership now believed public ownership would solve the country's problems. Moreover, the means by which the party could have challenged these policies were limited. Labour's income was much less than that of the Conservatives, so it could not compete on equal terms. Thatcher also exploited the resources of government: television advertisements announcing the sale of shares in privatized industries promoted the policy. Much of the popular press was, in addition, virulently hostile to Labour: the biggest selling daily tabloid, the *Sun*, probably better advanced the Conservative cause than the party itself. Furthermore, the British economy boomed in the very areas where Labour needed to win votes most. These were not, therefore, the best conditions for the party to set about immediately shaping preferences.

In any case, it would wrong to conceive Kinnock's response as purely accommodating. If Labour wanted to lead the voters in a certain direc-tion it had first to find out where they were and then take them step-by-step towards its preferred position. It was no good straightaway seizing the high ground and exhorting voters to follow: this was the approach that led to 1983. Thus, on becoming leader, Kinnock stressed Labour had to appeal to voters in words 'attuned to' and 'in touch with their realities'. This undoubtedly entailed compromise, particularly as Labour needed to focus on those Kinnock described as the 'modern working class' who were defined by their 'upward social mobility, increased expectations and extended horizons'. Even former Benn allies recognized Labour had to attract more middle-class support (Labour Party, 1983, 30; *The Guardian*, 25 June 1987; Jones, 1996, 116). As Kinnock put it, Labour needed to appeal to such voters' 'enlightened self-interest' and persuade them that, for example, helping the less well-off would also help them (Benn, 1994, 494–5).

This was not just a case of altering party propaganda: it also implied policy changes. Kinnock's 1987 Policy Review therefore sought to reassure voters that Labour was economically capable by making its acceptance of the market more overt than hitherto. If, in trying to rebuild support, Labour's stress on its 'prudence' attenuated criticism of Thatcherism, the leadership calculated that there was a greater chance voters might take the party seriously.

The Lessons of 1992

Labour's 1992 manifesto promised to restore the value of child benefit and once more link the state pension to wages; these measures would have increased spending by £3 billion. To finance this, Labour wanted to raise the employees' ceiling on National Insurance (NI) contributions. This was a modest package, and one criticized by the left for its paucity of ambition. The Conservatives nonetheless transformed Labour's proposals into a threatening 'tax bombshell' that many thought scared off affluent voters who might otherwise have supported Kinnock.

The result of the 1992 campaign was therefore desperately disappointing: Labour's vote rose but remained lower than in 1979 (Heath, Jowell and Curtice, 1994). The Policy Review encouraged voters to see the party as less extreme than hitherto; indeed, on most policies Labour was closer to voter preferences than the Conservatives. Yet, despite being in the midst of a recession, John Major still won the support of 2½ million more voters than Kinnock. The main reason for Labour's failure was that it had not fully escaped its association with division, weakness and failure: the party was still not 'trusted'. This led voters to believe Conservative propaganda for, while an objective assessment of

Labour's plans indicated that 80 per cent of people would have been better off, one exit poll suggested only 30 per cent believed they would benefit.

Kinnock's successor as leader, John Smith, broadly adhered to the view that to win power Labour needed what was referred to as just 'one more heave'. The hope was that Smith's level-headed public character would encourage doubters to trust Labour next time. Under Smith the party nonetheless dropped its tax proposals and reassured voters it had no intention of raising revenue 'irresponsibly'. Further than this Smith was unwilling to go, and he appeared to hope that Conservative unpopularity would deliver a Labour victory. This strategy was criticized by Tony Blair and Gordon Brown, who believed Labour should embark on a more active attempt to improve its appeal amongst affluent voters.

So far as most strategists were concerned, Labour's fate remained in the hands of well-off skilled or semi-skilled manual workers and those employed in routine clerical occupations (people often categorized as belonging to social classes C1 and C2). If they had done well out of the 1980s, they were also vulnerable to economic instability. To discover why so many had stayed true to the Conservatives, the Fabian Society commissioned a survey of marginal constituencies in the south and midlands, amongst those who voted Conservative but had considered supporting Labour (Radice, 1992; Radice and Pollard, 1993 and 1994).

Such voters echoed many apparently Thatcherite assumptions, although how far they owed their views to Conservative propaganda is impossible to judge. Whatever their origin, these opinions were not fertile Labour ground. In particular, they denigrated the redistribution of wealth for rewarding the lazy and penalizing hard workers. Attitudes to redistribution, however, largely depended on whose incomes were to be affected but, if they were to be taxed and 'scroungers' – or the 'undeserving' poor – were to benefit, these voters opposed it. Pride in their own achievement, combined with an appreciation of how vulnerable this was, led to a visceral loathing of 'scroungers' long familiar to historians of the British working class.

If they rejected equality of outcome, the idea of 'opportunity for all' was strongly endorsed, although the latter concept was associated with the Conservatives. Overall, their basic moral disposition was summed up by the endorsement of the Thatcher-sounding statement that 'my only responsibility is to my family' (although many qualified this with support for the idea that 'I'll help someone else if I have something left over'). This ambiguity was also evident in attitudes to government spending. Despite scepticism about the efficacy of devoting more tax-payers' money to helping the poor, they wanted more money spent on health and education (although they were unwilling to pay for it themselves).

Crucially, such voters considered Labour less economically competent than the Conservatives. Thus all those included in the survey thought they would have been worse off under Labour's 1992 tax and spending plans, yet they claimed not to oppose raising income tax in principle (but considered it should be levied on those whose incomes were considerably higher than their own). Moreover, if they saw Labour as more 'caring' on welfare issues, the party was thought incapable of spending extra cash efficiently. Similarly, while supporting more education spending, they considered Labour policy ineffective: it was too 'liberal' and soft on 'standards'. Finally, these Conservative waverers perceived Labour as being opposed to their own interests as it allegedly most favoured the poor, gays and ethnic minorities. If Labour was also considered to exhibit a preference for the 'working class' this brought it no advantage because, while by most measures many of those surveyed were working class, they did not think of themselves in that way.

These opinions did not change much, even after sterling's enforced exit from the Exchange Rate Mechanism (ERM) in September 1992 and the numerous tax rises that followed, even though these damaged the Conservatives' reputation for competence. However, by the time the final survey was undertaken in the summer of 1994 some changes beneficial to Labour were noted. Respondents, for example, considered the party's relationship with the unions 'more sensible' after the passing of 'one member, one vote'; the party's policies also no longer seemed a matter of 'spend, spend, spend'.

The Birth of 'New' Labour

If by 1994 an increasing number of voters saw Labour in more positive terms, the party was not guaranteed a General Election victory. Immediately prior to Blair becoming leader, Labour performed well in both local and European Parliamentary elections. Some see these victories as evidence that 'New' Labour was unnecessary as the party already had the 1997 election in the bag. Yet these triumphs were mainly due to disenchanted Conservative voters staying at home; and, of those who changed allegiance, by far the greater number switched to the Liberal

Democrats rather than Labour (Heath, Jowell and Curtice, 2001, 102–3, 107). Under Smith, Labour did nonetheless enjoy a significant increase in support. The number of those claiming to identify with the Conservatives, as opposed to simply being prepared to vote for the party, fell dramatically between 1992 and 1994 and had only marginally recovered by 1997. In contrast, those willing to say they identified with Labour increased markedly in 1992–4 but rose little thereafter. This implies that the fundamental shift from Labour to Conservative, sufficient to see the former win in 1997, had mostly occurred prior to the declaration of 'New' Labour. However, it only suggests this: had Blair not become leader and followed his strategy, many of Labour's newly acquired identifiers may well have slipped back into the Conservative camp (Crewe and Thompson, 1999, 69).

If the evidence is ambiguous, so far as Blair and Brown were concerned at the time of Smith's death matters were very straightforward: to secure victory Labour could not afford to stand still and wait for disillusioned Conservatives to flock to it. It was not unreasonable to assume that Major's party would recover ground by the time of the forthcoming election. It was similarly sensible to believe his government would reverse many of its tax increases prior to the contest, while the shock of leaving the ERM would have abated. Indeed, leaving the ERM gave the economy a boost and it was expected the next election would be held during a boom. Moreover, few could have predicted Conservative divisions over Europe would have intensified as the election approached. Had politics taken a more predictable course, Blair and Brown's outlook would have seemed eminently sensible.

Blair's favoured strategy was outlined in the conclusion to the first Fabian survey written by the venerable revisionist Giles Radice in which he wrote that, if Labour was to secure more support among aspirational voters, it had to assume a 'new identity' (Radice, 1992, 14–24). In particular, the 'outdated' clause four had to be repealed. As such voters thought of themselves as individuals, so Labour should describe itself in a way that resonated with this outlook. It needed to do away with any sense of being a party linked to a particular interest group (most obviously the unions). Citing Blair's own response to 1992, Radice suggested Labour should associate itself with advancing the interests of individuals and oppose those 'vested interests' that stood in their way. Radice appeared to outline a radical preference-accommodating strategy that left no room for shaping. However, he claimed Labour did not need to abandon its key policies; indeed, it was only by adopting this course that the party could win support for such measures. Accordingly, by strongly identifying with the individual, Labour's case for collectivist measures should become more credible. The party's support for the public sector would no longer be tainted by voters' suspicion that it was motivated by the desire to help the poor at their expense. Instead, they might accept the argument that certain forms of collectivism were beneficial to all individuals, including themselves.

Blair concurred with analysis that took Labour's post-1983 strategy to its logical conclusion. As he told Labour's 1996 conference, the party lost in 1992 because suburban dwellers wishing to 'get on in life' believed Labour wanted to stop them (*The Daily Telegraph*, 2 October 1996). He aimed to persuade them otherwise. To do that, Blair determined he had to stress Labour's acceptance of much of the Thatcherite legacy. His overall message was, therefore, that Labour under his leadership offered 'a degree of continuity as well as change'; the party was 'safe' on the unions, tax and the economy (*The Daily Telegraph*, 18 March 1997).

Kinnock had offered as much, but his message had not got through. Blair therefore appreciated the need to dramatize Labour's transformation to draw attention to those changes that had occurred under his predecessor. Blair's own leadership had given the public a sense that Labour had changed, but he appreciated this required entrenchment. He therefore started to refer to Labour as 'New' Labour, a conceit so insidious even Conservatives used the term. Moreover, at his first conference as leader Blair called for the revision of clause four. By ridding Labour of this symbolic link with the past, Blair forced voters to reconsider further their negative view of his party.

Images and symbols were important but, to ram the message home, it was decided that emblematic policies also had to change. Thus after some debate, Blair and Brown agreed to change the party's position on 'tax and spend'. Brown promised a Labour government would not increase the basic rate of income tax, increase its top limit or raise Value Added Tax. He also pledged to follow Conservative spending plans for his first two years as Chancellor. Significantly, the only tax-raising measure included in Labour's programme was one to be levied on privatized companies: this suggested Blair was not against tax increases, just unpopular tax increases.

The party altered its approach on other issues – in particular education and crime – so they reflected the more conservative outlook of target voters. Some of this implied a change of policy; the rest was just words. The education spokesperson, David Blunkett, talked of improving 'standards' in schools and even endorsed (but subsequently did nothing to advance) the reintroduction of uniforms. Jack Straw, who shadowed the Home Secretary, promoted curfews for the young, which in the end came to very little. He also made newspaper headlines by apparently attacking street beggars, although his speeches were actually sympathetic to their plight.

Few internal organizational reforms were introduced, as much had already been done. However, like his predecessors, Blair was alert to the need to refute charges that the unions controlled Labour. To that end, he repeatedly stated that, if elected, he would treat the unions on the basis of 'fairness not favours', and left to it to junior colleagues to imply he favoured severing the party's union link. The Labour leader similarly stressed his admiration for the market and sought the approval of business leaders. Indeed, Labour's first television broadcast of the 1997 campaign comprised a series of endorsements from a variety of entrepreneurs. Matthew Taylor, one of those responsible for applying this strategy, later revealed the party did this believing that knowing Labour was 'trusted by millionaire businessmen' impressed even the poorest of voters (*The Observer*, 2 April 2000).

In order to communicate his message more effectively Blair's press officer, Alastair Campbell, improved relations with those who owned the popular press, especially Rupert Murdoch, whose *Sun* counted as readers a sizeable slice of Labour's target voters. His approval was sought in the knowledge that (as Campbell put it) they were dealing with a man who 'basically wants to do us in' if it were possible. Blair also realized the likes of Murdoch supported him only because they believed he would form a harmless interregnum that would allow the Conservatives to sort out their affairs in Opposition (*The Guardian*, 17 February 1997; Ashdown, 2000, 357, 384). To the surprise of many, in the first week of the 1997 campaign, *The Sun* went so far as to call on its readers to support Blair.

By the time Major announced the date of the 1997 election, therefore, 'New' Labour had closed down most of the usual avenues of Conservative criticism months, if not years, before. Major's party still attacked Labour's proposal to enable workers to force employers to recognize their representation by a trade union if they voted for it yet, as the self-proclaimed 'entrepreneur's champion', Blair prevented this issue developing too far. The Conservatives also questioned Labour's commitment to follow their spending plans if this meant privatizing state assets. Labour dealt with this matter by bluntly arguing the party was now not tied to either state or private ownership: what mattered was what worked.

Labour's 'Landslide' Assessed

The dramatic reversal in party fortunes brought about by the 1997 election suggested it had been a special kind of contest. The swing from Conservative to Labour was 10.3 per cent, the biggest since 1945, while Blair's Commons majority was the largest for any party since 1935 and more than Labour had ever enjoyed. Furthermore, Labour could rightfully again describe itself as the 'People's Party': its unprecedented inroad into the middle-class vote was matched by levels of support within the working class not seen since the 1960s (see Table 4.2). What is more, according to Benn and others, Labour's landslide 'represented the wholesale rejection of the crude capitalist philosophy associated with Margaret Thatcher' (*Tribune*, 9 May 1997).

Closer inspection suggests Labour's success is better viewed more prosaically. The party's Commons majority was the product of a skewed electoral system: in return for 44.4 per cent of votes, Labour was rewarded with 65.2 per cent of seats. Even more soberingly, as turn-out fell to 71.2 per cent, Blair's party only enjoyed the active support of 30.8 per cent of those entitled to vote. That the result represented the voters' rejection of Thatcherism also requires qualification. Labour's victory was principally based on a disciplined focus on the concerns of Middle England: if the party had a mandate for change, it was for 'safe' change. As the Blair loyalist, Margaret Hodge, conceded, Labour politicians fought shy of discussing equality, for example, because they worried voters would see it 'either as being steeped in political correctness or as simply taxing them', and so 'stood back from our traditional political terrain' (Hodge, 2000, 34). Indeed, the party's policies made a sharp shift to the right between 1994 and 1997 so that, if Labour remained somewhat to the left of the Conservatives, it was actually positioned between them and the Liberal Democrats (Budge, 1999). As a result, Labour had moved much closer to the preferences of the notional 'median voter' on all the key issues of the day (Pattie, 2001, 41–7). However, it was Labour that had shifted position rather than the voters.

If voters had become critical of the Conservatives, their views remained inchoate as the fear of alienating potential supporters prevented Labour from giving them a strong lead (Crouch, 1999, 70–1). Thus, if it had won their votes, Blair's party won few hearts amongst the waverers: in 1997 their votes were enough. Focus groups convened by numerous national newspapers during the campaign confirmed the shallow nature of the party's support. NOP discovered, for example, that 46 per cent of those polled agreed with the statement 'I'm not enthusiastic about them [Labour] but they can't be worse than the Tories.' As a result, informed analysis suggested that Labour's support was especially vulnerable to disintegration once Blair had entered Downing Street (Norris and Evans, 1999, 271; Crewe, 2001, 71).

Some blamed Blair's pre-election strategy for this state of affairs. Conservative unpopularity had been such that 'New' Labour could have done more than simply offer watered-down Thatcherism. Moreover, by being so accommodating to the sensibilities of aspirational voters, Labour had probably given them added legitimacy. If, for instance, Blair had made the case to raise the top rate of income tax even by a modest amount he might have altered preconceptions and made Labour's vote more positive, and so more solid. Radice suggested that if Labour reinvented itself it could renew support for core policies: 'accommodate in order to shape' was his strategy, yet so rigorous had been 'New' Labour's accommodation of Middle England's outlook that any subsequent reshaping would be extremely difficult.

Blair countered such criticism by referring to the need to build a 'radical centre', a concept first introduced to Britain by Roy Jenkins as he prepared to establish the Social Democratic Party. Significantly, this was originally an American term used to characterize the position of affluent white working-class voters who had abandoned the Democrats for being (in their eyes) too left wing in favour of the more right-wing Republicans (Wallace, 1976). Thus, Blair stated, if 'you want to push through the kind of radical changes we're talking about, you have to drive it from the centre'. By this he meant Labour had to renew its appeal to Conservative waverers whose opinions many in the party might disparage, because without them the party could not win office. This was an apparently pragmatic electoral tactic, the merits of which many party members could appreciate. They were, however, disturbed when Blair went further and suggested these new policies were 'not just the route to power', they were actually 'right' as well (*The Guardian*, 29 September 1996 and 25 April 1997).

Nevertheless, one adviser claimed that if the Labour leader sometimes gave away 'a huge amount in language' he usually conceded 'almost nothing in terms of policy' (Draper, 1997, 78). For, other occasions, Blair intimated he adhered to the accommodate-to-shape strategy. Thus he suggested that by keeping to the exceptionally modest 1997 manifesto, his government could show it was trustworthy. As Blair stated in 1999, if people believed Labour was a 'competent economic manager', they would 'allow you to spend more money because they'll believe you'll spend it wisely and sensibly (*The Guardian*, 25 September 1999).

Accordingly, having reached this point, Blair assured his listeners he would then turn to voters and say: 'this is the direction, and we want to go further' (*The Guardian*, 1 May 1997). Prior to winning power such considerations were left vague: if Blair intended to move from mainly accommodating preferences to actually shaping them, he could not predict when this second stage would begin. It would also be self-defeating to admit openly that this was his strategy. Given some of his comments, a number in Blair's party nonetheless wondered if their leader's strategy had a second stage.

Maintaining the Coalition

If Blair was to secure a second full term he needed to keep Middle England and Labour's heartlands happy, but creating a level of support across the classes sufficient to give it power was a trick that had taken Labour 30 years to repeat; maintaining it would be no easier. In 1997 many voters had one object that kept them united and that was to be rid of the Conservatives; at the next election Blair would need something more positive to offer. Unfortunately, the interests of Middle England and Labour's heartlands were popularly believed to conflict. To give the former what they were said to want – low taxes and a balanced budget – was the opposite of what the heartlands were assumed to desire. The dominant view held that satisfying the various elements constituting the party's 1997 coalition would be a zero-sum game: for one group to win, the other had to lose. This matter was undoubtedly complicated further by the fact that those individuals conventionally categorized as Middle England were themselves divided along lines of occupation and gender and so, taken together, their social and political profile was indistinct at best (Crouch, 1999, 76–83). Balancing this confusing array of actual and perceived interests would therefore require astute political skills.

Labour's initial objective was to reassure the numerically decisive residents of Middle England that the party was as good as its word: Blair and Brown could manage the economy, stay within Conservative spending plans and not raise income tax. This was critical as Middle Englanders were the least committed of Labour voters. Thus, in the autumn of 1997, while the government could have abandoned a proposed Conservative cut in single-parent benefit and remained within spending limits, Blair decided to go ahead as the cut was meant to appeal to Middle England's social and fiscal conservatism. Perhaps as a result, the party's opinion poll lead increased markedly with the majority of Labour's post-election converts coming from the middle class (*The Observer*, 26 April 1998). Yet, if commentators praised Labour's success in extending its support, they criticized Blair's continuing reluctance to lead adherents away from Thatcherism (*The Guardian*, 15 January 1999).

The concerns of Middle England certainly coloured how certain government policies were presented and could determine their content. Echoing Blair's pre-1997 ambiguity, if this approach appeared merely pragmatic, some ministers actually seemed to believe in what they were saying and doing. Given the views exposed by the earlier Fabian surveys, it is not surprising that welfare and the problem of poverty brought this lack of clarity into particular focus. Thus Blair claimed that 'matching opportunity and responsibility' – the hallmark of his approach to welfare reform – was 'the only way to obtain consent from the public to fund the welfare state' (Oppenheim, 2001, 79). The Prime Minister knew he had to address two audiences when discussing poverty: the poor and those who spoke for them, as well as sceptical tax-payers. Thus he stressed the hidden costs of poverty – such as rising crime – to persuade affluent voters it was to their advantage that government tackled the issue. Like Kinnock, Blair hoped to appeal to their enlightened self-interest. Yet the punitive rhetoric employed by other Labour speakers only reinforced hostility to 'scroungers' and prevented the government building support for poverty reduction (Benn, 2000, 311–12; Howarth, 2001, 9). More typically, however, the government addressed poverty without drawing voters' attention to its policies: many argued however that doing 'good by stealth' left unchallenged some of Thatcherism's basic tenets (*The Guardian*, 15 February 1999).

Finding the Right Language

The importance of discovering a rhetoric that resonated with all members of 'New' Labour's coalition was more than a question of presentation. If successful, such a language could reshape how voters saw their own interests and enable the government to pursue policies they might otherwise have opposed. In Opposition, the party used a language that stressed its novelty and modernity but which was less appropriate once in office. Labour now needed to restructure how voters thought of themselves and their relationship to society (Marquand, 1998, 7–9).

The Prime Minister initially hoped the Third Way would achieve this end. However, the various policies identified with the Third Way did not enjoy consistent support from the same groups – what the working class liked, the middle class did not and vice versa – so it failed to give the coalition a greater sense of unity (Bromley and Curtice, 1999; Hills and Lelkes, 1999). Indeed, the very concept of the Third Way was to many in Middle England, as Blair's influential adviser Philip Gould noted, 'confusing and abstract'. On the other hand, some (such as the moderate left-wing junior minister, Peter Hain) complained of the lack of a language that connected with the heartlands (*The Independent*, 13 July 2000; BBC website, 21 October 2000). Instead of mobilizing them behind a common outlook, the Third Way appeared only to unite voters in confusion.

The Prime Minister attempted to find another means of giving his coalition a sense of cohesion. Thus in 1999 he sought to construct a new cleavage for the Millennium in which the 'forces of conservatism' based on 'privilege, class or background' were arrayed against those of 'progress' adhering to 'the equal worth of all'. On the former side were 'the cynics, the elites, the establishment'; on the latter, 'the forces of modernity and justice', those 'who believe in a society of equality of opportunity and responsibility' and 'who have the courage to change'. Deeming the class war over, Blair's new cleavage was dichotomized by the 'struggle for true equality' (*The Guardian*, 29 September 1999).

Blair echoed Labour's earlier efforts to pitch the 'useful people' against an indolent and privileged elite. In these instances rhetoric only imperfectly drew together disparate interests: Blair's definition of 'conservatism', in contrast, actually cut across the coalition he hoped to sustain. If the dividing line he sought to construct was, as the junior minister Charles Clarke put it, between 'those who seek change and those who oppose it', this found members of Labour's coalition on different sides of the rift (Clarke, 2000, 12). In particular, the Prime Minister attacked the 'conservatism' of public-sector workers who opposed his version of 'progress' (*The Guardian*, 21 October 1999). Moreover, at this stage it was not clear how Blair proposed to advance 'true equality', or what that term meant.

The Heartlands

As Wilson's fate in 1970 indicated, Labour could go too far in assuaging middle-class interests if these were perceived to be at the expense of the working class. Labour's long recovery from 1983 was based on the assumption that manual workers would remain loyal even though policy was retuned to appeal to others; yet party analysts suggested as early as

1992 that working-class voters were losing the incentive to support Labour (Shaw, 1994, 195).

Staggeringly low turn-outs at elections held in working-class areas were taken to indicate that those who had remained faithful to the party during the 1980s were deeply disappointed by Blair's government. Disenchantment was especially evident in the 1999 European Parliamentary elections, which saw 80 per cent of those entitled to vote remain at home, a disproportionate number of whom were formerly loyal Labour supporters. As a result, whereas Blair's party polled 28 per cent, William Hague's Conservatives took 36 per cent of votes cast. Elections for the Welsh Assembly and Scottish Parliament held at the same time also saw Labour fail to impress. Commentators speculated that Labour's coalition was beginning to break up: while extending its grip on the middle class, the party was losing working-class support (*The Observer*, 23 June 1999).

Concern that 'New' Labour had gone too far was brought to a head with the resignation in January 2000 of the previously loyal junior defence minister, Peter Kilfoyle. On leaving office, Kilfoyle promised to act as the government's 'critical friend' and in that capacity he would oppose tax cuts and support more spending on public services. Kilfoyle's disenchantment with the government's pursuit of southern middle-class voters, at the apparent expense of Labour's core vote, reflected that of many others. Even before 1997, however, Kilfoyle had warned against taking working-class voters for granted and attacked what he described as Mandelson's 'palpable contempt' for the poor (*Tribune*, 8 March and 9 September 1996). It is doubtful many 'New' Labour strategists took Kilfoyle's views too seriously before 1997; however, after 1999, the prospect of working-class abstention at the next General Election could not be so lightly dismissed.

Many Labour members agreed with Kilfoyle's claim that, in its third year in office, 'New' Labour had become a pejorative term in its heartlands. Labour, he asserted, required 'a quite distinct purpose' compared with that of its opponents so it could remobilize its established supporters (BBC website, 31 January 2000; *The Guardian*, 31 January 2000 and 1 February 2000; *The Daily Telegraph*, 5 February 2000). These thoughts were echoed, albeit from a different perspective, by Gould in a confidential memorandum written to the Prime Minister. He stated that the 'New Labour brand' had been 'badly contaminated' and was 'the object of constant criticism and, even worse, ridicule': it consequently needed to be 're-invented' (BBC website, 19 July 2000).

Blair responded by claiming that the 'whole country is our core constituency' and that if the heartlands were to be helped then votes had to be won in Middle England (BBC website, 6 February 2000). Thus, to choose between the interests of one or the other was, according to numerous 'New' Labour supporters a 'false choice' (Bradshaw, 2000). As Blair stated: 'Everyone in this country wants decent schools for our children [and] good health care when we are sick' (*The Guardian*, 7 April 2000). This particular insight would become the cornerstone of Labour's strategy to secure re-election.

In any case, survey evidence suggested that Labour's coalition was not as divided as many assumed. On key issues such as redistribution, public spending and taxation, voters in the middle and working classes enjoyed a level of agreement greater than that indicated by Kilfoyle. If on these matters working-class respondents were more to the left than those in the middle class, the difference was less than acute. Such voters were actually more at odds over social issues, such as the anti-gay Section 28 and whether asylum seekers should be allowed to remain in the country. As in the past, broadly speaking, working-class voters were more socially conservative whereas those in the middle class were more liberal (Evans, 2000). The charge that Labour's allegedly socially conservative agenda was designed to appeal to Middle England therefore seems ill-founded (Toynbee and Walker, 2001, 153–79). If anything, it was more attractive to Labour's core voters.

Early in the government's life, the Home Secretary Jack Straw had seen building more prisons and maintaining police numbers as vital to Labour's re-election prospects (Jones, J., 1999, 204–5). Like the economy, law and order had once been considered a Conservative preserve. Unlike the economy, Hague hoped to regain the initiative on the issue and made populist noises that won the enthusiastic endorsement of the *The Daily Mail*. That Labour was not going to let the Conservatives recapture the issue was made plain in the Queen's Speech delivered in December 2000, which initiated the last parliamentary session prior to the 2001 election. Containing four crime bills, this was seen as Labour's last attempt to appear tough on 'yob culture' before the campaign began. Despite the populist aspect of its social agenda, Labour also exhibited more progressive instincts: the government tried to revoke Section 28, only to be defeated by the inveterate hostility of the House of Lords.

A Change in Emphasis

Some observers feel that mid-way through his term in office the Prime Minister underwent a conversion in favour of increasing funding to the public services in preference to further tax cuts. His insight into how badly under-resourced were the likes of health and education supposedly led him to return to a modified version of 'Old' Labour's alleged obsession with 'tax and spend' (*The Independent on Sunday*, 26 November 2000; *New Statesman*, 27 November 2000). It is, however, much more likely that Blair and Brown entered government with their minds already set on painstakingly challenging Thatcher's tax-cutting agenda. Yet, if it was strategy rather than events that underpinned 'New' Labour's change of emphasis, then the latter would still dictate when the government felt it could make its intentions obvious.

Labour's 1997 manifesto certainly did its best to echo key voters' concerns about public spending. In particular, it criticized the 'myth' that 'the solution to every problem is increased spending', and described the level of public spending as 'no longer the best measure of the effectiveness of government action' (Labour Party, 1997c, 11–12). Thus during the government's first two years ministers appeared to make a virtue of not spending taxpayers' money. This changed towards the end of 1999 when Blair suggested Labour would enter the next election campaign committed to substantially increasing spending on public services (*The Times*, 2 September 1999). As will be indicated in Chapter 6, Labour's economic measures had met with widespread approval while it enjoyed the consequences of continued expansion. Labour was now trusted to run the economy, and it had the money to increase spending should it want to. Moreover, the electorate – not just the heartlands but also Middle England – was increasingly disconcerted by the parlous state of public services. Finally, while raising spending was popular, it would also throw the Conservative Opposition into relief as Hague was committed to cutting taxes.

Brown's March 2000 Budget signalled that the government intended partially to reverse the Thatcherite agenda by promising 'better public services for the many, not tax cuts for the few' (*The Observer*, 26 March 2000). The Chancellor's intention was made manifest when he unveiled the comprehensive spending review in July 2000. This included plans to spend an extra £43 billion on those services favoured by the public – health, education, transport and the police – over the next three years. Thereafter, just as he had once praised low spending, Blair highlighted the merits of higher spending (or 'investment', as he described it). Indeed, in November 2000 the Prime Minister claimed 'we are in a new era' in which government could tackle the destructive consequences of the Thatcher years, the most salient of which was 'chronic underinvestment'. Lack of spending, he now claimed, was the main reason for most of the problems experienced in the public sector (*The Guardian*, 23 and 27 November 2000).

The nature of the government's radicalism was nonetheless circumscribed: in particular, higher expenditure was not to be financed through raising income tax. In 1997 Labour promised not to raise income tax so as 'to encourage work and reward effort', the implication being that to increase personal taxation would undermine these qualities (Labour Party, 1997c, 12). In office the Chancellor did, however, raise taxes, not just through his 'windfall' levy on the privatized industries but through numerous consumption taxes (most famously on petrol); these were dubbed 'stealth taxes' because they were designed to go unnoticed. Ministers were sensitive to the charge that the Chancellor had increased the share taken by tax from the Gross Domestic Product. However, at the same time as Blair declared spending would increase, they conceded that the tax 'burden' had indeed risen since 1997. If it was happy to announce more spending, the government nonetheless remained shy of talking about tax, which after all was the means of paying for that spending (*The Guardian*, 5 November 1999 and 15 March 2000). Blair nevertheless claimed that government could 'invest in the future' without 'over-taxing people' (*The Independent on Sunday*, 24 September 2000).

What Did the People Want?

'New' Labour's cautious treatment of taxation was based on its perception of the public's attitude to the subject. The ubiquitous Fabian Society conducted an in-depth survey into what the public thought during the weeks following the government's announcement of higher spending which helped explain its sensitive handling of the issue (Hedges and Bromley, 2001).

According to the survey, most people thought Britain an 'overtaxed nation' and, even when it was pointed out that comparatively taxes were low, many simply refused to believe the evidence. Despite thinking taxes had increased recently, public services were widely regarded to have declined in quality; those surveyed sensed they were not getting 'value for money'. If there was some recognition that these services were under-resourced, this was off-set by the belief that inefficiency was rife. It was possible, therefore, that the public could be persuaded to support increases in income tax, but only if they believed the extra revenue would be spent effectively. This would be no easy task because few trusted politicians with their cash. Moreover, those favouring raising income tax did so on the understanding it would only affect the 'really rich': few wanted their own taxes increased. There was, however, little demand to cut taxes: when asked if government should spend more on the public services or cut taxes, 80 per cent favoured more spending. Yet the public was only in favour of raising taxes if they would pay for certain services: many resented spending on most welfare benefits which they thought supported 'scroungers', asylum seekers or other members of the 'undeserving' poor.

The Fabian Society's Commission on Taxation and Citizenship, the body that had commissioned this survey, believed it indicated that Labour could challenge popular views on tax (Commission on Taxation and Citizenship, 2001). If the public was presently sceptical about the utility of extra taxation, opinion was dynamic. However, government had to become more open about the merits of higher taxation and altering how some taxes were raised, in particular making the link between tax and spending more obvious through 'hypothecation'. This latter proposal would explicitly link revenue-raising with spending on particular services. More immediately, the Commission believed Labour could increase the top rate of income tax from 40 to 50 per cent for those on £100,000, a measure that would raise £3 billion and adversely affect only about 200,000 people.

Tax and the 2001 Campaign

As the unprecedented dip in Labour's opinion poll rating during the petrol tax protests of September 2000 indicated, taxation remained a contentious topic. The public endorsed disruptive actions undertaken by lorry drivers to give weight to their demand for cuts in petrol tax. As Brown was forced to concede ground on this issue, the eve of a General Election campaign did not appear the best moment to consider raising income tax.

In fact, despite the urgings of the Fabians, the Prime Minister reiterated his 1997 pledge not to raise income tax. The motives for Blair's insistence remain obscure. It is possible he decided that in principle income tax should rise no further. However, it is equally likely that, in light of the unsettled nature of public opinion, Blair calculated that the time was not yet right to tackle the issue. If Labour had convinced voters it was economically competent, they still thought public services inefficient. For selfish reasons the electorate wanted more money spent on health and education but remained sceptical about financing improvements personally. However, once voters could see that extra spending improved efficiency, they might be susceptible to the argument that increasing income tax would take the process a stage further.

As a result Labour's 2001 election campaign was curiously defensive (Fielding, 2002). Thus, when the Conservatives claimed there was a 'black hole' in Brown's financial plans, the party's response was uncertain. Conservatives asserted that if the Chancellor wanted to invest in public services ahead of economic growth after the next Labour government's first three years, he would either have to increase taxes or reduce spending. An uneasy Brown implied he would follow the latter course, but made no definitive statement.

Hague's party then focused on Brown's plans for NI. Labour's 1992 campaign had come unstuck when the Conservatives translated its proposed abolition of the ceiling on NI into a 'tax bombshell'. To avoid a repeat, in 1997 Brown promised to maintain the NI ceiling. The Conservatives claimed that one of the few means by which Brown could fill the notional 'black hole' during a second term was by abolishing it. As Labour's manifesto did not promise to maintain the limit, they alleged Brown wanted to get rid of it and so adversely affect 4 million members of Middle England. This was a clear attempt to evoke the 1992 'bombshell': *The Daily Mail* even produced a front-page headline that referred to Brown's 'Ticking NI Timebomb'. Afraid of the controversy's impact, Brown dissembled but did not explicitly deny Labour would abolish the NI ceiling.

Despite the Chancellor's fears, there was little evidence that Conservative attacks had any effect (*The Sunday Times* and *The Sunday Telegraph*, 27 May 2001). In any case, quite a number of voters now appeared to believe that, whatever Brown might say, taxes would go up under a second Labour government. What the public really resented was the way Brown had raised taxes through 'stealth', and not necessarily the fact that the overall tax 'burden' had increased (*The Daily Telegraph*, 11 May 2001; *The Sunday Telegraph*, 13 May 2001). It seemed that the public was now prepared to countenance an increase in tax because they believed Labour would spend the money wisely, yet Brown and Blair simply did not trust such evidence and not all survey data pointed in one direction. 'New' Labour's leaders recalled that, during the 1980s, opinion polls regularly suggested that the public wanted higher taxes in return for better services, but when general elections came around they voted for tax cuts.

Public Services: The New Agenda?

If guarded in relation to tax rises, 'New' Labour had become less nervous about higher spending. Indeed, the need to invest in the public services was now the major point of contrast between Labour and the Conservatives and lay at the heart of Blair's attempt to lead his 1997 coalition beyond Thatcherism.

As the Prime Minister conceded, in 1997 Labour's had been a largely negative mandate but in 2001 he wanted to 'win a mandate for change on our own terms' (Fielding, 2002). Blair sought the means to encapsulate 'New' Labour's purpose in terms that would appeal to all members of the coalition that had brought the party to power. For this purpose, the Third Way and the 'forces of conservatism' speech had been cast aside: Blair's focus on the need for public service investment now promised to imbue his rhetorical labours with a tangible quality they had previously lacked.

During the campaign the Prime Minister delivered a series of keynote speeches in which he hoped to establish a 'radical, modern social democratic' agenda for the second term. 'New' Labour's 'big idea', Blair revealed, was 'the development of human potential, the belief that there is talent and ability and caring in each individual that often lies unnurtured or discouraged'. Blair claimed to be beginning to 'exorcize the old Tory fatalism ... that extra spending was money down the drain'. The Prime Minister also criticized Thatcherism for its lack of 'compassion' and 'selfish individualism which failed to acknowledge the vital role of society in helping individuals to succeed'. In contrast, Labour wanted to establish a society 'in which everybody gets the chance to succeed'. To do this a Labour government would 'break down every barrier, every impediment', for 'no vested interest, public or private' should prevent any individual from developing his or her potential. Blair admitted that in its first term his government had only gone part of the way to achieving this end. Economic stability was not an end in itself but only the 'foundation' of progress. The specific means of manifesting Labour's 'big idea' was then to be 'sustained investment and far-reaching reform in our public services', for without this Labour would be unable to provide 'genuine opportunity for all'.

While Blair stated that 'inadequate investment and poor standards' went 'hand-in-hand', extra investment would not by itself improve public services. There also had to be 'real reform' of how these services were managed and delivered, in which there would be 'no predisposition towards public or private' provision. In particular, health and education had to be rebuilt 'around consumers'. As the Prime Minister reiterated: 'pupils do not exist for state schools; but state schools for pupils', and the 'patient doesn't exist for the NHS, but the NHS for the patient'.

Sometimes the Prime Minister liked to describe this agenda as exemplifying a 'new politics' but he was – as he conceded – really outlining an updated social democratic outlook. Thus he argued that a suitably modified state could improve people's lives and that, without such intervention, many would suffer. Within this schema, Blair wanted to appeal to the party's heartlands, those for whom adequately-funded public services offered the only real hope of improvement. Yet, as he knew only too well, this outlook also had to be couched in terms that would win the approval of Middle England. In 2001 increased investment without raising income taxes appeared the most electorally prudent means of achieving that aim.

Conclusion

Blair led 'New' Labour to power in 1997 and gained re-election four years later by creating and sustaining a socially diverse electoral coalition, something no previous Labour leader had managed. The precise implications of 'New' Labour's 2001 campaign will be discussed in the concluding chapter, but here it should be stressed that it was a much less overtly ' "New" Labour' campaign than the one conducted in 1997. Blair no longer complimented Thatcher but attacked elements of her agenda. If he reiterated the promise not to raise income tax, this was not accompanied by a rhetoric that implied 'New' Labour saw taxes as an evil to be condemned. Government spending had also been converted from an unpleasant necessity into something approaching an act of virtue.

The campaign was, moreover, conducted under the auspices of a rhetoric that echoed earlier party campaigns. The state was presented as the main means by which society could be moved closer to equality, and Labour was depicted as representing the interests of a majority drawn from across society. Since 1945 the role of the state had been redefined, while the precise means by which equality could be promoted had altered. Nonetheless, in essence, 'New' Labour's message was basically the same as in the past: a degree of collectivism was required to offset the shortcomings of individualism. Yet Labour's leaders dared not take public opinion for granted: if they believed collective provision was necessary they had to take account of a widespread mistrust in politicians' capacity to spend tax-payers' money to good effect.

Unlike Attlee in the 1940s and Wilson in the 1960s, Blair had managed the tensions inherent in maintaining a winning electoral coalition. The terms of this coalition had obviously changed over time: the working class remained a significant element and its support was crucial to victory, but the centre of gravity had shifted decisively towards the sceptical suburbs. The Prime Minister's political skills undoubtedly played their part. Yet 'New' Labour was also the beneficiary of Conservative misfortune and incompetence, while continued economic growth undoubtedly helped. Nonetheless, despite social changes that had only accelerated during the 1980s and 1990s, 'New' Labour was demonstrably pursuing the party's long-established electoral strategy. Blair had accommodated the preferences of the most vital parts of the electorate, albeit with an alacrity that disturbed many. Having won the trust of voters in Middle England, he appeared reluctant to radically reshape their key preferences. These were the acts of a cautious and conservative but recognizably social democratic Labour leader, and the party has followed plenty of those in the past.

5
Becoming Blair's Party? Labour Organization

Critics invariably argue that 'New' Labour is uniquely obsessed with what they term 'control freakery'. Echoing this charge, Peter Mair has asserted that the Labour leader seeks 'a degree of control within his own party without precedent in modern British political history'. According to Mair, Blair wants to create a party which articulates only one voice: his own (Mair, 2000, 21). Thus, where once power was dispersed between members, trade unions and the Westminster leadership, it now only resides in the leader's hands. In effect 'New' Labour is run by a handful of professionals based in London who owe loyalty to Blair rather than the party. Labour cannot now claim with any degree of seriousness to be a democratic organization: it is quite literally Blair's party.

Against these charges 'New' Labour partisans can argue that the party is more democratic than ever it was. Individual members now exert an influence on policy-making unrivalled in Labour history; they also enjoy more of a say in the election of their representatives, including the leader. If the unions no longer dominate proceedings to the same degree as before this is only because the members' voice has increased. In any case the unions continue to play a significant role within the party while, despite such changes, the annual conference remains Labour's sovereign body.

This chapter will suggest that neither perspective is entirely satisfactory. As it will make clear, the extent to which Labour was ever a pristine example of democracy in action should be seriously questioned. An assessment of Labour's founding 1918 constitution will indicate that the present leadership's desire to minimize internal dissent is not exactly unique. This constitution restricted the members' ability to influence policy, although they were still expected to help mobilize electoral support. In addition, while the constitution gave the unions a formally dominant position, in practice the party's Westminster leadership enjoyed effective autonomy. This freedom was undermined during the

116

1970s when many active members and some union leaders asserted themselves. Thus, after 1983, Neil Kinnock set about restoring the leadership's established position in order to facilitate policy change, yet it did not appear wise to simply restore the *status quo ante*. As a result, while reasserting the power of the leader, Kinnock and his successors also 'modernized' party organization to help it adapt to wider cultural changes. Consequently, as others have suggested, it will be argued here that although many of Labour's organizational forms have changed in the recent past, the substantive position has altered less than it might appear (Tanner, 2000).

Party Organization and Political Theory

Before focusing on the impact of 'New' Labour on the party's structures it is necessary first to locate the present within a wider perspective by briefly reviewing what leading students of political organizations have to contribute to our understanding of the subject.

It is generally agreed that during the last 30 years or so the nature of political activity across the West has undergone a profound change. Many observers have detected a decline in civic engagement: social change has transformed active, publicly spirited citizens into passive, private-centred consumers. If this process has reached its apogee in the United States, that country merely embodies the future which awaits us all (Putnam, 2000). In particular, the social foundations of popular political activity have been eradicated: the clear class cleavage that once gave partisanship its anchor has disappeared (Mulgan, 1994).

Partly due to these social and cultural influences, the nature of party organization is thought to have altered significantly (Mair, 1994; Katz and Mair, 1995). Indeed, modern political parties – in particular those of the left – have been in state of flux since their inception. From being 'mass' organizations whose leaderships were directly accountable to a large single class-based membership, they have mutated since 1945 into 'catch-all' parties in which leaders exerted greater authority over their members and appealed to a socially more disparate constituency. Over the last decade or so the emergence of a different set of attributes has been identified, prompting some to refer to the development of the 'cartel' party. While typologies such as 'mass' and 'catch-all' can never account for each and every detail in a particular party's structure, they nonetheless isolate dominant trends to which all parties are subject (to a greater or lesser extent). Thus the notion of the 'cartel' party is a potentially useful heuristic frame within which to set this chapter's discussion of 'New' Labour's organization.

The chief characteristic of the 'cartel' party that has most relevance here is the autonomy of the parliamentary leadership from their members. This centralization of power has paradoxically gone hand-in-hand with members being granted a greater voice in decision-making. This is less of a contradiction than it at first appears, for the leadership is considered to have ceded influence to the broader membership as they generally accept what they are told at the expense of more independently-minded activists. Thus, if increasingly democratic (in the sense that more members enjoy a greater say), the practical effect has been to grant the leadership freedom from party control.

The extent to which 'New' Labour fits the cartel model is questionable. Accusations of 'control freakery', however, suggest a *prima facie* case for believing Blair has acquired an unprecedented level of autonomy. Yet Labour's leaders have always enjoyed a dominant position within the party, or at least they have compared to their European counterparts (Webb, 1994). The extent to which Labour was ever democratic in the sense of having a leadership directly accountable to its individual members is therefore problematic. Indeed, given the relatively low number of such members, it is doubtful Labour was a 'mass' party in any descriptive sense (Bartolini, 1983). In fact, the authority who did most to elaborate the 'mass' party concept described Labour as only a 'semi-mass party' given the influence which the unions rather than individual members exerted over its affairs (Duverger, 1964, 3–4, 65). Moreover, it is questionable how far the leaders of 'mass' parties in general were ever truly accountable to their members. It was at the start of the twentieth century that the German social democrat, Robert Michels, claimed to have discovered an 'iron law of oligarchy' (Michels, 1962). This stipulated that even social democratic parties were fated to become dominated by their parliamentary elites.

Despite the above we should not dismiss the relevance of the cartel concept. If Labour's leadership always enjoyed considerable freedom and the accountability within social democratic parties was weaker than retrospectively imagined, this does not mean such features have not become even more entrenched of late. If Labour was never especially democratic, it remains important to ask whether the party has become less so since 1994.

The cartel model therefore usefully highlights the crucial relationship within any political party: that between its leaders and members. It is clear that party membership has declined across the West (Scarrow, 2000).

It is also evident that party leaderships increasingly focus their energies on campaigning, and many have noted the emergence of technically proficient professionals whose sole purpose it is to win elections (Farrell and Webb, 2000). As a result, the current significance and purpose of members has been keenly debated. This is because if social change means there are fewer members, some believe the rise of the 'electoral-professional' party means they may no longer be necessary (Panebianco, 1988). From the start, 'mass' party leaderships have tried to play off the benefits entailed by a large and active membership with its costs. For much of the twentieth century a healthy membership was seen as necessary to electoral success. However, a large and active membership was also a problem in as much as it increased the number of those who wanted a say in the making of policy. According to some, the cartel model has made recent changes in the relationship between members and leaders appear more straightforward and historically distinctive than they actually are (Scarrow, Webb and Farrell, 2000). Even so, it usefully denotes the sensitive point that relations between members and leaders have reached in all political parties, not least within 'New' Labour.

In order to address these issues, it is now necessary to look in some detail at how Labour was organized for much of the twentieth century: this inevitably means trying to understand the basis for Labour's 1918 constitution.

The Road to 1918

Prior to 1918 Labour was a federation of otherwise independent bodies rather than a party with its own bureaucratic structure and national membership. During this time Labour was, however, governed by a single National Executive Committee (NEC) composed of representatives elected by its constituent elements, affiliated organizations such as the Independent Labour party (ILP), the Fabians and the trade unions. Reflecting their importance, in particular the amount of money they contributed to Labour, the unions held a majority of NEC seats. These affiliated associations also sent representatives to an annual conference, which was Labour's sovereign policy-making body; once again, the unions cast the majority of votes.

As the First World War drew to a close Arthur Henderson, the party's secretary, was determined that Labour should substantially upgrade its organization so as to meet the challenge of what promised to be a very different post-war world (Leventhal, 1989, 79–117). Given the break-up of the party's alliance with the Liberals and the enfranchisement of all men and most women, Henderson and others considered that Labour needed to establish a presence in all of the country's municipal wards and parliamentary constituencies. If it was to contest general elections with any hope of aspiring to hold office, Labour needed its own national organization backed up by a large membership and adequate finance.

Some wanted Labour to be transformed into a fully membership-based party in which only those who paid their own dues could be considered members. This they believed would help mobilize the thousands of volunteers required to run local branches and get out the vote at elections. It also enjoyed the advantage of meaning the party could escape what Ramsay MacDonald described as the unions' 'intolerable' 'tyranny' (Marquand, 1997, 227–33). If the Labour Representation Committee had been established to encourage the unions to support left-leaning candidates, this did not mean everybody saw the arrangement as perfect. To those such as MacDonald, the unions were a sectional interest that could help as much as hinder Labour's development. Moreover, a party based only on individual membership might also make Labour more attractive to middle-class 'progressives' who took exception to the unions' overbearing influence.

Most union leaders opposed the creation of a membership-based party and were unwilling to bankroll an organization in which their influence was to be substantially downgraded (McHugh, 2001, 47–76). Despite his ambition to transform the party, Henderson appreciated that in the short term, without union funds and the electoral benefit of their close links with much of the urban working class, Labour would find it difficult to contest general elections. As a result the 1918 constitution was a compromise that allowed for the introduction of individual members and the continuation of the pre-existing federal structure. To win union support for this curious amalgam, Henderson was forced to give them an even greater say in the new body than under the old regime. Therefore the unions retained their majority on the NEC, which continued to be responsible for administration and policy development. Local parties were given a small number of NEC seats but, as such representatives were elected by a vote of the Annual Conference (where the unions still prevailed), they rarely reflected membership opinion. It was not until the 1930s that local parties were granted the right to elect their own NEC representatives at Conference free of union opinion (Pimlott, 1977).

While the continued formal dominance of the unions through the NEC and Conference disappointed some, for others in the leadership it was preferable to the creation of a party in which individual members exerted a significant influence. Indeed, the constitution was deliberately constructed to prevent newly enrolled members having an effective say in formulating policy. Sidney Webb, who drafted the constitution, thought constituency parties were 'frequently unrepresentative groups of nonentities dominated by fanatics and cranks and extremists' (McKenzie, 1964, 505). If such 'cranks' could determine policy, he feared they would transform Labour into an ideologically pristine but electorally marginal force.

The 1918 compromise therefore gave the unions a paper dominance granted on the understanding it would be used to guarantee the virtual dictatorship of the parliamentary leadership. Thus, for most of the following decades the unions protected the platform from hostile left-wing constituency activists and ensured that on most of the key debates of the day the activists lost (Minkin, 1978). While in theory exerting enormous power, union leaders rarely used it: as Lewis Minkin has concluded, restraint was the central characteristic of the union–party relationship (Minkin, 1992). This was because both party and union leaders respected a division of labour in which the political 'wing' of the labour movement did not interfere in industrial matters and the industrial 'wing' avoided embroiling itself in political affairs. Party leaders knew that to meddle in industrial affairs would only antagonize the unions, while union leaders were persuaded that if they threw their weight around at Conference they might harm Labour's electoral prospects. Such an independence of roles nonetheless became less tenable during the Labour governments of the 1960s and 1970s. By this point, government's ability to manage the economy often seemed to depend on the activities of trade unions. This led Harold Wilson and James Callaghan to seek wage limitations and even legislation to reduce strikes: if the leadership appeared to be turning on the union interest the active members promised to defend it. Moreover, the party's declining electoral performance suggested the leadership was no longer able to win power, which had been one of the key reasons why the unions had hitherto remained so loyal.

The Members

Under the 1918 constitution, party members were meant to do much of the work of mobilizing Labour's electoral support. However, they were also to enjoy very little influence over policy-making and none whatsoever over who would be their national leader. Even so, some officials hoped the 1918 constitution was not the last word on the matter and liked to think that Labour would eventually evolve into a fully membership-based party. Herbert Drinkwater, one of Labour's senior organizers, claimed that 'individual membership had in it the genesis of a revolutionary transference of weight and power within the party' away from the unions. For him the constitution was 'nowhere a final and last word regarding [Labour's] structure ... it will adapt itself to circumstances as it grows' (Fielding and McHugh, 2001). Yet while the party increased its vote there was little reason to change the constitution, especially as the unions also increased in size and influence. During the 1950s, when the electoral advantages of increasing the number of members became more obvious, the unions resisted, while even many existing activists did not welcome an influx of enthusiasts for fear they would disturb their own established positions of influence (Fielding, 2000c).

Denying those whom Webb feared would be 'cranks' much of a say at the national level, the 1918 constitution nonetheless gave them an inflated voice within local branches. This was because those keen enough to attend ward meetings and stand as delegates could control constituency party affairs through sitting on its general management committee (GMC). In contrast, those who stayed at home were left wholly unrepresented. Such activists always formed a small minority of the total, even during the 1950s when Labour's individual membership stood at its historic peak of one million. At this time, some inner-city ward gatherings attracted barely more than 3 per cent of members. Moreover, while the overwhelming majority of Labour's individual members were working class, even in heavily proletarian constituencies activists were disproportionately middle class (Fielding, 2001a, 249–52).

Labour's reliance on the exertions of a few over-worked enthusiasts did not necessarily promote electoral efficiency, especially in comparison with the better-funded and more professional Conservatives (Labour Party, 1955). Yet, many of those who did much of the hard work understandably demanded some reward for their endeavours. Victory for Socialism (VFS) was established in the mid-1950s and aimed to reduce union influence at conference and increase that of the constituencies. Those who led this organization believed activists held the key to electoral victory. Indeed, the reason for Labour's defeat in 1955, the chair of VFS asserted, was that there had been too few members willing to 'knock on doors' because they were dismayed at their leaders' abandonment of 'socialism'. Thus, he suggested, if Labour was to win future contests, it had to give 'the man [sic] who knocks on the doors a voice in deciding policy' as this would at least give members the enthusiasm to knock on more doors and so increase those willing to vote for the party (Fielding, 1997c, 44–5).

During the 1950s and 1960s, electoral inefficiency and activist discontent did not seem to matter much. Activists could send as many critical resolutions to Conference as they liked since the general secretaries of the major unions ensured they had no impact. Indeed, some revisionists keenly anticipated the time when television-based national campaigns would make activists irrelevant (Crosland, 1962, 143–63). During this period, it was believed activists posed nothing more than a problem of internal management. While revisionists doubted that their reliance on the unions was democratic, they reassured themselves that it at least ensured their point of view became party policy.

Uncertain Sovereignty

Being the result of compromise, the 1918 constitution was a very ambiguous document that did not always mean what it appeared to say; and when its meaning was clear this did not guarantee the party ever acted in the prescribed manner.

The constitution, for example, stated clearly that the 'work of the Party shall be under the direction and control of the Party Conference' and that the role of the Parliamentary Labour Party (PLP) was merely, 'to give effect as far as may be practicable to the principles from time to time approved by the Party Conference'. Many believed this meant Labour's sovereign body was its Annual Conference, or the 'parliament of the labour movement' as it was sometimes described. Whether this meant Labour was also 'democratic' depends upon one's definition of that term, especially given the preponderance of the union block vote and the fact that only a small minority of local members voted for constituency representatives. Nonetheless, most in the party liked to think the constitution placed MPs under the firm hand of the wider party (Attlee, 1937, 85–112).

The 1918 formulation was, however, less straightforward than it at first appeared. The statement that the PLP was 'to give effect as far as may be practicable to the principles ... approved by the Party Conference' gave MPs considerable autonomy to interpret the principle as well as the timing and form of its application. They might even argue that the principle was not 'practicable'. Some commentators consequently viewed conference's sovereignty to be entirely formalistic (McKenzie, 1964, 485–516), while others looked on the matter as more complex. Lewis

Minkin in particular argued that while the PLP often asserted its autonomy within the party it was bounded by the constitution, specifically the
role of conference and the unions' dominant role within it. This resulted
in an ebb and flow of authority within the party which largely depended
on historical circumstances (Minkin, 1978, 3–29).

It is certainly true that the extent of a leader's autonomy varied over
time. After 1918, the number of MPs increased, as did the likelihood of
the PLP forming a government: as a result this body was less willing to
take orders from the wider party. This process was furthered when MPs
elected MacDonald as chairman of the PLP in 1922: for the first time
this post-holder was referred to as leader of the whole party rather than
just of MPs. This confirmed Labour's adherence to existing parliamentary protocols, and was something McDonald stressed to reassure voters
beyond the party's working-class redoubts. Thus, the leader of the whole
Labour Party was elected by MPs only; should Labour gain a Commons
majority he alone appointed the Cabinet; and he also exercised the
patronage of the Prime Minister's office. Once installed in power the
Labour leader and the PLP as a whole gained prestige and power: they
could – and often did – claim to have a dual mandate to both the party
and the electorate, but one in which the party was definitely subordinate.

The power of Conference was reasserted in the aftermath of
MacDonald's 1931 'betrayal'. Clement Attlee, who became leader in 1935,
demonstrated how the position had altered by announcing he would
submit to the will of Conference even if he disagreed with it. Yet the formal position remained the same as under MacDonald: Conference established the principle whilst the PLP used its discretion to decide its
practicability. But the context post-MacDonald *had* changed: neither the
party nor its leaders wished to repeat what were taken to be the mistakes
of a virtually independent leadership. In any case, Attlee's time as Prime
Minister between 1945 and 1951 saw Labour achieve much that pleased
both unions and members; there was little of substance to criticize.

This position changed when Hugh Gaitskell became leader in 1955.
As a revisionist, he considered that many of the party's cherished
nostrums were outmoded; he also believed the unions and party activists
could be electoral liabilities. If Labour was to prosper, he wanted
to assert his independence and demonstrate to the voters that the PLP
at least was in tune with the modern mood. Yet, despite his intentions,
Gaitskell failed to revise clause four in the wake of the 1959 General
Election because party opinion was heavily stacked against him. The
defining moment of his leadership, however, came in 1960 when Conference, mobilized by the Transport and General Workers' Union, voted

in favour of unilateral nuclear disarmament. Gaitskell declared that he and the PLP would 'fight, fight and fight again to save the party we love'. In other words, he flatly rejected the decision. Gaitskell appeared to refute the very principle of conference sovereignty and pitched the PLP and Conference in direct opposition to one another. Despite – or because of – his defiance, in 1961 Conference changed its mind and rejected unilateralism. Gaitskell had thereby effectively shown the public where power in the party lay: with him. Despite that, he still had to spend much time and energy to change the mind of conference delegates: Gaitskell rejected the policy but not the institution (Williams, 1982, 335–80).

The Crisis of Control

The leadership started to lose control of the party during the 1964–70 Wilson governments. Economic weakness forced the Cabinet to follow policies bitterly opposed by active members and numerous trade union leaders. These measures led to a rise in unemployment and a curtailment of promised welfare spending; ministers made matters worse by attempting to reduce the unions' capacity to increase their members' wages. As re-election approached, Wilson even sought to introduce legislation that would have used the legal system to curtail unofficial industrial disputes. While still Prime Minister, Wilson could ignore the increasing number of occasions on which the platform was defeated at Labour's Conference due to the unions and constituency delegates making common cause. Nonetheless, he became vulnerable after Labour lost the 1970 election, especially as defeat was blamed on what many in the party regarded as Wilson's anti-working-class policies.

An increasing number of unions now looked on Labour's activists as those who might better serve their interests. The leaderships of some of the biggest unions had also been radicalized through their members' response to full employment. Workers now expected an ever-increasing standard of living, to which end the unions' ability to extract wage increases from their employers was vital. The last thing union members wanted was a Labour government preventing their officials pressing home this advantage. In addition, the party's membership underwent some important changes: the end of the 1960s saw an influx of young Marxist-influenced middle-class public-sector professionals who were intent on turning Labour into what they considered to be a truly socialist party (Whiteley, 1983, 53–80; Seyd, 1987, 37–75).

As a result of this new alliance, Labour's leaders found themselves on the defensive. The PLP was forced to establish closer links with the unions so policy better expressed their needs: a Trades Union Congress/ Labour Party liaison committee was established and drafted a 'social contract' in which Wilson promised measures to strengthen the unions' position and committed himself to a massive extension of public ownership (Wickham-Jones, 1996). Finding themselves unexpectedly in office in 1974, Labour ministers were reluctant to enact such policies. The government's position in the Commons was weak, while worsening economic problems forced ministers to do the bidding of the International Monetary Fund which strongly opposed Labour's manifesto. Moreover, union leaders considered ministers wanted to use the social contract as a means of imposing wage restraint rather than giving them more power in the workplace. Disillusion came to a head with the 1978–9 'winter of discontent', in which many public-sector workers went on strike in protest at the government's attempt to prevent them gaining what they considered to be reasonable wage increases.

By 1979, the party's activists were convinced that the only solution to the leadership's habitual 'betrayal' of party policy was to change the constitution and thereby reduce their autonomy. To that end, Conference voted for the automatic reselection of MPs. This meant that during every Parliament an MP would have to win the support of their GMC or be replaced: the aim was to force the PLP to reflect the wishes of their active members. The most notable innovation of this period was the creation of an electoral college for leadership contests. Hitherto only MPs had decided the matter, which meant left-wing candidates stood little chance of success. At a special conference held in 1981 it was agreed that MPs' votes should only count for 30 per cent of the total, leaving the constituencies with 30 per cent and the unions with 40 per cent. This was too much for some of the party's neo-revisionists who considered Labour had become a lost cause and so formed the Social Democratic Party (SDP). Late in the day they had supported one member, one vote (OMOV) for leadership elections but this was widely seen as disingenuous given their previous reliance on the unions (Crewe and King, 1995, 71–84). In any case, Labour's activists did not want to enfranchise all party members, just themselves.

By the early 1980s, the Parliamentary leadership consequently found itself advocating policies imposed by a Conference and NEC now dominated by an activist left controlled by the ex-Cabinet minister, Tony Benn, and supported by an unprecedented number of major trade unions. The aim of Webb's constitution had been inverted; and Labour was set to be out of power for nearly two decades.

Restoring Autonomy

While he put it in more diplomatic language in public, Neil Kinnock thought Labour's 1983 defeat was largely due to the fact that party policy had ceased to reflect the concerns of most voters. Labour had instead echoed the outlook of the party's active members and their union allies: their control of policy-making had condemned Labour to disaster (Labour Party, 1983, 30). Thus Kinnock considered restoring the Westminster leadership's lost freedom of action to be an electoral imperative. In addition, it appeared that many voters had abandoned Labour because they considered it dominated by the unions and militant left. Constitutional change was also required to demonstrate this was no longer the case.

In the years following 1983, Kinnock persuaded an increasing number of union leaders and activists that only his 'modernization' of policy could improve Labour's election chances. The argument that the programme put to the country in 1983 was not popular proved especially persuasive with the unions. They suffered damaging legislative reverses during the 1980s: in that context, any type of Labour government was preferable to one led by Margaret Thatcher. Thus, while they proved troublesome when the leadership accepted the bulk of Conservative industrial relations law, by the end of the 1980s the unions had largely resumed their supportive role. If willing to accept changes to policy, however, there was little union support for constitutional amendments that threatened to reduce their formal influence. Hence when Kinnock proposed introducing OMOV to the selection of parliamentary candidates in 1984 he was roundly defeated.

In addition, irritating though activists might be, party members as a whole were still considered necessary to the leadership as they contributed income and were especially useful in mobilizing support in marginal constituencies. Even before 1983 a few on the left began to appreciate that at least some of the party's electoral troubles were due to its organization having become detached from society. Local parties did not engage with the electorate but were instead preoccupied with internal affairs that left most voters cold (Labour Co-Ordinating Committee, 1982). Impressed by this thinking, Kinnock wanted to increase membership so the party could become more representative of the public, reduce his financial dependence on the unions and marginalize the activist left. In 1989 he aimed to enrol one million members, a feat the party had achieved once before in the early 1950s (Scarrow, 1996). At the same time Kinnock sidestepped what could still sometimes be a fractious and unreliable NEC by asserting his personal authority through building up the leader's office and establishing the Campaign Strategy Committee as well as the Shadow Communications Agency; these bodies were answerable only to him (Kinnock, 1994; Shaw, 1994, 108–23).

As a result, by the time Blair became leader, the party's constitution remained fundamentally the same as in 1983 although there were some important and hard-fought changes that had reduced union influence and increased the voice of ordinary members. John Smith ensured that OMOV had finally been applied to candidate selection; the proportion of the vote cast at Conference by the unions was set to be reduced to 50 per cent in 1996; the National Policy Forum (NPF) had been created; and the electoral college for leader and deputy contests had been revised so individual party members and trade unionists could enjoy a direct say. If the unions continued to enjoy a special place in the constitution it was more circumscribed than at any time in the party's history, and ordinary members had an unprecedented say in Labour's affairs. Had Smith lived, there would probably have been no further changes (McSmith, 1993, 294–311). It might be argued that there was now little need to alter the constitution as the leader's effective autonomy had been restored.

Before being elected Prime Minister, Blair did not indulge in further constitutional innovations except in one important respect. He used two referenda, the first to win support for his version of clause four in 1995 and the second to test membership opinion on the party's draft manifesto, *New Life For Britain*, in 1996. Both by-passed the party's established decision-making processes and were of dubious legitimacy. After announcing his desire to revise clause four, Blair called a special conference and invoked the electoral college, calculating that ordinary party members and trade unionists would endorse his initiative as a show of support for him personally. This would prevent a repeat of the reverse suffered by Gaitskell by sidestepping opposition from union leaders and activists (Rentoul, 2001, 257). On both occasions Blair won a majority, and on that basis asserted that this proved Labour members had changed in a way acceptable to the majority of voters. It is unlikely either indicated that for, while 85 per cent of members who voted supported the new clause, only 27 per cent of those eligible participated in the ballot. Furthermore, 43 per cent of members either registered their opposition or failed to vote on the draft manifesto.

The early years of Blair's leadership saw membership increase at an impressive rate, leading to speculation that a different type of person was now joining the party: one more likely to support 'New' Labour. Kinnock's attempt to raise membership had produced less than impressive results: by 1992 official figures placed it at only 280,000; and it stood at 305,000 in 1995 although it then rose to 405,000 by 1997.

Taking into account membership turnover, this meant that in the year Labour finally won power about 40 per cent of Labour's members had joined since the creation of 'New' Labour. It was assumed that this influx was largely of a certain type. As Robin Cook informed the Liberal Democrat leader, Paddy Ashdown, they were 'the sort who came to you with the SDP ... very nice people – professionals, etc.' As a leading member of the Labour left Cook was uncertain about the quality of such members as, 'when we started mentioning delivering leaflets and knocking on doors, their eyes glazed and they said they had Rotary meetings to go to'. 'I am not at all sure', he stated, 'there is enough substance here on which to build a sustainable political movement, especially if things start to get tough, as inevitably they will' (Ashdown, 2000, 423).

While a number of prominent former SDP members (such as David Marquand) rejoined Labour, not all the new intake fitted this profile. Survey evidence in fact suggested they were no more likely to be middle class than existing members, although they did appear closer to the leadership on the crucial issue of nationalization; in contrast, only two-fifths of new members agreed with the direction Blair was taking the party. Yet members old and new were sufficiently pragmatic – or desperate – to consider that whatever they thought about him, Blair deserved their support, as he looked likely to return the party to power (Davey, 1996; Young, Henn and Hill, 1997; Seyd and Whiteley, 1998; Webb and Farrell, 1999).

A Partnership for Power?

There was no guarantee this conditional support for the leadership would be sustained once Labour had won office. Indeed, wiseacres predicted there would be an inevitable falling out between leader and party if a 'New' Labour government stuck to the letter of its manifesto: it was one thing to reluctantly endorse policies as the price worth paying to win power, and quite another to uncomplainingly support them once they were being applied. In such conditions, Blair might come under internal pressure and find his autonomy reduced by the combined force of active members and the unions. Despite claiming the party had changed irrevocably, some 'New' Labour partisans feared a repeat of the late 1970s. This possibly explains Blair's support for a radical change to the party's constitution; his fear of future conflict might also illuminate why these reforms failed to live up to the more idealistic expectations of those responsible for drafting them.

Prior to the 1992 General Election, officials close to Kinnock sought to place Labour's constitution on a new footing. This led to the creation of the NPF, which consisted of members appointed from different levels of the party (including the trade unions). Parallel with the Annual Conference, the NPF examined major policy statements and proposed amendments. The hope was this would make policy-making more deliberative and accountable: in order to facilitate the expression of disagreement and foster consensus-building, discussions were closed to the media. As a result, since first meeting in 1993 the NPF remained an unknown quantity to most; and leadership critics saw it as an attempt to undermine the sovereignty of Conference. Nonetheless, if aware of its shortcomings, some on the left viewed the NPF as an important innovation that should be developed further (*Tribune*, 21 October 1994).

After Smith's indifference, Blair gave fundamental reform a fresh impetus and encouraged the party's General Secretary, Tom Sawyer, to draft proposals under the title of *Partnership in Power* (PP), which were endorsed by Labour's 1997 Conference (Labour Party, 1997a, 1997d). Sawyer hoped to achieve a number of objectives, the most important of which were: first, to sustain leadership accountability while guaranteeing it some autonomy; and second, to integrate members into policy-making at the same time as minimizing conflict between party and government. His ultimate aim was to construct a new party culture, at the centre of which would be a genuine 'partnership' between leaders and members. This partnership would nonetheless be based on members recognizing some fundamental truths: their leaders had ultimate responsibility for policy-making; members could not act as 'watchdogs' over the leadership; and, while disagreements were to be expected, members had to be 'supportive rather than antagonistic' (*New Statesman*, 12 July 1996). By altering the party's procedures Sawyer hoped members would gain a better sense that their views were being taken into account, and that this would encourage them to take a more responsible attitude when their leaders made decisions of which they disapproved.

Despite what certain critics said, Labour Party policy-making by the middle 1990s was no more or less democratic than it had ever been. As one the observer put it, by this period the notionally sovereign Party Conference had become a 'safety valve' for those excluded from the 'real policy-making process'. If it was meant to articulate grassroots opinion and ensure it was taken seriously, Conference was a palpable failure (Taylor, 1993). As has already been pointed out, for much of the century so long as the leadership retained the support of enough union leaders, Conference endorsed policy with little demur. Conference had never given individual members much of a say and there had been few occasions in which activists sitting on GMCs made a substantial contribution to policy-making. The classic route was for each constituency to send a resolution to be scrutinized by the Conference Arrangements Committee (CAC). This body amalgamated resolutions submitted on similar topics into one coherent proposal that could be discussed by delegates; but during amalgamation the meaning of most resolutions was usually lost. Moreover, even if a resolution was discussed with a wording that retained most of its original sense, a few union leaders could prevent it being passed. Conference debates were, in addition, hardly based on the Platonic model, being often brief and ill-informed. Sawyer's reforms at least promised to promote a more thoughtful discussion of policy and allowed for the participation of every member who wished to be involved.

Since 1998, Labour policy-making has therefore taken the following route (see Figure 5.1). First a Joint Policy Committee (JPC), chaired by the leader and comprising equal numbers of ministers and NEC members as well as a smaller number of those elected by the NPF, decides which policies should be discussed by the party. This initiates a process that lasts two years. The development of specific policy proposals becomes the responsibility of different policy commissions on which sit three members each from the government and NEC, and four from the NPF. These commissions take submissions from a variety of interested groups as well as from local policy fora, which all members are entitled to attend. Having made such consultations, each commission issues a draft report which is debated by the NPF, NEC and finally Conference. The main place to debate any proposals is, however, the NPF which is constituted by representatives from the constituencies, regions and various affiliated bodies, most notably the unions, as well as MPs, MEPs, councillors and NEC members. In the second year the commission submits a final report to the NPF after all members have been given time to discuss it. This report is then debated in the NPF, which may amend or produce alternatives to be debated at Conference. It is only after Conference has endorsed the report that it can become Labour policy.

Sawyer was careful to stress that Conference remained Labour's sovereign body in this new process. The function of the NEC was, however, substantially reconstructed and it ceased to make policy, becoming a purely administrative body. The unions also lost their majority on he NEC while individual members could directly elect their own representatives, although these only accounted for six out of 33 seats, half the number held by the unions.

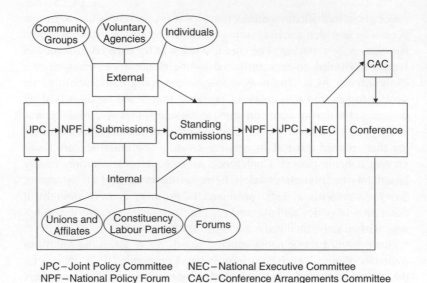

JPC – Joint Policy Committee   NEC – National Executive Committee
NPF – National Policy Forum   CAC – Conference Arrangements Committee

Figure 5.1   Policy-making in the Labour Party after 1997
Source: Labour Party (1997a), 17, reproduced with the permission of the Labour Party.

Debating Change

Press commentators generally assumed PP was designed to achieve only one purpose: to create 'a party run from the centre, by the centre, for the centre' (*The Guardian*, 18 February 1997). If that might have been the aspiration of certain figures in the leadership, it was not the intention of all those who drafted the proposals. Moreover, some in the party hoped reform would actually promote a more participatory and effective organization. Before looking at the impact of the new regime, it would therefore be useful to survey the debate surrounding Sawyer's proposals. This not only indicates the range of opinions about the development of 'New' Labour but helps indicate why the reforms had the effect they did.

Many of those associated with Blair's closest adviser, Peter Mandelson, wanted leadership autonomy to increase because they considered this would enhance Labour's electoral performance. To achieve that end they argued that the more pliable individual members should be given more influence at the expense of activists and the unions. This meant extending OMOV to all aspects of party activity and reforming (or even abolishing) constituency GMCs, the Annual Conference and the NEC.

The belief that members and their leader should be separated by as few levels of bureaucracy as possible was not simply based on the desire to be rid of the unions and activists. Mandelson considered it a matter of fact that 'the era of pure representative democracy' was drawing to a close. Social change meant voters no longer deferred to political elites but wanted to be more directly involved through mechanisms such as the internet and referenda (Routledge, 1999, 277–8). As others close to Blair pointed out, the era of traditional political parties was nearly over (Mulgan, 1994). Therefore, it was futile for Labour to try and attract more members and encourage them to participate within the existing organization. The emergence of more private-centred lives meant few would join and even fewer would become active in the established manner. Labour should instead transform itself into a 'post-activist' party in which the 'deadweight' of internal bureaucracy was replaced by a looser conception of membership which did not entail attending meetings (Clifton, 1994).

This perspective was embodied in the report produced by the Labour Co-Ordinating Committee's (LCC) commission on party democracy, which announced that Labour 'must become a party of individual members' and cease being one of 'obscure representative structures' (Labour Co-Ordinating Committee, 1996). It should mobilize electoral support rather than 'act as a focus for opposition' to the leader; to that end, the most salient recommendation was for the Annual Conference to be converted into an American-style convention with few decision-making functions. If the LCC exposed the illusion that individual members ever exerted much influence on policy-making, it merely wanted to formalize their impotence. Thus the role of members should be to 'legitimize' leadership decisions: if they were to be allowed 'consultation' through question times with ministers, they were not to be allowed the chance of subjecting them to a binding vote. If the LCC welcomed PP, it considered the proposals did not go far enough as they stopped short of seeking to change the operation of local parties (*LCC Activist*, Spring 1997).

Veterans of earlier attempts to reduce leadership autonomy had a different perspective and rejected Sawyer's proposals wholesale. The only NEC member to vote against PP (the MP, Dennis Skinner) described it as a 'continuation of the process' started by Kinnock 'of taking power from the grassroots and giving it to the centre'. It was consequently 'all about transferring the real power upwards, to the leadership' (*Tribune*, 7 February 1997). Such critics based their opposition on three chief propositions. Despite what Mandelson said, they first of all believed active members were representative of Labour's electorate and so served to keep their leaders in touch with voter opinion (*Keep the Party Labour Newsletter*, January 1997). Second, they assumed that if members were treated as individuals they would produce outcomes favourable to the leadership because those 'acting collectively are infinitely better informed, stronger and more progressive than individuals isolated from one another' (*Tribune*, 19 April 1996). This meant existing means of airing members' views, such as GMCs and Conference, should not be replaced by giving votes to those who sat alone at home. Finally, as it was feared reform would emasculate the union influence, it would deny the party 'the experience and feelings of millions of working people' (Mortimer, 1997).

Between these two groups stood those who rejected the centralizing implications of recent reforms but recognized the deficiencies of relying on activists alone (Fisher, 1994). This was a wide-ranging body of opinion, partly orchestrated by *Tribune* which, despite its other criticisms of 'New' Labour, thought PP a 'genuine attempt to strengthen and extend internal democracy' (*Tribune*, 7 February 1997). It was given further shape by Labour Reform, a group established in 1996 by members drawn from across the party. Indeed, some junior shadow ministers also hoped PP would produce something more than a new way to legitimize leadership autonomy.

This diverse group believed Labour's organization needed to promote 'participation, democracy and openness at all levels of policy development'. A Blair government would only be sustained in power by members' 'active support'; and this would be forthcoming only if they could make a tangible contribution to policy (Black, 1996). In fact they considered Labour could only be 'managed through a participatory democracy in which accountability and communication' were a genuine 'two-way process between the leadership and the grass roots' (*The Guardian*, 20 January 1997). To that end, they supported the extension of OMOV but criticized Blair's use of referenda as not conducive to the promotion of real debate (Fisher, 1996). Yet they did not consider it necessary to reform established procedures and institutions, and were happy with the continued union role. However, if the proposed reforms were to work it was considered imperative that the NPF be made more open and accountable so it could bridge the 'yawning gap' that had previously divided members from Labour ministers (Fatchett and Hain, 1997).

It is clear that Sawyer, as a man who supported Benn in the early 1980s, was aware of the need to encourage greater participation but, as someone who became one of Kinnock's closest allies and was appointed General Secretary by Blair, he also believed the leader needed to be free to take key decisions. In trying to reconcile these two approaches, it is not surprising PP touched the concerns of both the LCC and Labour Reform. Nonetheless, like all constitutional changes, the effect of the one approved by Conference in 1997 was to be influenced as much by the intentions of those who proposed them as by the actions of those who would implement them.

Assessing the New Regime

According to Liz Davies, who served on the NEC between 1998 and 2000 as a members' representative, the NPF did not inaugurate a new era of partnership but instead 'reduced the policy-making process to one exclusively shaped by deals done behind closed doors' (Davies, 2001, 80). Davies was a critic of 'New' Labour who eventually left the party, but other less partisan observers echoed some of her concerns (Seyd and Whiteley, 2001; Sturgeon and Hurley, 2001).

First, the new procedures and machinery seemed too top-down to most. It was the JPC that determined those policies to be reviewed and the leader effectively controlled that body. Moreover, most discussions took place within the commissions, which also had responsibility to write the reports; the leadership determined the membership of each commission. In addition ministers with responsibility for the area under debate usually chaired these bodies; NPF members found it difficult to challenge the authority of what were usually highly articulate and persuasive advocates.

Second, the format of both the NPF and local policy fora was criticized for stopping participants gaining a clear idea of how their own contribution influenced policy. As they employed the workshop format in which observing officials noted the content of discussions, there were few means of checking which points were forwarded to the relevant commission, let alone whether such views were taken seriously. This lack of clarity was particularly serious as one object of reform was to ensure members believed they contributed to policy. The lack of accountability of NPF members was also criticized: only 54 out of 175 NPF delegates represented members, and none was elected by OMOV; they were all Conference appointments.

Finally, the protracted nature of policy deliberations, originally meant to be a positive feature, made organizing opposition more difficult. It had been far easier to mobilize Conference votes in a one-off contest, but the new regime extended the period of debate to over two years, thus testing dissidents' resources to their limit. Moreover, the fact that discussions were not open to the media – again for ostensibly good reasons – meant NPF meetings were barely reported, so party members often did not know what had occurred.

All new systems have their problems and Labour's procedures were at least subject to review. Nonetheless, the initial view was that reform had made little difference to how most members viewed policy-making. Indeed, it may even have increased their alienation from the process for, if the Party Conference had only been spuriously democratic, many nonetheless felt it still generally represented their views; the NPF, in contrast, was soon looked on with cynicism. Thus while in 1997 Patrick Seyd and Paul Whiteley discovered that 35 per cent of members thought their leaders did not pay much attention to their members, by 1999 the figure was 53 per cent (*The Guardian*, 11 October 1999). Very few members had direct experience of the NPF and, while many representatives did their best to keep in touch with the wider party, the process seemed distant and obscure. Moreover, local policy fora were initially said to have generated large and enthusiastic gatherings of ordinary members. Seyd and Whiteley discovered that in 1999 around 11 per cent of members had participated in the policy forum process, which was a relatively impressive figure. Attendances, however, declined as it became difficult to state with any certainty what impact such discussions had on policy. Perhaps not surprisingly, after retiring as General Secretary, Sawyer believed his proposals had not been developed in a satisfactory way (*The Guardian*, 16 May 2000; *The Independent*, 5 June 2000). Possibly as a result of the distrust generated by reforms, attendances at Conference also declined to such an extent that, in 2000, as many as 200 constituencies failed to send a delegate. By the end of Labour's first term in office, the number of members who could be bothered to vote for their representatives on the NEC similarly fell (to under one-third).

Many in the party complained that the leadership was able to manipulate the new procedures to circumvent outcomes that might better reflect membership opinion. Yet, had they been so minded, the unions could have challenged the leadership but for the most part they chose not to. Davies was particularly critical of the 'shabby deals' made by union representatives at NPF and NEC meetings to secure their own ends (Davies, 2001, 88–91, 174–5). Tony Robinson, another NEC member elected by the members (albeit one normally less critical of the leadership), made a similar complaint. At the NPF meeting held in Exeter prior to the party's 2000 Conference, he accused union representatives of holding meetings with ministers that excluded constituency members. Robinson noted how familiar it would have seemed to anybody who had attended conferences in the 1970s (Robinson and Turner, 30 May 2001). Indeed, another NEC representative considered the unions had managed to create a 'parallel forum' (Black, 2000).

On those few occasions when they decided to oppose the leadership, the unions proved an effective adversary. At the 2000 Conference the public service unions, UNISON and the GMB, supported a motion calling for the link between pensions and wages to be restored (Davies, 2001, 180–3; Jones, 2001, 28–36). Whereas the CAC could have ruled this out of order for not being a 'contemporary' motion, union representatives on that body ensured it was accepted. It is important to bear in mind the context here: the government was in a uniquely weak position, having alienated public opinion by increasing the basic state pension by just 75 pence, while its opinion poll lead had been lost as a result of the popular fuel protest. If this gave the unions confidence to press on with their case, the thing that should be stressed is that the constitution still allowed them to. Union representatives on the CAC ensured the issue was placed at the top of the ballot of such motions, which meant it had to be debated. Ministers lobbied to have the motion withdrawn and, while it was not, the proposal put to Conference called for an 'immediate and substantial' increase in the pension but made the demand for a link to wages more ambiguous. The NEC nonetheless opposed the resolution but Conference supported it by a ratio of 60:40; as a result, although ministers stated the vote would have no impact on government policy, within a few weeks they had announced a more generous rise in the pension.

Selecting Candidates

Candidate selection has long been recognized as an important means of influencing policy: this was why activists lobbied for the mandatory reselection of MPs in the 1970s and early 1980s, and why Smith introduced OMOV to the process a decade later. When Blair became leader, however, candidate selection still remained the exclusive preserve of local members, although for some years the NEC had possessed powers in relation to by-elections and constituencies that had failed to select a candidate on the eve of a General Election campaign.

Given that Blair's government set about devising devolved bodies and introducing different forms of election, more innovative selection procedures became necessary. In drafting such methods the ostensible aim of officials was to improve the quality and diversity of Labour's candidates, and in particular to increase the number of women and those from ethnic minority backgrounds. Some suspected that under the cover of this noble aim, 'New' Labour actually wanted to centralize control of selection (Shaw, 2001b).

Officials generated a number of procedures that were applied to the selection of candidates for the Welsh Assembly, the Scottish Parliament, the Greater London Authority and the European Parliament, as well as for the London mayoralty and the Welsh and Scottish party leaderships. Each method gave all members a say either at the start or at the end, and utilized vetting panels whose members were appointed by the NEC. Such panels had first been used in the late 1980s when a series of by-elections revealed the poor quality of candidates sometimes selected by local parties when left to their own devices. The role of these panels was nonetheless subject to dispute as many saw them as the means by which the leadership could impose its will. Panellists subjected applicants to a variety of written and oral tests as well as a formal interview; while the criteria used to judge applicants were entirely proper, the suspicion was that in practice certain panellists aimed to exclude those opposed to 'New' Labour.

The European Parliament was already well established in 1997 but, as part of an agreement with the Liberal Democrats, Labour replaced the existing first-past-the-post system with one based on proportional representation in time for the 1999 elections. This entailed a new selection procedure in which local parties nominated candidates for short-listing; successful applicants were then interviewed by eleven regional panels. These panels also had to rank successful candidates, which was a vital task as ministers had decided to use 'closed' regional lists in which electors could vote for a party but not discriminate between individual candidates. The Liberal Democrats had supported an 'open' list system, as this would have allowed voters to order candidates irrespective of party. Consequently, those placed at the top of the party list were much more likely to be returned than those at the bottom. Many Labour MEPs had opposed the revision of clause four and it was possibly no accident that only three of the 24 who had stood against Blair on this issue were re-elected (Coates and others, 1999). Suspicion was not allayed when one union official bragged on publication of the list of candidates that 'We have done in the left' (*The Guardian*, 23 August 1998). A similar situation pertained in Scotland where applicants for the devolved

Parliament were vetted and interviewed before being put to a membership ballot. Some considered it questionable that the leading left-wing MP, Dennis Canavan, was prevented from reaching the ballot because he was said to be 'just not good enough', although other, less abrasive, dissidents were successful (*The Guardian*, 7 May 1999).

If it was not clear how far officials used the new procedures to eliminate potential trouble makers from the Scottish and European Parliaments, their desire was more obvious when it came to the selection of the Welsh party leader and London's mayor. In 1998 Ron Davies had been elected leader of the party in Wales and so became prospective Labour leader of the principality's soon-to-be-elected Assembly. At the end of the year, however, he was forced to resign over a personal matter (Flynn, 1999; Morgan and Mungham, 2000). Davies had defeated the MP, Rhodri Morgan, under a mechanism designed by Welsh officials to ensure the former's victory. After Davies' resignation they turned to the junior minister, Alun Michael, even though Morgan had confirmed his desire to become leader. If the national Labour leadership endorsed this preference, it was the Welsh party, and in particular those leading trade union officials who still controlled the organization, that opposed Morgan with such gusto. It was moreover the Welsh party that created an electoral system once again designed to prevent Morgan's victory. This took the established form of a three-part electoral college similar to the one that had elected Blair. Yet, while the membership and representatives' sections were to be determined by OMOV, the affiliated section dominated by the unions was not. Unlike the college that returned Blair, the unions were not obliged to consult their members, as it was feared they would back the more personable Morgan.

A similar electoral college was designed for comparable reasons by London party officials to select Labour's candidate for mayor (D'Arcy and McLean, 2000). At one stage a single ballot of all members based on OMOV had been mooted, but this was rejected in favour of a college in which the unions were allowed to decide whether they would consult their members. The purpose of this was to prevent the election of Ken Livingstone. If the system to defeat Morgan had been created in Wales, the attempt to stop Livinsgtone was definitely orchestrated by Number 10. Blair and other 'New' Labour partisans saw his leadership of the Greater London Council as embodying all that had been wrong with the party in the 1980s. Since becoming an MP Livingstone had hardly tempered his views, and he regularly attacked Gordon Brown's approach to the economy. Blair feared that if he became mayor, Livingstone would use his position to wage a war against the government.

Despite their different genesis, both schemes produced the same result. In Wales Michael beat Morgan despite failing to win a majority of members' support, largely thanks to those unions who did not ballot their members. In London Frank Dobson, Blair's favoured candidate, also narrowly defeated Livingstone due to union backing in the face of members' opposition. Michael's leadership saw the Welsh party perform badly in Assembly elections held in 1999, and within the year he had resigned to be replaced by Morgan. Angry at being denied the chance to become mayor under Labour's colours, Livingstone successfully stood as an independent and, for good measure, beat Dobson into third place. In the wake of these reverses the NEC agreed that future ballots would all be subject to OMOV, while Blair claimed that the experience of the early 1980s had 'almost scarred me too much', leading him to over-react to the prospect of a Livingstone victory (*The Observer*, 9 April 2000; *The Guardian*, 6 May 2000). The leadership realized that such overt attempts to manipulate selection procedures not only antagonized their members but also alienated many voters.

The selection of MPs remained fully in the hands of local members after 1997, although the national party now compiled a list of suitable candidates for nomination (something also attempted in the early 1960s). The selection of Parliamentary candidates for the 2001 General Election was largely problem-free except in St Helens South. Shaun Woodward was a Conservative MP who had defected to Labour in 2000 and since then, supported by party officials, he had tried to win selection as candidate for a winnable Labour seat. Unfortunately few members wanted to be represented by a man who helped devise Conservative strategy for the 1992 General Election. Rather suspiciously, immediately after Blair announced the polling date, the MP for St Helens South announced his immediate retirement. Misgivings were further aroused when the NEC, as it was empowered to do in such circumstances, drafted a shortlist for the seat that included Woodward but excluded the names of the strongest local candidates. Even so, Woodward still had to face a ballot of members and, on the second attempt, by a majority of four he was elected as their candidate. While some claimed he had been imposed on local members, this was not true: the NEC had manipulated events to best advantage but it was the members who had the final say.

There is therefore much evidence to endorse the claim that Labour officials often stage-managed the new procedures as best they could to ensure the selection of candidates of whom they approved. It would nonetheless be wrong to think this desire unique to 'New' Labour: in fact, the leadership's reliance on the ability of union officials to engineer certain outcomes sometimes recalled 'Old' Labour at its worst.

A Twenty-First-Century Party?

In 1999 the NEC published a consultation document under the title *21st Century Party* (TCP), which was designed to increase the participation and effectiveness of party members (Labour Party, 1999). By this stage many saw any internal reform as motivated by the leadership's desire to increase control. Indeed one anonymous party official claimed TCP would 'break the stranglehold of leftwing "cliques"' in constituency parties. If this gloss reflected the hopes of some, it did not echo the intentions of the MP, Ian McCartney, who was largely responsible for the document (*The Guardian*, 23 September 1999). For over a year, under the auspices of the 'Healthy Party' initiative, McCartney had investigated the best means of regenerating moribund parties in safe Labour seats (*The Observer*, 20 June 1999). Thus TCP was but the most concrete expression of a long-standing concern about the introverted nature of local parties and the extent to which they had been left behind by social change.

If the advance of individualism had caused the membership of all parties to decline, this did not mean that membership had diminished in importance. Many in the party recognized that local campaigning could make a decisive difference to the outcome of elections. This meant parties should become more involved in their communities and evolve into more 'permeable' organizations (Wheeler, 1995). Such disquiet had been expressed with increasing frequency since the early 1980s and led a few constituencies to experiment. As some saw it, local parties should abandon 'boring' matters such as policy and become more 'fun' places (*Tribune*, 28 October 1994). In Blair's Sedgefield, membership subscriptions had been reduced in 1993 leading to a membership of 2,000 (Smyth, 1996). In Ipswich activists tried to cure the problem of low attendances at meetings by abolishing their GMC and holding gatherings open to all members (*Tribune*, 20 January 1995). A similar initiative was undertaken in Enfield Southgate; there activists also closed down its GMC and placed the emphasis on social and new-member events, the object being to create a party that was 'inclusive, truly democratic and active' (Chapple and Sutton, 1999).

Some feared TCP represented an attempt to emasculate local parties: by ridding them of their established structures and putting the focus on social and campaigning activities, it would prevent members from criticizing their leaders. Indeed a new type of member might emerge: one for whom politics was simply about agreeing with their leader. This undoubtedly had been the ambition of the now-defunct LCC: as members should have no real say in policy-making the LCC wanted their energies directed outwards to mobilize support for their leaders. Few in the unions liked the idea of losing GMCs as these were still bodies on which they could influence events at the grassroots level. Yet even those uncertain of the need to abolish GMCs conceded that local meetings were often deeply tedious. If the party was to attract more members and if they were to contribute to the party's success, Labour had to take account of what they wanted to do, and that did not simply mean just discussing policies and procedures.

Not all those parties experimenting with new formats enjoyed unalloyed success. Sedgefield might have 2,000 members but, as most paid a reduced rate while the constituency was still obliged to pay the national party the standard affiliation fee, the party was constantly fundraising to make up the shortfall. How far this marked an advance for the party was unclear. Nonetheless, having consulted with the wider party, the NEC planned to initiate official pilot schemes to explore such alternatives systematically (*The Guardian*, 16 March 2001). On the basis of past performance, change at the local level will be slow in coming, if it comes at all (it was not long after the party had been established that members first complained about 'boring' meetings and lack of participation). In the 1950s and 1960s the sense that the party had been left behind by social change and so needed to rethink its local structures had also been articulated. The passive resistance of the unions and many active members was one factor in explaining why nothing much changed (Fielding, 2000c). At the start of the twenty-first century Labour's position at the grassroots was much worse than 40 years before, and (for a variety of reasons) the leadership wanted reform but even under 'New' Labour this was no guarantee of change.

Change, however, was certainly required for, despite the government's re-election in 2001, organization at the grassroots was described by one Labour Reform stalwart as 'weaker than at any time in its history' (*Labour Reform Members' Briefing*, July 2001). Moreover, membership was reported to have fallen from its 1997 peak of 405,000 to about 280,000, which was lower than when Blair first became leader (*The Daily Telegraph*, 28 January 2002). Despite the hopes of some, those joining the party during 'New' Labour's earliest days made little difference to local party culture. Indeed, while hard to verify, the majority of those who left after 1997 were probably the party's most recent recruits. Thus,

Labour in the country appeared to be mainly run by long-standing members, most of whom were alienated from their leaders: if this was not an unprecedented state of affairs, it did not suggest much hope for the future.

To help improve poor government–party relations, after his re-election Blair created the position of Party Chairman, which came with a seat in Cabinet. Such a post was mooted at various times: among the first to propose this innovation was Mandelson (Mandelson and Liddle, 1996, 223). Some suspected that the chairman would be mainly concerned with 'spinning' a good case in the media. That the MP appointed was Charles Clarke, one of the authors of an early call for a more outward-looking party, indicated he would devote his energies to more basic matters (Labour Co-Ordinating Committee, 1982). Indeed, Clarke immediately committed the party to end 'control freakery' and promised to ensure members had a genuine policy-making role (*The Guardian*, 5 July 2001).

Conclusion

Directing their members' energies outwards and away from policy-making is one of the hallmarks of a cartel party, something 'New' Labour has yet to fully achieve. For this and other reasons it must therefore remain an open question how far events since 1994 have made Labour any more of a cartel party than it was before.

It is certainly doubtful that the party has become any more democratic in the sense that its policies accurately reflect the views of its members. Before 1997 some 'New' Labour partisans hoped to give members a greater say in the party's affairs, but only because they seemed pliable and a more legitimate platform on which to base the leader's effective autonomy. The unions appeared tainted and it was feared that too close an association with them would alienate suburban voters (Ludlam, 2001a, 115). Since 1997, however, the members have shown that they cannot always be relied on to make what the leadership considered were the right choices. Thus, the unions have retained a position not too different to the one held in the 1950s: to protect the leadership from the members (Ludlam, 2001c).

Therefore, despite the predictions of some, the unions retain a significant if paradoxical place in the party. This is best illustrated in the case of the Amalgamated Engineering and Electrical Union (AEEU). The AEEU has a long history of being controlled by leadership loyalists and its present General Secretary, Sir Ken Jackson, upholds that tradition.

Thus the AEEU proved helpful in both London and Wales when officials felt they could not rely on the members, yet Jackson opposed further constitutional change because he saw it as a device to reduce union influence; he described PP as marking the limit of what he was prepared to accept and threatened to withdraw funding to make his point (*The Observer*, 28 September 1997). Indeed, while the proportion of Labour's income contributed by the unions as a whole has fallen from about 90 per cent at its peak to about 30 per cent, even this would leave a large hole in the party's finances should it be withdrawn. The unions have in any case successfully adapted to the new constitution and now use the NPF to further their own interests; none more so than the AEEU which has fought hard to prevent the party supporting the introduction of a more proportional system to Westminster elections.

If no more democratic, it is arguable that Labour is little more subject to the leader's will than previously. At the very least, members have the ability informally and indirectly to influence their leaders in much the same way as Conservative members are said to have done in the past, despite the lack of any mechanism to hold their leaders to account (Kelly, 1989). Moreover, it may be that the members' formal voice is now heard and acted on more than in the very recent past at least. At the NPF gathering held before Labour's 2000 Conference, ministers made important concessions on policy that were reflected in the content of the party's 2001 manifesto. As Ann Black (of Labour Reform and a member of the NEC) stated, there was 'more flexibility, more willingness to move positions and more willingness to listen' than had once been the case (*The Independent*, 21 July 2000).

6
Managing the Economy

Many observers consider the critical difference between 'New' Labour and the party in the past to be their respective attitudes towards capitalism. Labour historically has been viewed as antagonistic to capitalism since it was based on private ownership and therefore thought to work against the collective interest. This disposition led the party to extend common ownership in the belief that only when the economy was run by government could it operate to the advantage of the working-class majority. In contrast, 'New' Labour is thought to consider that in a modern, globalized economy no government can do no more than make the labour force fit to do capitalism's bidding. Thus, from being a constraint on the exploitative and at times destructive forces unleashed by capitalism, Labour under Blair has become its champion. In particular, although established largely to defend the interests of trade unionists against those of their employers, since 1994 Labour has been accused of privileging the welfare of business over that of the workers.

It is certainly true that much of the rhetoric employed by 'New' Labour was designed to stress the extent to which it had embraced the market. Hence the new clause four committed Labour to promoting market 'dynamism', while the 1997 manifesto declared 'healthy profits' to be 'essential' (Labour Party, 1997c, 15). This emphasis did not slacken as 'New' Labour grew into office. As Patricia Hewitt stated, not long after being appointed Secretary of State for Trade and Industry in 2001, the government was 'unashamedly pro-business' (Hewitt, 2001a).

Chapter 3 provided the context for an understanding of Labour's historical attitude to capitalism and promoted a view that challenged the one described above. In particular, it questioned the importance of the party's formal commitment to common ownership. The chapter then reconsidered the motives of post-war Labour governments and suggested that most ministers believed limited state ownership and Keynesian fiscal manipulation would make capitalism more efficient, not weaker. It concluded that the hostility of Labour governments – rather than certain party members – to capitalism has been much exaggerated.

The party's leaders were acutely aware of the need to promote the success of a mixed economy in which the free market predominated. Some in fact believed the market should enjoy a determining role, and did not need Margaret Thatcher to tell them when the time had come to reconsider their attachment to Keynesianism. Although the party temporarily assumed a much more antagonistic attitude to capitalism in the late 1970s and early 1980s, Neil Kinnock's Policy Review restored the established position.

Despite appearances, therefore, 'New' Labour drew much of its inspiration from the developing perspective of the party's post-war leadership. The achievement of the Thatcher–Major administrations undoubtedly contributed to its economic thinking, but it needs to be borne in mind how far the last Labour government had laid the foundations for policies which some identified as exclusively Thatcherite. As a consequence of this confluence of influences, those who have studied the Blair government's economic record have understandably assumed a variety of perspectives. Philip Stephens, for example, believes Blair's strategy represented 'a momentous shift for a party of the left' as it erased the 'old dividing lines between right and left' (Stephens, 2001, 185). This view was echoed by David Coates' assessment that Labour's industrial and employment policies were 'remarkably similar' to those of its Conservative predecessor (Coates, 2001b, 133–4). In contrast, Michael Moran and Elizabeth Alexander consider Blair's approach marked a 'clear break' both with that of previous Labour governments and those adopted by the Conservatives under Thatcher and Major (Moran and Alexander, 2001, 120). Finally, while Andrew Gamble and Gavin Kelly argue that Labour's policies exhibited elements of both change and continuity, they think its attitude to the state was in sharp contrast to that of the Thatcher–Major governments. Indeed, 'New' Labour's more positive view of government intervention places it, they believe, 'squarely in the long tradition of economic revision' which has been a major feature of the party's post-war progress (Gamble and Kelly, 2001, 183).

This chapter will make its case by looking in some detail at the rationale for 'New' Labour's economic policies, as well as the policies themselves. This means first looking briefly at the context in which the government came to power. The chapter will then sketch out the rationale for Labour's approach to the economy, looking in particular at the importance of 'globalization'. The crucial significance of macroeconomic stability, which appears to imply a stress on government non-intervention, will be emphasized. The extent to which this appearance is misleading will be demonstrated by the importance of the state's active promotion of competition and productivity within the 'New' Labour schema. Two key areas, which some take to vindicate the notion that Blair's party has abandoned Labour's historical approach, are industrial relations policy and the respective roles of the public and private sectors. In the final section, these areas will be highlighted to suggest that, notwithstanding some considerable differences of emphasis, as Gamble and Kelly suggest, 'New' Labour's approach enjoys a surprising degree of continuity with that of earlier Labour governments.

The Context for Economic Policy-Making

The development of a political party's economic policy is not a discrete activity undertaken in isolation from other considerations. It is usually formulated with at least one eye on its potential to foster a successful electoral coalition, as a reputation for competent economic management can influence voters' affiliations (Moran and Alexander, 2001, 108–12). The relationship between policy and popularity was especially acute for Labour in the 1980s and early 1990s as the party appeared to lack sufficient economic credibility with key voters. As made plain in Chapter 4, one of the purposes behind the assertion of 'New' Labour was to encourage those who had voted Conservative in 1992 to believe in the party's ability to run the economy. It was meant to address affluent voters' broad satisfaction with economic progress under Thatcher and Major, and their fear that Labour would undermine this by conceding too much influence to the unions and raising taxes irresponsibly.

The need to reassure voters was reinforced by the leadership's belief that it also had to overcome the ingrained scepticism of those running the international financial markets about any type of Labour government. Such speculators favoured a stable fiscal environment based on low inflation, modest government spending and limited tax rates. Their assessment of how far government policy might harm their investments could determine the success or failure of any economic strategy. If the markets lost confidence in a government, they might bring about the collapse of the national currency which would in turn throw all forms of activity out of kilter: interest rates would rise, imports become more expensive and unemployment increase. Thus, the leadership considered it imperative to appease such nervous sensibilities.

It is moot exactly how far 'New' Labour's policies were adopted simply to assuage these two audiences, but at the very least presentation was strongly influenced by the leadership's desire win them over. As the substance of policy did not much change as a result of Blair's leadership this meant the party had to employ rhetorical exaggeration. The revision of clause four was the primary example of how far the leadership would go to over-sell the proposition that Labour had embraced the market. Thus, if in certain respects the emphasis of policy did alter under Blair, change was nonetheless more apparent than real.

The nature of the contemporary British economy also needs to be taken into account when attempting to understand why 'New' Labour followed its particular path. The economy's sluggish rate of growth, something the Conservatives had failed to overcome, remained a problem and one that would have been familiar to Harold Wilson. Yet the basis of economic activity had changed dramatically since Labour was last in office. Manufacturing had been displaced by services: the former accounted for less than one-fifth of those in employment whereas the latter comprised about three-quarters of all workers. Moreover, the main areas of growth appeared to be based around digital information technologies that spawned modestly-sized units of production requiring small numbers of highly skilled workers. In Britain at least, the era of dominant mass-production 'metal-bashing' industries had long gone. If for no other reason, Labour's policies had to change to take account of this new reality.

The Importance of Labour

Blair and Gordon Brown had established the intellectual basis for 'New' Labour's economic approach well before the former was elected leader (Blair, 1994; Brown, 1994). If this outlook owed much to the immediate concerns of Kinnock's Policy Review, it also derived from their particular interpretation of Labour's long-established precepts. What is most striking about this joint elaboration of the party's enduring 'values' is the extent to which it stressed the importance of the economy. Some considered this meant 'New' Labour's purpose was reducible to crude economic considerations. It more probably marked Brown and Blair's desire to make Labour's vision appear practical to a sceptical audience. That they defined the role of the state under a Labour government in terms surely designed to appeal to those who believed in the free market could have been no coincidence.

In particular, both men asserted that 'globalization', a term we shall investigate below, made the possession of a sufficiently skilled and educated labour force vital to Britain's prosperity. Brown went so far as to describe labour, rather than capital, as 'the driving force of the modern economy'; 'the skills of the workforce', he stated, 'are the key to economic progress'. They argued that the country lagged behind its main rivals because, by comparison, British workers lacked the necessary expertise. The reason for this, Brown and Blair claimed, was the Conservatives' over-reliance on the market, for only government could help the country fully adapt to the challenges provoked by global economic change.

According to Blair's notion of 'social-ism', self-interest and the general welfare of society were inextricably linked as it was based on the belief that a 'strong and active society' was 'necessary to advance the individual'. Central to the fulfilment of these complementary interests, according to Brown, was enabling individuals to realize their full potential. This was a long-standing social democratic end that (on one reading at least) implied greater equality. It had, however, now become a key economic objective due to the extent to which 'individual liberation' arose from 'the enhancement of the value of labour'. Moreover, in this scheme, government had a duty to intervene to ensure everyone achieved their latent promise. Brown qualified the nature of such intervention by asserting that government should foster 'personal responsibility' rather than become a substitute for it. This marked it out from the kind of direct macro-level intervention practised by previous Labour administrations. Instead, Brown proposed state involvement at the level of the individual, although this would inevitably have social consequences. 'Our guiding theme', the future Chancellor announced, 'is not what the state can do for you but what the state can enable you to do for yourself'.

Brown described this approach as constituting a 'new economic egalitarianism' from which both individual and society could benefit. This, Blair asserted, betraying the political aspect to such rethinking, allowed Labour to 'capture the ground and language of opportunity for itself' by promoting economic policies that were 'entirely consistent' with the party's 'traditional' principles. Consequently, in his first Budget speech Brown stated that the 'dynamic economies of the future will be those that unlock the talent of all their people, and our creativity, our adaptability, our belief in hard work and self-improvement ... are precisely the qualities we need to make Britain a strong economic power in the twenty-first century'. In this economy where capital, inventions and raw materials were all mobile, Brown claimed, 'Britain has only one truly national resource: the talent and potential of its people' (*The Financial Times*, 3 July 1997).

Globalization

Central to the Brown–Blair approach was their belief in 'globalization'. It would be wrong to think 'New' Labour unique in imagining Britain had to take account of the world economy. Due to the country's dependence on international trade, every post-war government (irrespective of its affiliation) had been acutely aware of external forces. It was because he believed the prevalence of strikes harmed exports that Wilson introduced *In Place of Strife* in 1969. James Callaghan provoked the 'winter of discontent' in 1978–9 because he considered high wage costs hurt the country's international competitiveness. In fact the need to keep currency speculators happy by pursuing policies they at least did not consider disastrous was never absent from the minds of Labour's postwar chancellors. Nonetheless, 'New' Labour's adherence to what it took to be the requirements of 'globalization' was generally taken to distinguish Blair and Brown from their predecessors.

Blair considered 'globalization' both 'inevitable' and even 'desirable' (Blair, 1996, 118–29). Although the Labour leader employed the term in an unproblematic way, like other means of understanding economic change 'globalization' was a contested term: analysts keenly debated its meaning and some even denied its existence. The conventional view of 'globalization' proceeds from the basic assumption that since the 1970s the ability of individual states to influence their economic environment has drastically declined. First, the power of financial speculators was said to have increased: the abolition of exchange controls, in conjunction with advances in computer technology, meant governments had either to accept speculators' judgement or see their currencies collapse. Second, employers supposedly became more able to relocate their operations: countries with high taxes and wages were considered in danger of seeing companies take flight to societies with lower costs. Finally, the level of international trade was said to have risen and so put a premium on the national economy's competitiveness. Few observers disputed that government capacity had diminished over the past three decades, but a number doubted 'globalization' was an irresistible force. Advocates of 'hyperglobalization' nonetheless believed the nation state had become irrelevant (Ohmae, 1995). Yet, if international financial markets had become more powerful, some questioned the extent to which companies had become footloose and how much more important was global trade. Indeed, sceptics believed 'globalization' was more smokescreen than reality, a concept designed to buttress the assertion of capitalist interests (Weiss, 1998; Hirst and Thompson, 1999).

'New' Labour's view was probably closest to those who charted a path between 'hyperglobalist' and sceptical positions and thought governments retained an important economic role, albeit one more circumscribed than in the past (Held *et al.*, 1999). As Jack Straw declared after becoming Foreign Secretary in 2001, 'globalization' had been 'created and shaped by the choices and decisions of us all'; thus national governments acting together could influence its development (*The Guardian*, 10 September 2001). Clare Short had anticipated this perspective in her capacity as Secretary of State for International Development. Welcoming the wealth created by greater global inter-dependence, she conceded that while the forces it unleashed were not always positive, they could be managed by stronger international institutions (Short, 1999, 55–7, 60–1).

It would be wrong, therefore, to believe (as its many critics do) that 'New' Labour can be placed 'squarely within a prevailing neo-liberal global orthodoxy' (Wilkinson, 2001, 136). At times, however, that did appear to be the case. Thus, Brown could assert that as 'globalization' meant 'greater competition at home is the key to greater competitiveness abroad', so it was the 'openness of the economy, not its closed nature', that was the 'driving force in productivity growth' (Owen, 2001, 209). This rhetoric was only partly due to the undoubted belief that, according to one 1996 Labour policy document, no country could escape the 'challenge of a new more competitive global economy' (Labour Party, 1996). It also derived from the fact that while they believed 'globalization' described something real and new, Brown and Blair appreciated that it could also be used as an ideological battering ram. Citing its apparently inflexible dictates might convince doubters in their own party that there was no alternative to an accommodation with the market. The impossibility of escaping 'globalization' was also a useful means of impressing on business leaders the crucial importance that they overcome a long-standing problem within the British economy: its lack of international competitiveness.

Stability

'Globalization' was also used to justify 'New' Labour's adherence to macro-economic stability, which Blair and Brown presented as the single most crucial precondition for success. This emphasis on stability was seen by some as distinguishing the Blair government from its Labour predecessors and most obviously associating it with the outlook of the outgoing Conservatives (Driver and Martell, 1998, 72–3). As with analysis of other aspects of 'New' Labour's economic approach, this rather exaggerated matters.

Blair outlined his belief in stability during the 1995 Mais lecture in which he drew useful comparisons between 'New' Labour and Conservative policy (Blair, 1996, 75–97). The Labour leader noted that the Thatcher governments had reversed what had been the conventional wisdom for much of the post-war period. This stipulated that macro-economic policy, through Keynesian demand management, could stimulate growth and so maintain full employment; in contrast, micro-economic policy (such as that relating to the labour market and levels of investment) was the key to controlling inflation. The Conservatives in contrast believed macro-economic policy – by keeping interest rates at a sustained low rate – was the key to maintaining inflation, whereas micro-economic policy promoted growth. Within this schema the only substantive role left for government was the setting of interest rates as micro-economic policy was best left to a market unhindered by state meddling.

Blair agreed with this new emphasis, accepting the argument that demand management had forced the economy to take a series of dramatic lurches in direction, creating ever-increasing levels of inflation that ultimately undermined Britain's competitiveness. Moreover, such volatility, he believed, had also inhibited long-term investment as companies needed to be confident in the future course of the economy if they were to risk their capital. The Labour leader noted, however, that the first steps towards this new paradigm had been taken not by Thatcher but by the preceding Callaghan government: to suggest that this was a uniquely Thatcherite policy was therefore misleading.

Blair consequently committed his government to a macro-economic policy designed to keep inflation 'low and as stable as possible'. Indeed, the supposed greater mobility of capital fostered by 'globalization' meant the need to attract investment was more imperative than in the 1980s. Thus Blair asserted that the control of inflation was of greater importance than even the Conservatives had claimed. Indeed, getting the framework right was, he asserted, the 'biggest single thing that will encourage business to invest'. Labour would therefore be more vigilant in maintaining low inflation than were the Conservatives. Indeed, one of the Labour leader's criticisms of the Conservative application of macro-economic policy was that they had been too lax and manipulated interest rates to improve their electoral popularity. His final criticism was more crucial: the Conservatives had neglected micro-economic policy due to their over-commitment to a free market. Blair instead believed that a successful micro-economic policy required continued government intervention.

In its first Queen's Speech the Blair government declared its 'central economic objectives' to be 'high and stable levels of economic growth and employment, to be achieved by ensuring opportunity for all'. The promise of a 'high and stable' level of employment was deliberately taken from the 1944 White Paper on employment. This had defined the aim of the Attlee government and those administrations that followed until 1979 as being the active promotion of full employment. Yet the 'essential platform' for 'New' Labour's objective was to be an economic stability embracing low inflation, along with 'prudent' tax rates and spending financed out of taxation rather than borrowing. There would be no direct and little indirect macro-economic intervention, as implied by the 1944 White Paper. The commentator, Will Huttton, was not alone in believing such stability incompatible with achieving full employment (*The Observer*, 1 June 1997). Against these views Brown argued that in the global economy nothing was possible without stability, while domestic political constraints had also to be taken into consideration. As he stated in 2000, the government simply had to work 'within an institutional framework that commands market credibility and public trust' (Stephens, 2001, 192).

The first step towards generating this trust saw Brown give the Bank of England freedom to set interest rates within days of winning the General Election. Blair had intimated that some such measure would be introduced in his Mais lecture although no details were forthcoming. This was meant to dramatize how far 'New' Labour had moved on from the 1940s, for in 1945 Attlee had nationalized the Bank whereas in 1997 Blair seemed to return it to a state of independence. This was, however, not quite true. The Chancellor retained the power to set the annual inflation target, which Brown declared was 2.5 per cent. The Bank – or more specifically the Monetary Policy Committee (MPC) – merely set interest rates designed to achieve that target. A majority of MPC members were, moreover, appointed by the Chancellor (one of them being the leading trade unionist, Bill Morris). This meant that while Brown was free to exert private pressure on the MPC, if things went wrong he could distance himself from its decisions. Furthermore, this was – comparatively speaking – no revolutionary act. Most major economies, including those run by social democrats, had fully independent central banks: it had not done the Germans much harm. In addition, if Britain were to join the European single currency, it would have to get used to the existence of independent bankers fixing interest rates.

Pursuing 'Prudence'

As further evidence of 'New' Labour's commitment to stability, the Chancellor adhered to two self-imposed 'golden rules'. The first stated government could only borrow to make capital investments, not to cover current spending. The second stipulated that, over the economic cycle, public debt had to be held at a 'stable and prudent level' which Brown defined as no more than 40 per cent of the Gross Domestic Product (GDP). Central to these rules was Labour's approach to 'tax and spend'. As indicated in Chapter 4, Blair had felt it necessary to commit his government to adhere to Conservative spending plans for its first two years and stick to existing income tax rates throughout its full term.

Even its own supporters believed the Major government's spending plans had been set at unfeasibly low levels. In office Labour ministers tried as best they could to circumvent the consequences of these spending levels, while remaining true to the essence of Blair's promise. Even so, these two years of abstinence helped cause spending during Labour's first term to fall as a share of GDP, from 41.2 per cent in 1996–7 to 38.8 per cent in 2000–1. The other influence on this relative decline was economic growth: government spending in absolute terms did not fall, but rose. However, the economy expanded even faster. As a result, calls on spending abated: the need for unemployment relief was reduced as more people found work. Government also repaid debts accrued during the Major years, so interest payments declined. There was in addition an unexpected problem: civil servants used to the previous regime proved incapable of spending all those funds given to them by the Chancellor. However, as a result of the 2000 Comprehensive Spending Review (CSR), Labour planned to increase expenditure by 3.8 per cent annually during the first three years of its second term. As the economy was due to grow by only 2.5 per cent this meant spending would once more rise as a share of GDP (Clark and Dilnot, 2001, 7–17).

True to his pre-election pledge Brown did not increase direct tax during Labour's first term: indeed, he cut lower-paid workers' income tax and National Insurance contributions, aiming to make employment more remunerative than living on state benefits. Nonetheless – and despite having attacked the Conservatives for their 22 tax rises between 1992 and 1997 – Brown increased numerous taxes to fund Labour's schemes. The party had entered the 1997 campaign pledged to levy a £5 billion 'windfall' tax on the privatized utilities. If raising income tax was deemed politically impossible, the windfall tax was popular with voters. Companies such as British Telecom had done remarkably well after leaving the state sector. Their 'fat cat' managers were widely reviled for the continued inefficiencies of some of their companies' services while they rewarded themselves with high salaries. The public saw the tax as righteous, especially as they were left untouched and most of the money raised was to be spent on reducing youth unemployment.

Brown increased other taxes in areas he hoped the public would not notice. For example, he abolished dividend tax credits and advance corporation tax which, all told, generated £7 billion in 2000 alone. He also imposed higher taxes on consumption, most infamously on fuel. Finally, Brown phased out mortgage interest tax relief and the married couple's allowance. These supposedly hidden (or 'stealth') taxes were only obscured for a time, and in the autumn of 2000 the country was brought to a halt by protests against the cost of petrol, which caused the Chancellor to concede ground. Thus, as a result of Brown's measures – and in contrast to the rhetoric of Labour's 1997 manifesto – the share of national income taken by tax in 2000–1 was 40.5 per cent of GDP, 2.9 per cent higher than in 1996–7. Yet, as with the relative decline in spending, this increase was partly the result of economic growth. More people in work meant more people paying tax; a tight labour market caused the salaries of those already in employment to rise and, with it, the amount such workers paid in tax. Thus, the money raised by income tax increased even as the rate remained the same (Clark and Dilnot, 2001, 7–17).

So disciplined were public finances under Brown that the government even reduced the public debt and placed government finances in what has been described as 'historically good shape' (Clark and Dilnot, 2001, 11). The Chancellor also reordered finances in a profound way, linking medium-term spending targets to outcomes so as to promote efficiency within departments. In addition the 1998 CSR introduced a three-year planning cycle to avoid the short-termism of previously annual spending rounds. Such reforms made an explicit connection between the money given to ministers and what they achieved with it, the monitoring of which was to be undertaken by the Treasury. The longer time frame in which to plan departmental spending was also meant to promote greater efficiency and consistency. By adopting such measures, the government hoped in addition to reassure sceptical voters that Labour ministers would spend their taxes wisely.

The EU and the Economy

On being elected in 1997, one of Blair's first acts was to adopt the European Union's (EU) Social Chapter, which was part of the 1991

Maastricht Treaty and something that the Major government, strongly supported by most employers, had refused to implement. The Conservatives believed the Chapter increased labour market regulation and so constituted a threat to Britain's economic efficiency. The Chapter's most salient measures were twofold: first, it allowed a working parent to obtain three months' unpaid leave on the birth of a child; second, it obliged companies with more than one thousand employees in at least two EU states to establish works councils. The role of these councils was to inform and consult workers on matters pertaining to trans-national issues: their powers were in truth very limited. Moreover, the measure only affected 300 of Britain's largest companies, 40 of which had already established such councils voluntarily.

By implementing the Chapter, Blair pleased the trade unions at little cost while indicating that 'New' Labour was more positive about the EU than the Conservatives. Nonetheless, aware of the views of many employers, the Prime Minister promised to oppose further measures that might restrain labour 'flexibility'. Consequently, in concert with German and British employer representatives, he attempted to block the introduction of a binding directive on companies employing over 50 workers to create consultation councils (Taylor, 2001, 261–3). Other proposals emanating from the EU that promised to increase what he considered unnecessary regulation were also rejected or watered down at Blair's behest.

Indeed, during the first term ministers did their best to prevent the EU having much of an influence on the running of the British economy. In some ways this disposition was not so very different from that of the Conservatives, and it contrasted with the tone adopted by Labour under Kinnock after 1987. As part of the Policy Review, Labour had abandoned the policy established in time for the 1983 election: namely, that it would take Britain out of what was then known as the European Economic Community (EEC). The left had opposed membership of the EEC because they saw it as a capitalist club with powers to prevent a radical Labour government from assuming the controls necessary to transform the British economy. In contrast, Kinnock assumed a more positive attitude, because he saw Europe as a means of restraining the unremitting advance of the free market under Thatcher (George and Rosamond, 1992).

If 'New' Labour remained generally positive about the EU, it was almost as wary as the Conservatives about the greater willingness to regulate evident in other EU states. Ministers feared this might be translated into EU directives that would undermine the British economy's one clear comparative advantage: a more 'flexible' labour market. It is certainly true that elements in both the left-led French and German governments favoured using the EU to challenge the dictates of the global economy. Some were also keen on an EU-wide job creation scheme conducted along Keynesian lines.

Just like any government, 'New' Labour sought to influence the EU in directions thought to favour the British economy. For the first term at least the nature of the economy also meant not joining the European single currency when it came into being in 1999. Most Conservatives saw membership as a threat to Britain's national sovereignty as it entailed having interest rates set by the independent European central bank rather than by national politicians. In contrast to this dogmatic position, Labour's view as set out by Brown in the autumn of 1997 was that there was no constitutional impediment to entry. There were, however, a number of practical problems that had to be worked out; in particular, the fact that the British economy was out of kilter with the rest of the EU. Once Britain and others in the EU found themselves at the same place in the economic cycle then entry would be less problematic (Bulmer, 2001, 246). A further reason for 'New' Labour's caution was the opposition of most voters to entry, something encouraged by leading tabloid press barons. As Blair was committed to winning a referendum before entering the single currency and despite favouring entry, he was reluctant to challenge popular opinion head-on. The Prime Minister appeared to hope that once the single currency had become an established success, Britons would see membership as inevitable and on that basis support it. In the meantime, the government acted as if it anticipated entry, even if it was not expected any time soon (Deighton, 2001, 317).

Micro-Economic Policy

If Brown and Blair considered macro-economic stability to be the crucial precondition for growth, they only saw it as a first step (Brown, 2000a). Ministers looked to micro-economic policy as the particular means of achieving 'New' Labour's basic aim: to increase the economy's trend rate of growth.

All post-war governments tried to accelerate growth; but, whether influenced by demand management or its *laissez-faire* successor, the economy stubbornly stuck to an average annual rate of about 2.5 per cent, some distance behind the country's major competitors (Fielding and

Tonge, 1999, 39–41). This problem had preoccupied earlier Labour governments although they aimed to solve it through macro-economic means. Attlee's nationalization programme was predicated on the belief that as utilities such as coal, gas, electricity and the water supply would be run more efficiently in public hands, productivity in private concerns dependent on their goods and services should increase. Until the change of heart under Callaghan, all Labour governments had supposed that demand management would create a period of sustained growth sufficient to produce a dramatic break-through in performance.

One of the post-war British economy's more intractable problems was that its productivity – the amount of profit generated by an individual worker – was inferior to that of most other major industrial nations. The implications of this fact have been widely but inconclusively debated, with even the means of measuring productivity remaining contentious. However, it is generally agreed that British productivity has been consistently lower than in the more regulated economies of Germany and France, and much lower than in the less regulated United States. In the former economies labour was relatively expensive so employers were encouraged to invest in capital equipment to offset employment costs. In the United States, while wages were much lower, this proved no bar to higher productivity. There was therefore no obvious solution to Britain's 'productivity gap'. Most analysts nonetheless focused on two possible ways out: more investment in human capital through training and education, and greater investment in physical capital. The need for more training was certainly something 'New' Labour embraced with enthusiasm. As noted above, Brown and Blair believed this would enhance individual potential and economic growth. The next chapter will highlight training and its importance to 'New' Labour's conception of equality.

Competitiveness

If training was considered an important means of advancing productivity, so was increasing competitiveness. The Blair government's emphasis on the need to increase competition in the market was widely thought unique, as previous Labour administrations were considered largely uninterested in such matters (Owen, 2001, 215). In fact Attlee's ministers saw improvements to industry's supply-side performance as vital to economic survival. They had employed a variety of means to improve productivity, in particular sponsoring the creation of the British Institute of Management to encourage the adoption of more efficient means of managing labour and capital. The government also created Development Councils intended to bring together workers' and employers' representatives in specific industries to find ways of improving production methods (Tiratsoo and Tomlinson, 1993). In addition, as one Labour publication of the time put it, ministers also sought to help private industry become more efficient by encouraging it to get rid of 'restrictive practices, price rings and rigged markets' (Mercer, 1991, 76). Monopolies and cartels were seen as inhibiting competition and, as Harold Wilson declared while in charge of the Department of Trade, 'competition is the public's natural safeguard' (Mercer, 1992, 60).

Attlee's ministers favoured encouragement rather than compulsion to achieve their aims in this field. Some consider the government's reluctance to legislate betrayed the party leadership's unqualified commitment to private enterprise, although others dispute that view (Tiratsoo and Tomlinson, 1993, 163–70). In any case, whether the means were flawed or not, few historians now dispute that the Attlee administration was dedicated to improving competitiveness and productivity so as to make business better able to prosper on the international stage. If anything, the Wilson governments of the 1960s were even more concerned with such matters, although they were no more successful.

Due to its administrative responsibilities the Department of Trade and Industry (DTI) was the Blair government's main means of increasing productivity. Peter Mandelson, who was briefly Secretary of State at the DTI, went so far as to describe it as the 'department for the future' (Mandelson, 1998a). The DTI's approach was best encapsulated in the 1998 Competition Act, largely the product of Charlie Leadbeater, author of an enthusiastic study of the 'new economy' (Leadbeater, 1999). The Act was preoccupied with fostering expansion in the high-growth 'knowledge-based' economy, especially that part which employed digital technologies. It was rather dismissive of what it took to be the low-growth manufacturing sector, largely because it now only accounted for a small proportion of the nation's output.

Once considered to be the party of industry, Labour did not propose trying to reverse long-standing and powerful processes that had forced manufacturing to decline. Indeed, mainly based in export sectors, during Labour's first term manufacturing suffered from the high value of sterling. Corus, formerly British Steel, cut back on production in south Wales; the car makers, Ford, moved out of Dagenham while Vauxhall left Luton; and Marks & Spencer abandoned domestic clothing suppliers in favour of cheaper products abroad. When BMW proposed selling off the Rover car business in the Midlands, the government gave some support to a management buy-out, but little else was done to challenge market forces. On this matter the global economy was deemed to have spoken. Thus, while some questioned whether the 'knowledge economy' was all it was claimed to be, the DTI considered that this was where help should be most concentrated. As Mandelson put it, 'knowledge' was 'the only source of competitive advantage' (Mandelson, 1998b; Hirst, 2000, 82–8).

The help government proposed offering was, however, of a very particular sort. As Stephen Byers declared when Secretary of State at the DTI, government should act merely to 'ensure the market functions properly' (*The Guardian*, 3 February 1999). Thus, instead of trying to 'second-guess boardroom decisions', Mandelson defined the DTI's role as removing those impediments preventing entrepreneurs from exploiting technological advances to the full. In this regard he wanted Britain to become more like he imagined the United States to be, telling a New York audience how he saw their country as promoting 'an enterprise-orientated, risk-taking, failure-tolerant business culture that enables you constantly to innovate and constantly adapt to changing economic conditions' (Mandelson, 1998a). Britain, he claimed, needed more entrepreneurs as 'they are the real agents of economic change'. Government would therefore help reshape the market to make the job of the entrepreneur easier; indeed, 'enterprise' should be promoted at every opportunity (Mandelson, 1998b; MacIntyre, 1999, 416–17, 423–5).

To this end government policy aimed to create what Brown hoped would be 'the most pro-competition policy in the world' based on the notion that greater competition at home was the key to superior competitiveness abroad (Brown, 2000b). Competitive markets were considered the optimum means of ensuring resources were put to best use: as Brown put it, they were the 'sharpest spur to innovation, efficiency and improvement'. Yet, as the market could not be relied on to always produce competitive outcomes, government had to construct a regulatory framework to prevent or overcome restrictive practices (Brown, 2000a). As they were considered to promote efficiency, the DTI therefore reduced obstacles to company mergers. The Competition Commission, which had powers to prevent such unions, was made independent of ministers and given but one criterion against which to make decisions: a merger could only be stopped if it would reduce competition. It was made easier for declared bankrupts to return to business as it was believed that those who had failed in business would actually be better equipped to succeed in the end. The Office of Fair Trading was granted extra powers to root out anti-competitive practices and outlaw cartels; in addition, it was allowed to levy more severe financial penalties on offenders who now were liable to jail terms.

Ministers believed that if companies were to become more competitive they needed to increase the proportion of their profits that went into capital investment, an issue Labour governments had tried to address in the past. A hoped-for consequence of sustained macro-economic stability was that entrepreneurs would gain the confidence to invest for the longer term. The government introduced measures designed to encourage this tendency further. It reduced the marginal rate of corporation tax and created a tax credit for small and medium businesses to foster greater investment in research and development. To that end, an Enterprise Fund was established to provide venture capital to entrepreneurs denied access to conventional sources of finance who wished to translate especially innovative ideas into practice. While a modest measure, it was hoped the Fund would encourage the private sector to become more involved in such high-risk – but potentially high-yield – investment opportunities.

The 'Soft Approach'

Despite its importance, some critics contend that Labour's rhetoric in this field was not matched by its measures, which were comparatively modest and rarely involved compulsion (Coates, 2001b, 134). As we have seen, Attlee's administration has faced similar criticism. For example, it was clear that not all 'New' Labour ministers approved of the legislation that underpinned corporate governance as this gave shareholders a pre-eminent position. For a brief time in Opposition Blair had tentatively suggested that companies had responsibilities to other 'stakeholders', such as employees and local communities, although he soon retreated when business leaders claimed he was trying to impede profit-making. However, it was widely believed that the legal imperative for directors to ensure that investors received a decent annual dividend meant companies often focused on short-term profit rather than long-term investment. A major review of corporate governance was initiated in 1998, but did not report until after the 2001 election. Most of its recommendations were useful but limited rationalizations of company law. However, the review did at least suggest that while company directors should remain accountable to shareholders, they also needed to take 'due account' of wider interests such as their employees, suppliers, customers and the community as a whole (DTI, 2001). How the review will be translated into legislation remains to be seen.

It is certainly true that during its first term 'New' Labour was unwilling to force businesses to change their practices through legislation. This may have been because ministers remained sensitive to the charge of over-burdening companies with regulations that might restrict their ability to generate a profit. Instead, ministers preferred to persuade business leaders of the need to change. Thus, while a minister for corporate responsibility was appointed, his role was limited to simply encouraging companies to consider being more 'altruistic' (*New Statesman Special Supplement*, 6 November 2000). Hewitt justified what she admitted was the government's 'soft approach' by stating that it was better to work slowly for 'cultural change' through dialogue than to use the 'blunt instrument' of regulation (Hewitt, 2001a). Whatever the rationale, the shareholders' interests remained paramount.

Trade Unions and the Workplace

During the 1997 campaign, Blair assured *Sun* readers that no government of his would be 'held to ransom' by the trade unions. 'We will not cave in to unrealistic pay demands', he stated: voters could support Labour safe in the knowledge they would not be giving the unions power through the back door (*The Sun*, 4 April 1997). Blair was aware key voters were concerned that an incoming Labour government would repeat the experience of the 1974–9 administration, which was widely perceived as having been utterly beholden to the unions. What they did not want was another 'winter of discontent'. In fact, the public-sector strikes comprising that period had been the result of the Callaghan government's determination to prevent unions gaining pay rises in excess of 3 per cent: hardly the act of ministers indebted to union 'barons'. Blair, however, had long before calculated it was better to distinguish his party from an inaccurately drawn version of the past rather than to challenge that picture detail by detail. In any case, he agreed with one part of the popular memory: shop-floor militancy during the 1970s had harmed the economy (Blair, 1996, 78).

To reassure doubters further, Blair promised to retain most of the legislation introduced by the Thatcher and Major governments that had severely restricted union power. The most crucial of these was the 1982 Employment Act, which made union funds liable to sequestration if their actions during a dispute were deemed to be illegal (Taylor, 2001, 247).

On becoming leader in 1994 Blair had, however, inherited a number of proposals that promised to restore some of that lost influence. These he described as 'based not on favours to the unions, but basic fairness'; they would not, he stressed, compromise the labour market 'flexibility' established during the 1980s. There was nonetheless unease amongst the 'New' Labour hierarchy about the possible electoral ramifications of these proposals, and efforts were made to obscure them from view. When the Conservatives raised the question of union recognition during the 1997 campaign, workers in Millbank Tower were temporarily gripped by panic (Fielding, 1997a, 30–1).

While many consider 'New' Labour's attitude to the unions to be barely distinguishable from that of the Conservatives, even one normally critical commentator conceded that the Blair government produced a 'quiet workplace revolution' (Taylor, 2001, 252). One reason this transformation was so muted was that ministers did not want voters to look too closely at measures Thatcher would have opposed tooth and nail. Blair's attitude to the unions' role in the economy was at heart little different from that of his predecessors. Labour leaders had always wrestled with the problem of having to represent the unions (so as to maintain party unity) and the nation as a whole (in order to win power and manage the economy). Moreover, in order to make capitalism work, Labour prime ministers had often felt it necessary to ask the unions to accept policies that were not in their immediate interest. The Wilson and Callaghan governments were consequently marked by ongoing conflicts between Cabinet and the Trades Union Congress (TUC). Indeed, as far back as the 1920s, Ramsay MacDonald had been prepared to break strikes if he considered it necessary. In 1969 Wilson even attempted to introduce legislation to restrict unofficial strikes, something Blair noted with approval (Blair, 1996, 82).

Although the post-war 'beer and sandwiches' era had seen Labour governments seek union cooperation – usually to limit wage demands – to achieve certain economic objectives, that was mainly because they were powerful and located in industries of strategic importance. Full employment meant that, had they wished to, some unions could have forced employers to concede exorbitant pay awards or could have simply stopped production. The decline of union authority since the 1970s, as much due to the changing structure of the economy as Conservative legislation, meant Blair was no longer obliged to seek their support as a matter of urgency. Thus, for both electoral and practical reasons, the new Labour Prime Minister was undoubtedly more distant from the unions than his predecessors. He had not abandoned them, however.

If Blair's 'fairness not favours' formulation was a retreat from the position the unions had enjoyed in the 1970s, compared to the Conservative years it marked a welcome advance. While suspecting Blair leant towards the employers' arguments rather than their own, union leaders were at least taken seriously as lobbyists for a cause once again seen worthy of consideration. Moreover, they knew that the Prime Minister's attitude was partly based on evidence that wavering voters remained nervous at seeing Blair support the unions too enthusiastically (Gould, 1998, 352–3). In any case, many unions had come to terms with their reduced status while the TUC under its General Secretary, John Monks, had embraced competitiveness, profitability and the idea of partnership with employers (Allen, 1998; Monks, 2000). Yet, if the Prime Minister welcomed Monks' approach, he doubted that all his union affiliates had similarly moved on (Taylor, 2001, 250–1).

Speaking for his Prime Minister, Mandelson had indicated the terms on which the unions could gain 'legitimate influence' within the government. They had, he said, to demonstrate above all 'flexibility', in terms of hours, skills, pay and even numbers of workers (MacIntyre, 1999, 419–20). If this sounded like surrender to some trade unionists, 'New' Labour ministers talked of the need for 'partnership' and referred to the rewards employers and unions could achieve if they only cooperated. To that end the DTI sponsored the Partnership at Work Fund, which promoted joint approaches to solving business problems (although fewer than one hundred such partnerships had been established by the end of the first term). Some have questioned the *bona fides* of this approach. David Coates, for example, has suggested that Labour in power showed a marked preference for the sensibilities of capital rather than labour. Blair is consequently accused of supporting a 'partnership' in which the employers held the whip hand (Coates, 2001b, 133–4). Yet, if still weaker than in the 1970s, as a result of Labour's first term the unions' position within this 'partnership' had undoubtedly been strengthened.

'New' Labour was also thought too keen on 'flexibility' for most union leaders' liking, although the party criticized the Conservatives' interpretation of the concept because of the way in which it promoted workers' insecurity. The party's 1997 manifesto proposed, instead, 'flexibility plus' to better equip employees to deal with some of the consequences of 'globalization'. This included the promotion of better skills; minimum standards as well as fair treatment at work; and welfare-to-work measures. Many union leaders remained concerned that 'flexibility', even as defined by Labour, still meant employers could pay their workers as little as possible and sack them whenever they wanted. To offset this, the unions lobbied the government to introduce as a quickly as possible the promised 'fairness at work' legislation. This embraced rights for part-time workers; protection against unfair dismissal; and, most crucially, a minimum wage and the right of unions to be recognized by employers.

Labour's manifesto stated that when a majority of the 'relevant workforce' voted in a ballot, employers should recognize a union for negotiation purposes. This, it argued, was only fair and would promote stable industrial relations from which all could benefit. Many employers, however, opposed the proposal, something the Conservatives exploited during the 1997 campaign. Labour's uncertain response demonstrated the extent to which the leadership remained uncomfortable with a policy that, while hardly returning Britain to the 1970s, some saw as reducing 'flexibility'.

Fairness at Work

Blair hoped the Confederation of British Industry (CBI) and TUC would agree a voluntary code as he did not want to introduce legislation, but this proved impossible as neither side wanted to make significant concessions. The unions saw recognition as invaluable to increasing membership; employers viewed any help to the unions as threatening profitability. The devil was in the detail. First, it was unclear how a 'relevant workforce' could be defined: in a factory, would shop-floor and office workers be lumped together, or would they need separate ballots? More significantly, would a union require a simple majority of those voting in a ballot or, as the CBI argued, a majority of all employees whether they voted or not? Of equal significance was whether smaller employers would be exempted and, if so, what size did the workforce have to be to be able to hold a ballot?

During the course of negotiations preceding the publication of the *Fairness at Work* White Paper in May 1998, union leaders and many Labour MPs feared Blair was too concerned to mollify the employers. They lobbied ministers hard to make their case. In particular, the unions wanted recognition to be granted through ballots that only required a simple majority of those participating. Anything else, they argued, would weaken the practical impact of this part of the legislation. In the event, Blair insisted that a ballot had to win the support of 40 per cent of all those in a designated bargaining unit. While this threshold severely disappointed the unions, it was at least made subject to a later review. Moreover, defeat was offset by the concession that, if over half of employees already belonged to a union, recognition would be granted automatically. Furthermore, a union was allowed to define the composition of the bargaining unit initially, although this was subject to an employer's appeal. Nonetheless, workplaces with fewer than 20 employees were exempted from the legislation, thereby excluding 5 million workers from the possibility of union recognition via this new route.

Employers' representatives resisted *Fairness at Work*: despite Blair's position on the ballot, many had become used to the freedom granted by the Conservatives and disliked being forced to negotiate with a union. Under Thatcher's tutelage, employers had also been able to sack union members almost at will, a power the White Paper now denied them. Nonetheless, after intense lobbying, the 1999 Employment Relations Act was passed with qualified support from both employers and unions. The eventual recognition process had been made more laborious and difficult as a result of employers' pressure. Thus a union could now only achieve automatic recognition if half of employees were already members so long as the independent Central Arbitration Service believed it would not disrupt 'good industrial relations' (Ludlam, 2001a, 124–6; Taylor, 2001, 252–7).

In 1999 Mandelson claimed Labour's legislation had corrected a 'basic imbalance' against employees. This was one of the more malign legacies of the Thatcher years 'New' Labour ministers were willing to discuss at this stage in the government's term (MacIntyre, 1999, 423). Certainly, after over a decade of decline, union membership began to increase during Blair's first term, reaching 7.3 million in 2000. This rise should not have been surprising as the total number in work also increased due to economic growth. More significant was the fact that, as a proportion of those in work, the share of union members at last stopped falling and remained steady at just under 30 per cent. It is too soon to make a definitive judgement about the impact of union recognition legislation, but the early signs are that it has helped recruitment. It is particularly significant that the proportion of female union members in the workforce has grown since the introduction of the legislation (TUC, 2001). Women are disproportionately employed in unskilled, part-time and low-paid occupations among which the unions have long found recruitment difficult. While the unions had made a special effort to win over female workers well before 1999, their new power to force hostile employers to recognize them must have helped.

The unions also saw the promised minimum wage as a vital means of reversing some of the impact of Conservative labour 'flexibility', especially in parts of the service economy where female part-time workers dominated. Numerous employers, however, viewed it as an unnecessary threat to their profits and claimed it would increase unemployment. The impact of the minimum wage depended on how it would be applied. Most employers favoured £3.50 per hour, while the unions backed at least £4.00. It was calculated that the former figure would affect 15 per cent of the workforce; the latter would improve the position of 24 per cent. Labour established a Low Pay Commission to investigate the rate at which the minimum was to be set and suggest whether there should be any exemptions, such as those based on age. In the end it was set at £3.60 but lower for those under 21 years of age, although both were subject to regular review.

Arguments about the minimum wage assumed a similar character to those regarding union recognition. Critics on the left and in the unions argued it had been set too low. They discounted the fact that initially employers had mostly opposed the principle of a minimum, arguing that it would price workers out of the labour market. The establishment of a minimum wage was, therefore a victory of principle that challenged free market orthodoxy, while in practice many of the lowest-paid workers in the country enjoyed some benefit.

As Blair reminded voters even as the above measures were being introduced, the British labour market remained less regulated than those in most other major European economies. This he saw as a clear competitive advantage, and in that sense embraced a view shared by Thatcher and her followers. Yet he had also set in train a process that would in all likelihood continue to improve the position of unions in particular and workers in general: this was something free market enthusiasts detested with a passion.

The Market and the State

As noted in Chapter 3, Labour's historical association with common ownership was not as straightforward as it can be made to appear: whereas some members saw nationalization as a panacea, others were less dogmatic. In particular, when Attlee nationalized 20 per cent of the economy, he acted largely in the belief that this would improve efficiency, an assumption apparently tested by wartime experience and one shared by some leading Conservatives.

If at mid-century even many outside Labour's ranks considered limited public ownership an appropriate economic tool, the same could not be said of the 1990s. By the end of the twentieth century, the Conservatives' privatization programme was generally considered to have been a success (*Economist*, 13 June 1998). First, sales had benefited the Treasury to the tune of £90 billion. Second, transferring publicly-owned companies to the private sector transformed most from loss-makers requiring state subsidy to profit-makers generating substantial tax revenues. Third, customers often benefited from improved services and lower prices. Finally, managers were now free to generate investment unconstrained by Treasury discipline. Not all privatized concerns adhered to this rule: the rail industry was probably the biggest exception. The introduction of competition and profit-seeking was considered inappropriate to some utilities. Moreover, a few doubted that all post-privatization improvements were due to a change in ownership: technological advance was often the cause. In addition, the need for profit often resulted in redundancies and a decline in the conditions of service of those workers who remained. Despite such drawbacks, by the late 1990s most European governments had begun to sell off their assets, including the French administration led by Lionel Jospin's *Parti Socialiste Français*. As with nationalization earlier in the century, those on the left and right looked on privatization as a legitimate tool to further economic growth.

If Labour's attitude to the market had initially been somewhat hostile, the Attlee government marked a turning point as ministers subsequently accepted the permanent existence of the private sector and tried to make it work. During the 1970s neo-revisionists even suggested that the market should be given back some of the freedom lost in the 1940s. The Policy Review confirmed this view by accepting that Thatcher's privatization programme should not be reversed. Furthermore, by the mid-1990s many who led 'New' Labour considered 'globalization' had undermined the capacity of the man in Whitehall to know best. As the businessman and future junior minister, David Sainsbury, stated in 1996, 'the complexity and speed of most product markets today' meant that 'there is no way that even the most able civil servants can make decisions about the strategies that companies should pursue' (Sainsbury, 1996, 113). Thus, when Labour entered office in 1997, party policy accepted that in many cases markets (albeit ones subject to proper regulation) could be more efficient than state control.

For an incoming government unwilling to raise income tax and faced with massive under-investment in the public services, selling some assets to the private sector looked a sensible way to raise revenue. Within months the new government had completed a National Assets Register, which identified resources that could be sold off and indicated how best the remainder could yield more revenue. After this Brown announced he would be selling £12 billion of existing government resources to private investors. Many Labour MPs blanched: to them this was the mark of Thatcherism. Brown argued, however, that the government was not relinquishing control of concerns such as the air traffic control system but merely creating what were termed public–private partnerships. These would, moreover, generate much-needed capital investment while not over-burdening government finances. The Chancellor was therefore using a supposedly Thatcherite technique for collectivist ends: any money raised would be invested in the country's infrastructure to the benefit of all. In contrast, the Conservatives had sold industries wholesale and most receipts financed tax cuts for the well-off. Thus Brown's approach was presented as at once pragmatic – in the sense that he employed what were considered the best means possible – and principled, in so far as he used such means to further the party's established ends. To assess 'New' Labour's approach in more detail the rest of the chapter will concentrate on three particular cases: the publicly-owned Post Office and London Underground, and the recently privatized Railtrack.

The Post Office

Labour entered office confronted by a Post Office in need of substantial investment if it was to compete in what had become a highly competitive market. In their 1997 manifesto the Conservatives promised to retain the Post Office in the public sector: it was, after all, a profitable and popular industry that contributed funds to the Treasury. However, by the late 1990s it was clear the Post Office required more commercial freedom than was allowed under existing arrangements if it was not to lose market share. Margaret Beckett, Labour's first minister at the DTI, together with the Communications Workers' Union, wanted the Post Office to become an independent but publicly-owned company free to raise capital from private sources. In contrast, the Treasury sought a partial privatization that would see the government divest itself of 49 per cent of the company. This would have given the Treasury's coffers a much-needed short-term boost while guaranteeing it a future income stream (*The Observer*, 21 June 1998; *The Guardian*, 1 September 1998). Opponents of this proposal speculated that even if just part-privatized, some of the Post Office's social functions – such as maintaining uneconomic branches in isolated villages – would be curtailed.

The future of the Post Office was complicated when Mandelson replaced Beckett as it then became part of an ongoing dispute between himself and the Chancellor. In the end, however, the Post Office was allowed greater commercial freedom and permitted to borrow money from private sources (MacIntyre, 1999, 417–20). The Treasury disliked granting the Post Office too much freedom to borrow as any amount would still be counted as government borrowing; Brown insisted a maximum figure be specified. Thus the Post Office was granted circumscribed commercial freedom, designed to allow it to raise enough funds to compete on better terms with its private rivals. This appeared a satisfactory compromise between the putative advantages of market freedom and the need to maintain certain social responsibilities. However, ministers refused to rule out future changes of ownership and postal unions remained convinced that what was now called Consignia would eventually be split up and sold off (*Tribune*, 12 October 2001).

The Tube

The London Underground had long been in state of disrepair that compromised efficiency and safety. Despite this, Conservative governments refused London Transport the necessary funds to invest in the system, and by 1997 Major's solution was to privatize. The incoming Labour government was therefore faced with a dilemma. John Prescott, the Cabinet minister in charge of transport, wished to invest in the service to the tune of £13 billion, but the Treasury was as resolute under Brown as it had been under his Conservative predecessors that this money should not all come from hard-pressed public funds. Prescott was forced to find a compromise that would generate private capital while maintaining the Underground in public hands. Given Railtrack's record, to be outlined below, few believed privatization was the best solution to rail transport. Prescott therefore developed complicated schemes designed to meet these two criteria, initially proposing to split the system into track and trains and lease these out under the supervision of London Transport. This at least allowed the minister to claim that he was not advocating 'wholesale privatization' (*The Guardian*, 17 June 1997).

In the end, the government agreed to lease the Underground's tunnels, tracks, signals and stations for up to 30 years to three private companies, while London Transport retained control of the trains. Thus the system would remain publicly owned but still give private companies the incentive to innovate and invest. As Brown saw it, contractors would bear the burden of risk in ensuring improvements were delivered on time and at cost, something he claimed they were better equipped to do than public-sector managers (Brown, 2001b). He also believed the scheme would substantially reduce the Treasury's financial burden, in his eyes probably its greatest merit. Yet, opponents argued, the lack of a central authority responsible for the whole of the Underground would create an unsafe and unreliable system. Some experts also believed it would in the end cost the tax-payer more than if the system was left completely under direct public control (*The Financial Times*, 5 July and 25 August 2001).

Whatever the precise merits, Labour's solution was unpopular with commuters and contributed to Ken Livingstone's victory in London's 1999 mayoral election. Indeed, such was the public's disapproval that the main architect of the scheme, the Chancellor, disavowed responsibility for it (*The Financial Times*, 26 July 2001). Most damningly, the process of creating a mechanism to deliver increased investment had been so protracted that the Underground was in a worse state in 2001 than when Labour first assumed office.

The Railways

Rail transport was the last of those industries nationalized by Attlee to remain in public hands. In the 1940s Labour had taken the network out of the private sector, deeming it to have 'failed the nation', and few disagreed with this analysis: rail nationalization was one of that government's least contentious measures (Cairncross, 1985, 469–70; Morgan, 1984, 97, 136–9). Conservative ministers had taken a keen interest in the operation of the industry since at least the First World War. During the 1920s the government even helped the more than 100 rail companies amalgamate into four: indeed, at this time the future Conservative leader, Winston Churchill, supported public ownership as the best way to encourage efficiency. During the Second World War the four companies were placed under state control so when nationalization came in 1948 it made little obvious difference. Nonetheless, despite its poor record in private hands, from a very early stage Labour's opponents exploited any problem on the tracks to castigate the very principle of public ownership. As both Labour and Conservative governments starved the railways of adequate investment, British Rail largely continued the poor performance of its private counterparts: there was much to criticize.

The Major government finally decided to privatize the rail network for two reasons. First, the Conservatives assumed it would be better run in private hands and so would eventually cease to be a drain on the public purse; second, they hoped to create a trap for 'New' Labour. By ensuring the railways were not owned by the state by 1996 the Conservatives forced Blair to make a difficult choice. He could either enter the forthcoming election campaign promising to re-nationalize the industry and possibly alienate key voters, or refuse to do so and provoke an internal party revolt. As the main aim was political, ministers rushed the measure through; to ensure a quick sale they sold the railways at a knockdown price and established a weak regulatory regime. The Conservative scheme also cut British Rail into many pieces: Railtrack took over the major part, being responsible for operating and maintaining the track. Twenty-eight franchises were also made available to companies wishing to tender for passenger or freight traffic. Once they were established these companies in turn sub-contracted maintenance and other operations to about 100 firms. These private operators, most notably Railtrack, were to receive public subsidies, but ministers expected market disciplines would soon reduce the amount required to keep the system going. Many Conservatives secretly hoped the companies would reduce the railway system to little more than the profitable Intercity routes.

Initially Blair promised that if British Rail was privatized Labour would take it back into public hands. At the party's 1995 Conference he blandly asserted that 'there will be a publicly owned, publicly accountable railway system under a Labour government'. As late as 1996 party members approved a draft manifesto committing the leadership to a 'publicly-owned, publicly accountable railway system', albeit with the caveat 'as economic circumstances' allowed. Yet, once the Conservatives had divested the state of direct responsibility, true to his cautious electoral strategy the Labour leader refused to take it back into public hands (Rentoul, 2001, 269–70). If he was afraid of arousing suburban fears of 'Old' Labour, there were also practical considerations. Not only would re-nationalization have been expensive, but there was no certainty private ownership would produce a worse service. As there were many risks associated with the industry, perhaps it was better to see how private operators managed it. Moreover, Blair considered there were more pressing issues to deal with on assuming office; once in power he fought shy of fundamental change, seeing it as an issue for a second term (Toynbee and Walker, 2001, 189).

Labour's 1997 manifesto criticized privatization for fragmenting the network, but merely promised to 'improve the situation as we find it, not as we wish it to be' and ensure the existing system was run in the public interest by strengthening regulation (Labour Party, 1997c, 29). Broadly speaking Labour continued the same transport policies as its Conservative predecessor: this meant accepting the country's dependence on road transport (Foster, 2001; Ward, 2002). There was, however, some support for increasing the role of rail for both environmental and economic reasons: the fact that only 6 per cent of passenger journeys were taken by train put a great strain on the roads. The post-privatization railways had actually seen the number of passenger journeys increase by 30 per cent and ministers wanted to encourage this development.

The new popularity of rail transport exacerbated the consequences of long-standing under-investment: delays and overcrowding increased. To overcome these problems more capital was needed. Railtrack was, however, reluctant to make the necessary commitment since as a private company it was obliged to maximize shareholder interests. As a result, not only was investment for the future neglected, so, it appeared, was day-to-day safety maintenance. The latter contributed to a fatal accident at Hatfield in 2000, which in turn caused massive disruption on the network. Prescott's response was to stiffen the regulation of the industry (*New Statesman*, 11 December 2000). Some argued, however, that as the reintroduction of the market was at the heart of the problem, tighter regulation was no solution (Wollmar, 2001).

As a result Railtrack became a byword for all that was wrong with privatization. Its directors were generously remunerated for running a worsening service; shareholders profited from public funds being poured into the company; and passenger safety was imperilled. Commuters became irritated due to the proliferation of delays and cancellations, while ticket prices rose. The government hoped to silence critics with its strategic plan for transport, which promised to invest £30 billion in the railways over ten years. If regulation was set to increase, however, further improvements would only come through public–private partnership (Labour Party, 2001, 11–12). Yet it was increasingly apparent that Railtrack was an ineffective partner: despite two-thirds of its income coming from government, it still lost money and looked set to do so for many years. Indeed, immediately after the election, Railtrack directors effectively asked Stephen Byers (the new transport minister) to sign a blank cheque to prevent the company collapsing. The private sector could not manage the rail network without a massive and ever-increasing public subsidy: in October 2001, Byers called in the receivers to take over the company.

For much of 2001 ministers had privately debated the future of the railways. They considered but rejected re-nationalization. The financial implications were huge, as the government would have been obliged to compensate shareholders and assume responsibility for the company's debt. This would have meant spending about £10 billion just to regain control of the track. Instead of placing the company into public owner- ship a half-way house was conceived: to transform Railtrack into a pri- vate trust run by a board independent of government. As a not-for-profit organization, it would be obliged to invest all returns back into the system rather than distribute some to shareholders. This model was derived from Welsh Water, which had recently assumed responsibility for water provision in the principality from a private company. The Treasury had opposed this take-over at the time, as officials believed such a trust would be under little compulsion to increase efficiency. Subsequent experience indicated otherwise.

Some on the left saw Railtrack's failure as marking the end of what they took to be ministers' Thatcherite assumption that the market was superior to the public sector. What they saw as a virtual re-nationalization led to the prediction that it would set a new course for the govern- ment's attitude to the market (*The Guardian*, 9 October 2001; *Tribune*, 12 October 2001). It was, however, doubtful that the end of Railtrack represented such a change in direction. The government's proposals for the Underground, which entailed the substantial involvement of the pri- vate sector, were finalized in the weeks prior to Railtrack's collapse. Moreover, there was no question that the more successful train operators would have their franchises revoked.

Railtrack had long been the privatized sector's weakest link. Some claimed it failed not because privatization was wrong in principle but because its application to the railways had been so badly thought out (*Economist*, 11 October 2001). As Blair stated, if Railtrack was a 'very bad privatization', that did not mean the private sector was inherently inferior (*The Guardian* website, 12 September 2001). Thus if their experience with Railtrack indicated to ministers that in some instances the private sector was an inappropriate means of delivering certain serv- ices, this was not something they did not already know. The reason why Byers called an end to Railtrack was less to do with an ideological shift and more with cash limits (the same reason Labour had come to terms with privatization in the first place). Instead of reducing its dependence on public funds while improving services, something promised by the Conservatives in 1993, the company achieved the reverse and, having given it a more than fair chance 'New' Labour was unwilling to bear further political and economic cost.

Conclusion

Economic growth during 'New' Labour's first term in power was calculated to have been between 2 and 3 per cent: this lay within parameters set by previous post-war administrations. It is, however, doubtful that in only four years any government can make a dramatic impact on any economy, especially as many of the measures introduced by 'New' Labour will take at least a decade to have effect. The government was nonetheless fortunate to operate in a period of sustained growth: 2001 was the British economy's ninth successive year of expansion. Ministers claimed credit for this but, as the process had begun under the Conservatives, more dispassionate analysts believed the ground had been prepared by the maligned Major administration.

The question of how far 'New' Labour continued policies set down by the Major and Thatcher governments has of course been widely debated. This chapter has suggested that, despite the rhetoric, 'New' Labour's broad approach to the economy demonstrated significant continuity with those of previous Labour governments. Some of the particular policies were undoubtedly different, due to the perceived failure of the past, the transformation of both domestic and international contexts, as well as changes wrought by nearly two decades of Conservative government. Thus 'New' Labour was much more sceptical about macro-economic intervention and placed a greater emphasis on the market to deliver growth than did those administrations run by Attlee, Wilson or Callaghan. Yet, despite being widely depicted as marking an accommodation with the Thatcher-Major years, Blair's policies might be better conceived as developing thoughts first sketched out by Labour's neo-revisionists in the 1970s in light of the experience of the 1980s.

As Peter Mandelson informed the CBI in 1998, whereas in the 1960s 'to be modern was to believe in planning', 'to be modern now' meant 'to make markets work better' (Mandelson, 1998b). This desire to be 'modern' might seem superficial; however, it encompassed the aspiration to remain relevant and credible to voters and those who controlled the world economy. For, to put the matter crudely, if the party was going to achieve anything it first had to accept the need for macro-economic stability as that is what both expected. The craving to be 'modern' also meant embracing those changes generated by capitalism rather than resisting them in the name of what were thought to be long-dead causes. The need to take advantage of – and even further extend – capitalist development in order to turn it to the advantage of one's political ends was an outlook the revisionist social democrat Eduard Bernstein had first outlined in the 1890s.

To some, 'New' Labour had gone too far in its regard for the market. Even sympathizers suspected that, for example, policy on the London Underground betrayed a prior and flawed assumption about the superiority of the private sector (Commission on Public Private Partnerships, 2001, 104–18). Despite claiming only to support 'what works' the government, one of its own MPs claimed, remained unconsciously trapped within Thatcherite beliefs (Whitehead, 2000). Yet, if the market had advanced centre stage and state intervention had shuffled to the wings, the former as much as the latter was considered to be merely a means and not an end. Thus society had to become fairer as a result of economic progress. This meant certain standards had to be imposed on the market by government: fairness at work legislation was one example of that viewpoint, although in most other areas ministers assumed what Hewitt described as the 'soft approach'. Moreover, 'New' Labour's belief in the central importance of a skilled and educated labour force meant its economic policy not only sought to promote efficiency but was also supposed to enhance individual potential. With that in mind, the next chapter will study in greater detail how far the government's policies affected Labour's long-standing ambition to reduce inequality.

7

Advancing Equality?

One of the most frequent charges made against 'New' Labour is that it abandoned the pursuit of equality. In contrast even to revisionist predecessors such as Hugh Gaitskell, Blair is said to want to create a society in which the reduction of inequality plays no obvious part (Brivati, 1996, 442–3). If the accusation were true this would mean 'New' Labour had turned its back not only on the party's past, but also on contemporary European social democracy. Historically, Labour has aspired to advance the cause of equality: indeed, many commentators believe this has been the party's pre-eminent purpose (Ellison, 1994). Moreover, according to the political philosopher Norberto Bobbio, the commitment to promote equality remains the principal distinguishing feature of all parties on the left (Bobbio, 1996).

Critics consider 'New' Labour abandoned the advancement of equality due to Blair's adherence to Thatcherism, one of whose aims was to shift responsibility for welfare from the state to the individual. They also suppose that many of the party's policies were influenced by an American experience in which low levels of government intervention and dire levels of poverty were taken for granted (Lister, 1997; Munby, 1998). Neither Stephen Byers' statement that the 'reality is that wealth creation is now more important than wealth distribution', nor Peter Mandelson's earlier comment that the government was 'intensely relaxed about people getting filthy rich', did anything to allay such suspicions (*The Guardian*, 3 February 1999; Taylor, 2001, 258). Indeed, they merely confirmed the view that Labour ministers were uninterested in reversing the massive social disparities that had emerged during the 1980s. Labour, it seemed, believed it should simply echo Conservative policy and just focus on creating a successful economy in the vague expectation that its benefits would eventually trickle down to the poor.

Many held to this position, despite the fact that leading 'New' Labour figures publicly committed the party to establishing a more equal society. Indeed, so seriously did the Blair government take the matter that it even issued annual poverty reports against which progress could be measured.

Moreover, while open to American influences, ministers also looked to the experience of social democratic governments in Australia and Europe for inspiration (Driver and Martell, 1998, 109; Annesley, 2001, 212–14; Wood, 2001, 50). Nonetheless, Blair argued that, due to social and economic change, his administration could not pursue equality through policies associated with earlier Labour governments. This was because the welfare state had to be reformed and its priorities recast so it could better address the issue in terms relevant to the 1990s. More than a few simply did not believe his assurances, and argued that Labour's refusal to redistribute wealth through higher income tax was a better indication of Blair's intentions (Lister, 2000, 9).

Some critics appear to consider that, prior to the creation of 'New' Labour, the party believed in the ambitious equality of outcome; and that it has only been since 1994 that it embraced the more modest equality of opportunity. However, Chapter 3 argued that revisionists such as Anthony Crosland actually advanced a form of equality which stood somewhere between that of outcome and opportunity. The purpose of the present chapter is to examine how far 'New' Labour remains committed to equality. The new clause four and the Third Way will be highlighted as a means of understanding how much of a break Blair has made from previous party thinking on this critical issue. The chapter will then focus in some detail on education and employment in order to assess the practical impact of the 'New' Labour government. The penultimate section will look at the less-regarded inequalities based on differences of gender, race and sexuality. The chapter will then conclude with an appraisal of how far Blair's first term has advanced the cause of equality.

The Thatcher Inheritance

Before considering 'New' Labour's attitude to equality it is necessary briefly to consider the impact of Thatcherism on the issue. The Conservatives won four general elections by adhering to a strictly *laissez-faire* view of the welfare state and employing a rhetoric that underlined the need to, above all else, extend individual 'freedom'. The party asserted that the post-war welfare state had created more problems than it solved. It was, first, a moral hazard as it undermined liberty by imposing high taxes on those who worked hard while featherbedding 'scroungers' too idle to get on their bikes and look for work. It was, second, economically inefficient. As those high taxes required to pay for welfare were disincentives to hard work, they contributed to the country's economic problems. If the tax 'burden' was alleviated, initiative and enterprise would be unlocked and entrepreneurs encouraged to create wealth. Thus Conservatives predicted that the contraction of the welfare state would increase the number of jobs in the economy and so reduce the number of those depending on state handouts. The party considered it preferable and more efficient for those who could afford it to assume greater responsibility for their own welfare. Therefore, under the auspices of Margaret Thatcher and John Major, successive governments encouraged the growth of private pensions and health schemes, their ultimate object being to transform the welfare state from a universal service provider to an emergency relief station used only by those in direst need.

The Conservatives principally extended their idea of freedom by cutting income tax and reducing the state's welfare role. After a massive slump at the start of the 1980s the British economy grew thereafter, but unemployment remained high so welfare spending rose, despite ministers cutting the real value of benefits: as a result, poverty increased. This situation was only exacerbated in 1988 when the Chancellor, Nigel Lawson, cut the top rate of income tax from 50 to 40 per cent. Indeed, one of the main consequences of Conservative policy was that Britain experienced a bigger increase in inequality than any other advanced country apart from New Zealand. This reversed a process of increasing equality that had started with the Second World War. The extent to which this reversal originated in changes to the labour market rather than government action is debatable, but Conservative tax cuts at least exacerbated the trend (Glennester, 2001, 384). Thus, between 1979 and 1997, after housing costs are discounted, the real incomes of the poorest 10 per cent of the population fell by 13 per cent, while they rose by 65 per cent for the top tenth. In the same period, those on or below half average household income after housing costs, the conventional measure of poverty, virtually tripled from 5 to 14 million, or from 9 per cent of the population to 22 per cent. The number of children in poverty grew slightly more, from 1.4 million to 4.2 million, or from 10 to 31 per cent of all children (Lister, 1997, 12). Despite this, most comparatively well-off voters failed to see poverty as an important issue, unless Labour's proposals to alleviate the problem threatened their incomes.

'New' Labour and Equality

Mandelson is credited with ensuring that a direct reference to 'equality' was taken out of a late draft of Labour's new clause four (MacIntyre, 1999,

276–7). The final version nonetheless committed the party to creating 'for each of us the means to realise our true potential', as well as building a 'community in which power, wealth and opportunity are in the hands of the many not the few'; and to promote 'the opportunity for all to work and prosper', along with an 'equality of opportunity' that 'delivers people from the tyranny of poverty'. Thus, the clause would appear to include a firm promise to reduce poverty and, at the very least, promote equality of opportunity. The wording was such that it is not obvious that this was to be the limit of Labour's ambition. Given that at the time of writing in Britain, 'power, wealth and opportunity' were undoubtedly held by the 'few' rather than the 'many', some redistribution appeared to be implied. The new clause therefore gave only a few clues as to Blair's specific intentions. Such ambiguity was undoubtedly deliberate as it allowed 'New' Labour to assuage the susceptibilities of party activists while not alarming Middle England.

This ambiguity was not made much clearer once 'New' Labour entered office. The uncertainty found in the comments of the party's leading lights may have been deliberate, but it might also have been due to the very slipperiness of the idea of equality itself, something which all serious students of the subject are acutely aware of. First, just before being elected Prime Minister, Blair stated that he believed in 'greater equality', a declaration that required clarification before its true meaning could be deduced. It was instructive therefore that Blair supplemented his comment by declaring that if the next Labour Government 'had not raised the living standards of the poorest by the end of its time of office it will have failed' (Annesley, 2001, 202). Raising the poor's living standards was consistent with established Labour aims. It was, however, also compatible with a rise in inequality, as an absolute increase in the living standards of the poor did not preclude the rich seeing their incomes accelerate even faster. This was certainly something Crosland would have criticized. The second example is taken from Mandelson, a man usually careful with his words. Soon after Labour's 1997 election victory, he asserted that the government wanted to make Britain a 'more equal society', an aim he stressed would not just rely on the 'redistribution of cash from rich to poor', something 'others artificially choose as their own limited definition of egalitarianism' (Mandelson, 1997, 7). Despite appearing to criticize redistribution, he nonetheless did not say it would not be employed to reduce inequality. Crosland would undoubtedly have approved. Finally, in 1998 Blair declared that the Third Way reasserted the centre-left's claim that, without a 'fair distribution of the benefits of progress', societies risked falling apart (Blair, 1998a, 20). While applauding the case for sharing the benefits of progress, Crosland would possibly have been as unsure as other readers about Blair's meaning; what constituted a 'fair distribution' was not immediately apparent.

Real Equality of Opportunity

If sometimes publicly uncertain as to precisely what kind of equality they favoured, 'New' Labour speakers were more sure about the sort they opposed. Echoing earlier revisionist declarations, Blair and Gerhard Schroeder made it very clear that the Third Way did not entail an equality of outcome. This they associated with 'conformity and mediocrity' and the imposition of intolerable tax burdens (Blair and Schroeder, 2000, 161). In contrast, Labour was firmly dedicated to equality of opportunity: this was after all one of the new clause four's more lucid claims. As Blair declared, 'people should be able to rise by their talents, not by their birth or the advantages of privilege'; he was, in that sense, 'committed to meritocracy' (Blair, 1996, 173). It might be argued that, compared to that of outcome, opportunity was the easiest form of equality to achieve. If so, Gordon Brown claimed Britain still lacked a sufficient degree of such equality so that instead of 'hankering after an unrealisable equality of outcomes', the party should take achieving equality of opportunity more seriously. Moreover, 'New' Labour's version of opportunity was, Brown claimed, more radical than the concept criticized by the likes of Crosland. Due to its focus on learning and training after the age of sixteen, the party sought what he described as a 'lifelong' or 'recurrent' equality of opportunity. This would entail 'not one but many opportunities' so individuals could not be 'permanently condemned to failure' as in the past. According to Brown, it was:

> a denial of any belief in equality of opportunity if we assume that there is one type of intelligence, one means of assessing it, only one time when it should be assessed and only one chance of succeeding. But we still have to act on the consequence of recognising these facts: that people have a richness and diversity of potential, that their talents take many forms, not just analytical intelligence but skills in communication, language and working with other people, and that these talents can develop over a lifetime ... I favour a rich and expansive view of equality of opportunity, with a duty on government in education, in employment and in the economy as a whole to consciously and relentlessly promote

opportunity not just for some of the people some for the time but of opportunity for all the people all of the time.

Consequently, Brown asserted, 'New' Labour's was a form of equality 'stronger and more suited to the 1990s' than was Crosland's (Brown, 1996 and 2001a).

Brown's finessing of the concept of equality of opportunity did not prevent critics from attacking 'New' Labour's commitment to reducing inequality. Roy Hattersley, who claimed to speak for the deceased Crosland on this matter, considered Blair's embrace of meritocracy to be part of his 'alien ideology' that had nothing in common with social democratic principle as it would leave poverty untouched (*The Observer*, 24 June 2001). Such critics looked back to Crosland's 'democratic' equality but overlooked his rejection of outcome and ignored the reasons why other revisionists criticized his outlook in the 1970s. They also closed their eyes to Anthony Giddens' clarification of 'New' Labour's rhetoric. Giddens made it as clear as it was possible to be that the Third Way's pursuit of equality of opportunity did not imply a neglect of outcome. Indeed, he suggested, it made it even more necessary. This was partly because the promotion of greater opportunities would, if not corrected by government action, widen inequalities of outcome. It was, Giddens announced, unacceptable to allow the material success or failure of one generation to enhance or undermine the opportunities of the next. This meant redistribution remained on the agenda, especially – something that would have been familiar to Crosland – in relation to inheritance taxes (Giddens, 1998, 101–4 and 2000, 89, 101–2). Acknowledging that a meritocracy would not achieve greater equality in itself, the minister, Margaret Hodge, also conceded that ultimately, 'some of us will have to have less for others to have more' (Hodge, 2000, 36, 41).

Many of 'New' Labour's critics refused to take such statements at face value. Instead, they continued to believe that the party's attitude to equality was evidence of Blair's accommodation with Thatcherism. If nothing else, this belied an ignorance of contemporary Conservative thinking. For, according to David Willetts (one of his party's leading intellectuals), egalitarianism was 'the key anti-Conservative concept'. Echoing the views of many colleagues, Willetts described economic inequality as 'part of the natural order', beyond the control of mere politicians. Moreover, he believed that the deliberate pursuit of equality, such as that embodied in Labour's 1995 clause four, entailed a degree of government meddling that could only have dire consequences (Willetts, 1992; Gray and Willetts, 1997).

Despite Giddens' subsequent clarification, in relation to equality at least, Blair's warning that the Third Way was a 'work in progress' remained all too true. As Mark Leonard, a commentator sympathetic to the enterprise, stated, the Third Way was unclear about whether inequality was 'axiomatically bad' or if increasing inequality within a fluid society rising in prosperity was 'acceptable'. This ambivalence was compounded, Leonard suggested, by its 'fuzziness' on redistribution and lack of a principled position on the appropriate level of taxation (Leonard, 2000, xviii–xix). Perhaps, as was the case with clause four, such obscurity was deliberate; or it may have been that some of these were questions any politician would have been foolish to prescribe too far in advance: *The Future of Socialism*, after all, did not contain an exact view on optimum tax rates. As with all matters of doctrine, the meaning of clause four and the Third Way would be fully revealed in action, in the operation of the welfare state during Labour's time in office. However, as we shall see, even after 1997 certain matters remained clouded.

A 'Modernized' Welfare State

According to Blair, unemployment was the biggest cause of inequality; and the best guarantee of earning a 'decent wage' was 'employability', something Brown considered 'the key to a cohesive society' (*The Observer*, 27 April 1997; *The Guardian*, 30 May 1997). Those who established the post-war welfare state also believed in the necessity of a fully employed population and recognized that without this, their vision was unsustainable. 'New' Labour had, of course, disavowed the demand management and state intervention Clement Attlee and his contemporaries had thought necessary to maintain full employment. Instead, the party now considered that a suitably reformed welfare state could itself help generate full employment through fostering skills meant to enhance the individual's employability (Kelly and Oppenheim, 1998, 36).

Beveridge's welfare state had to be modernized because, in what Brown described as the 'information age', there was now a premium on the ability to acquire 'knowledge and to use it creatively', which meant that all workers should be 'educated, responsive to change and involved' (Brown, 1996). In this context, Blair believed that the object of the welfare state was now to 'equip citizens with the skills and aspirations they need to succeed', including the 'core skill' of 'entrepreneurship'. Instilling these qualities would be part of welfare's new remit to promote opportunity, while at the same time still protecting the weak and ensuring everybody gained from economic growth (Blair, 1998b, 10–11).

Thus, instead of simply compensating the workless with what would inevitably be meagre benefits, Blair wanted the welfare state to 'enable people to help themselves' and find employment. As Brown stated, welfare should create 'pathways' out of unemployment and poverty rather than 'trapping people in persistent dependency'. So far as David Blunkett was concerned, 'passing cash from one section of the community to another' merely confirmed the poor in their poverty (*The Guardian*, 29 July 1997; Driver and Martell, 1998, 107; Blair and Schroeder, 2000, 161). To that end Brown wanted his Budgets to 'make work pay' and 'redistribute in favour of work and opportunity' by manipulating the tax and benefits system to give those on benefits the incentive to take up work. 'New' Labour's focus was therefore not on increasing benefit payments; Blair wanted to move away from the idea that achieving a more equal society could be based on government paying people 'a few more quid' (*The Observer*, 27 April 1997). This, in truth, was not an idea to which Beveridge had ever adhered.

Such a perspective placed a heavy premium on government helping the most demoralized sections of the unemployed, such as those living in deprived communities where long-term and even second-generation unemployment was commonplace. If the policy was to succeed, such people required help to recapture their desire to seek – and their ability to find – work, for it was believed these had been eroded by years of Thatcherite neglect (*The Independent*, 16 July 1997). Brown, in fact, claimed to want to build welfare around a revived 'work ethic', for one of the consequences of Conservative rule was that it had undermined belief in this principle (*The Observer*, 11 and 18 May 1997; *The Guardian*, 26 June 1997).

The immediate influence on 'New' Labour's vision of a modernized welfare state was the final report of the Commission on Social Justice, itself a recapitulation and development of contemporary centre-left thinking. John Smith had established the Commission in the wake of Labour's 1992 defeat. Possibly fearful of the consequences should its recommendations prove controversial, he ensured it was formally independent of the party. Reporting after Smith's death, the Commission confirmed that all basic needs should be met by the state and remained convinced government should continue to reduce inequality. Yet, in relation to this objective, the report recommended that government needed to assume the role of an 'enabler' to active individuals rather than be the agent of change itself. It envisaged the creation of an 'intelligent welfare state', one responsive to change and engaging with it. This reformed welfare state would, in contrast to Beveridge's 'safety net', be a 'spring board' for those in need. In this way the pursuit of social justice could also promote economic efficiency (Commission on Social Justice, 1994).

It is probable the Commission merely encouraged 'New' Labour in directions the leadership would have taken in any event, as the report's proposals and metaphors were already familiar to Brown and Blair. They were nonetheless keen to develop many of the Commission's themes, especially the need for 'rights' to be matched by 'responsibilities'. According to Anthony Giddens this was the 'prime motto for the new politics' (Giddens, 1998, 65). Some considered 'New' Labour's assertion of this principle seriously eroded those social rights supposedly established by the post-war welfare state. They pointed to the fact that the Conservatives had first made the 'right' to access a welfare benefit dependent on the 'responsibility' of recipients actively to seek work with the 1994 Job Seekers' Allowance (JSA). Both parties, they argued, now sought to impose sanctions on those most in need. Moreover, as with the Conservatives before them, 'New' Labour's leaders only seemed willing to force the poor to exercise their responsibilities. Paying higher income tax for the good of the wider community was, some argued, also a duty, but not one properly enforced (Lister, 2000, 10–11). It was true that 'New' Labour's public elaboration of the theme often stressed its authoritarian aspect; this was at least partly due to electoral considerations. Critics exaggerated the unconditional nature of the 'rights' established by Attlee, however: social democrats had always been keen to buttress benefits against exploitation.

Despite the apparent importance of welfare reform, some doubted it had been conceived in more than outline prior to Blair becoming Prime Minister (Rentoul, 2001, 373–90). Employing the rhetoric of 'reform' was an easy way to assure key voters that 'New' Labour would not feather-bed the lives of 'scroungers'; working out in detail how change would be manifested proved more of a challenge. Frank Field's appointment as minister in charge of the issue indicated that the direction of policy remained to be determined. While agreeing with Blair and Brown's general outlook, Field favoured a system of relatively generous universal benefits based on compulsory insurance. He believed means-testing demoralized people by reducing their incentive to save because it rewarded those who failed to look after their own interests, confident government would bail them out (Field, 1996; Driver and Martell, 1998, 88–9). The Chancellor in contrast considered universal benefits to be both expensive and ineffective: they meant raising taxes but would not deliver help where it was most needed. Blair seemed caught between the two. In such a situation, close textual analysis of the Third Way was of little help and the matter was resolved when the man with most political weight – and the apparently cheapest option – exerted his authority. Field was sacked in 1998.

During this period of uncertainty, some initiatives were launched that indicated the nature of the government's approach to welfare policy and how it proposed to tackle poverty. The creation of the Social Exclusion Unit (SEU), described by Mandelson as 'the most important innovation in government we have made', was one such (Mandelson, 1997). Its object was to focus on what was popularly referred to as the 'underclass', that core of about 10 per cent of the population said to be responsible for most crime, drug abuse and single parenthood. While most people experienced poverty as a temporary phenomenon, members of the 'underclass' were trapped in that state for much of their lives. This was thought to be partly because such recidivists lacked the essential desire for education and employment: no matter how much extra in benefit they were paid, without some intervention they and their offspring would remain on the margins of society (Driver and Martell, 1998, 90; Giddens, 2000, 104–8).

The SEU proceeded from the assumption that existing government money was not being spent wisely on this group: if more funds were not necessarily required, new approaches were. As a result, critics saw this as social policy on the cheap, a band-aid to cover disadvantages that called for basic income tax-financed surgery (Benn, 2000). While others conceded the SEU employed praiseworthy methods, they still underlined the need for extra investment (Salmon, 1998). The real value of benefits had certainly declined under the Conservatives, but the more proactive approach advocated by the SEU promised to prevent people from slipping into a life based on the dole by tackling minor problems before they had the chance to develop. This entailed addressing conditions in especially deprived areas, invariably 'sink' council estates located on the edge of industrial towns or within the inner cities. Given the SEU's pre-emptive approach, this meant focusing in particular on the young. For example, as it appeared truancy at school was an early predictor of future unemployment and criminality, Sure Start was introduced to help children acquire key learning skills even before they entered primary education. Moreover, to try to ensure such schemes enjoyed sustained success, they relied on fostering local initiative, thereby challenging the paternalistic approach embedded in Beveridge's original conception of the welfare state (Social Exclusion Unit, 1998).

Yet even this apparently most innovative of approaches to welfare had been anticipated by long-forgotten initiatives undertaken at the behest of ministers and civil servants working within the Wilson governments of the 1960s. Both the establishment of Educational Priority Areas and Community Development Projects were predicated on the desirability of social workers helping residents of particularly deprived areas to take more responsibility for their own lives, the idea being to help the poor liberate themselves from dependence on the state (Halsey, 1974). While apparently ignorant of such schemes, the leaders of 'New' Labour would have heartily endorsed their aims.

Not Taxing but Spending

For the first two years of its life, Blair's government did not increase overall public spending due to the party's commitment to stick to Conservative budgetary plans. As the 1997 manifesto had stated, 'New' Labour ministers would be 'wise spenders, not big spenders'. This did not, however, prevent priorities being altered: extra resources were shifted to health and education from other departments. It was nonetheless clear that once the two years had elapsed, additional spending would not be financed through increases in income tax. While Brown imaginatively tapped other sources of revenue, for the most part economic growth would finance extra spending on welfare and public services. The 1997 decision had been dictated by Blair's desire to dissociate Labour from 'higher, indiscriminate and often ineffective' spending (Blair, 1998b, 15). The Labour Prime Minister appeared to believe that raising income tax was not just electorally unwise but was also economically hazardous, confirmed by his assertion that public expenditure as a proportion of national income had 'more or less reached the limits of acceptability' (Blair and Schroeder, 2000, 164). Blair's insistence on repeating the 1997 pledge not to raise income tax at the start of the 2001 campaign seemed to indicate that this was now entrenched 'New' Labour policy.

Many considered Blair's hostility to raising income tax denied his government funds needed to properly tackle poverty. It seems Brown and Blair disagreed about the need for the 1997 and 2001 tax promises: according to some accounts the former thought Labour should retain the power to raise the top rate. Those close to Blair, however, argued that increasing income tax was not necessarily the best means of generating revenue: to put up rates would not automatically achieve the desired result as evasion would increase. In some instances, they thought cutting taxes might better supplement government income (Giddens, 2000, 96–103). Nonetheless, whatever its impact on government revenues, it is probable that by not capping the rising incomes of the rich through increasing the top rate of income tax, Blair's government allowed inequality to grow.

Instead of raising the top rate, Brown cut income tax for the poor. He increased the amount above which an individual would start to pay tax and lowered the initial rate from 20 to 10 per cent. In addition, the Chancellor introduced numerous tax credits available to those on low incomes with children, in particular the working families' tax credit and a childcare tax credit that met up to 70 per cent of care costs. As a result, it was calculated that the incomes of some low-wage families would nearly double (Oppenheim, 2001, 81). Such measures were reinforced by the minimum wage but somewhat offset by Brown's reliance on regressive consumption taxes (Metcalf, 1999). By focusing on tax relief rather than raising benefits, however, the Chancellor not only made work more remunerative for the low paid but also avoided Conservative charges that he was using tax-payers' money to make life easier for the idle. Brown's redistribution of income to the families of the working poor also complemented the government's objective of abolishing child poverty within 20 years. This emphasis on families was based on the belief that young children growing up in poverty did less well at school and so found securing suitable work difficult in later life. In other words, unless government took some action, those born into poverty were likely to remain in poverty (Hodge, 2000, 35–6; Brown, 2000c and 2001a; Wincott, 2001, 227–38).

Despite Blair's pre-election rhetoric about not paying 'a few more quid', selected benefits were raised well above inflation. Given the government's concern with child poverty, it was unsurprising that it increased child benefit by one-third. Pensions were, however, a less straightforward issue. When the Attlee government introduced a universal state pension, it was at a time when to be old was to be poor. By the 1990s this relationship had been attenuated: if one-third of pensioners languished in poverty another third were so affluent, due to their accumulated assets and private pensions, that they paid income tax. Attlee had set the state pension at a very low rate, meaning many recipients relied on means-tested benefits to supplement their income. The Labour government of 1974–9 broke with tradition and tried to end this dependence by linking the pension to average earnings. The Conservatives subsequently cut the real value of the state pension by setting it against slower-rising prices.

They did this, first, because of the projected cost – pensions were due to account for 10 per cent of the Gross Domestic Product (GDP) by the middle of the twenty-first century – and, second, they wanted more individuals to seek private solutions (Johnson, 2001, 64–5, 70–1).

At the 1992 election Labour promised to increase the basic pension and set it once more against earnings, but that commitment was placed under a question mark by the party's defeat. As it entered office, the leadership had not finally decided whether to stay true to this earlier pledge or, given pensioners' income disparity, target spending and rely on those who could afford it to continue to supplement the basic pension by private means. The former course was popular in the party and supported by many leading unions. It was, however, very costly and Brown argued it would give affluent pensioners more cash which they did not need, and still deny their poorer counterparts funds sufficient to meet their basic requirements.

After much controversy, the government introduced a Minimum Income Guarantee that significantly increased means-tested income support available to poorer pensioners. It promised that this – but not the basic pension – would be linked to earnings so that by 2003 it would have risen by up to one-third in real terms. The amount of savings a pensioner could hold and still be eligible for the scheme was also increased. For the longer term, the government established a second state pension for the poorest that would eventually double the value of the basic pension. Finally, it inaugurated a regulated 'stakeholder' private pension scheme for those on low incomes which enjoyed substantial tax relief to encourage saving. Such initiatives left affluent pensioners untouched and targeted spending on those in most need, combining income redistribution with an increased stress on the individual's responsibility to save for the future. If this confusing array of additional schemes was not an outcome that could have been deduced from a close reading of the Third Way, it was nonetheless consistent with its overall intention of reconciling the party's established priorities with new social realities (Glennester, 2001, 387–90; Johnson, 2001, 72–4; McCormick, 2001, 92–4).

The Importance of Public Services

'New' Labour's emphasis on the importance of effective public services – in particular health and especially education – to its wider objectives became increasingly obvious the longer it held power. Moreover, if Labour promised to be a 'wise' rather than 'big' spender, by the time the party sought re-election it effectively claimed to be both. Indeed, the Third Way accepted that to ensure 'excellent' services, government had to increase 'investment' – a politically astute synonym for spending – while driving through 'reform' so as to achieve 'higher standards' (Blair, 1998b, 15–16).

As he reiterated during the 2001 campaign, Blair saw the public services as a vital 'foundation' to achieving 'genuine opportunity for all' and so was 'social justice made real'. At the time, most attention was focused on his supposedly controversial emphasis on reforms designed to ensure health and education would be rebuilt 'around consumers'. The public, he stated, had to be given greater choice and enjoy guaranteed minimum standards (*The Guardian* website, 12 September 2001; Fielding, 2002). Public services, therefore, had to satisfy the public's expectation of high quality delivery whilst they also furthered the party's aim of increasing equality: they had to serve both the affluent and the poor. It should be recalled that post-war revisionists thought social cohesion best served if hospitals and schools were used in common by those from diverse backgrounds. Blair's stress on 'standards' was designed to facilitate that end.

The Prime Minister's suggestion that, if deemed efficient, the private sector could be involved in delivering public services antagonized some. 'Reform', however, did not just mean private involvement; it also implied new forms of management that would address one of the most widely noted features of the public services: too much discretion for service providers. Ministers agreed that professional autonomy had its merits, but only within a framework in which performance could be measured and value for money gauged. This was certainly not the case when Labour took office: too few public services were held accountable to those who used and funded them. If the Conservatives introduced consumer-orientated reforms, it would be wrong to think the desire for greater accountability and efficiency is uniquely Thatcherite. For, if the affluent could opt out of badly run public services, those on modest incomes could not: it was the poor who suffered most from inadequate delivery (Hodge, 2000, 39–40). Thus, it could be argued, raising standards within the public services was a vital equality issue.

Health

Labour came to power wanting to reduce health inequalities, abolish the Conservatives' National Health Service (NHS) reforms and enhance delivery. The rise in poverty during the 1980s had seen health disparities increase in step: at the end of the 1990s it was calculated that a boy born into a poor family would die nine years before his most favoured equivalent. Recognizing the importance of the issue, one of the government's first acts was to establish the means to identify and reduce health inequality (Exworthy and Berney, 2000). This was a complex undertaking, whose outcome would take many years to become manifest: significantly, it was something in which the Conservatives had expressed no interest.

The government's immediate aim was to improve health care delivery. According to a World Health Organization survey, immediately prior to 1997 the NHS was a comparatively inefficient health provider. This was not surprising, for it consisted of an unwieldy bureaucracy of one million employees managed in a paternalistic climate by largely autonomous professionals. As a result, patients enjoyed a variable service that could be shockingly bad: in too many cases geography determined whether patients lived or died. If persistent under-funding had exacerbated variation of service, there was no guarantee extra investment would in itself reduce it (Dixon, 2001, 30–1).

Hoping to improve efficiency, the Conservatives had introduced various market-style reforms that Labour sometimes spuriously described as attempts to 'privatize' the NHS. However, by the late 1980s, the party was beginning to see the merit of 'putting patients first'; in effect, treating them as consumers by, for example, offering them booked appointments in out-patients (Gould, 1989, 169–72; Labour Party, 1989, 52). Most pertinently, the Conservatives had introduced a general practitioner (GP) fund-holding scheme to encourage doctors to act like consumers by 'buying' services from local hospitals, now styled independent 'trusts'. To induce GPs to participate in the scheme, members were granted preferential treatment over those who remained aloof: the latter's patients therefore suffered. Labour abolished fund-holding but replaced it with a virtually identical format, except that all GPs were now obliged to participate, thereby eliminating discrimination. This reform was, however, under-pinned by a different ethos due to the statutory obligation to cooperate rather than, as under the Conservatives, compete (Driver and Martell, 1998, 93–6; Dixon, 2001, 32–7). The result was that those closest to their patients' needs were given greater influence over the provision of local services, which was something the Conservatives had also wanted to encourage. This set the tone for subsequent reforms which devolved responsibility but only within a nationally established framework of common standards of treatment that could be measured and so used to identify 'failing' parts of the NHS (Glennester, 2001, 399–402).

As one authority put it, due to the government's spending constraints, health was an area where Labour in power 'promised most but delivered least': for much of the first term, the NHS experienced more 'reform' but little extra 'investment' (*The Financial Times* website, 8 August 2001). Labour's first two years in power nonetheless saw health expenditure rise by an average of 2.2 per cent in real terms per year, although that was less than the 3.1 per cent increase experienced during the Conservatives' eighteen years in office. Subsequent announcements meant spending during the entirety of Labour's first term actually rose by an average of 4.8 per cent. Moreover, Labour promised to increase spending further during the first half of its second term: between 1999/2000 and 2003/4, it was set to rise by 6.4 per cent every year. This was an unprecedented commitment and markedly higher than the NHS's historical average increase of 3.5 per cent. Britain has always spent a much smaller proportion of its GDP on health compared to other leading industrial economies: this gap will have been reduced, but hardly eradicated, by 2004 (Clark and Dilnot, 2001, 18–21). Yet in January 2000 Blair promised that health spending would eventually reach the European average: the implication must be that investment in health is not only set to be sustained, but to increase further during the latter half of Labour's second term.

Education: The Key Public Service

Even during its first two years, Labour engineered annual spending increases for education of 2 per cent in real terms, higher than the 1979–97 Conservative average rise of 1.5 per cent. Overall, the average yearly rise in Labour's first full term was 3.6 per cent, and between 2001/2 and 2003/4 it was set to rise by 5.6 per cent. This generosity should not have come as a surprise for Blair had famously made his three top priorities for government 'education, education, education'; he had also placed one of his most able colleagues, David Blunkett, in charge of the Department for Education and Employment. As the Department's mission statement was revised to read, its purpose was now 'to give everyone the chance, through education, training and work, to realise their full potential, and thus build an inclusive and fair society and a competitive economy' (Smithers, 2001, 410). Education would, in other words, reduce inequality and promote economic efficiency; for 'New' Labour, it was the key public service.

Many consider that, apart from spending, 'New' Labour's approach to education differed little from that of its Conservative predecessor

(Smithers, 2001, 405). This may possibly be due to the fact that in many respects the Thatcherite agenda was itself a continuation of approaches that had emerged during the last Labour administration (Stedward, 2001, 169–70). There is certainly much evidence to support this view. It was, after all, James Callaghan who in 1976 focused attention on the importance of raising basic standards; and under his auspices ministers issued a Green Paper stressing the need for all schoolchildren to gain a 'basic understanding of the economy and activities ... which are necessary for the creation of ... wealth' (Ellison, 1994, 47; Morgan, 1997, 502–3, 540–1). Indeed, the importance of education to the development of Britain's economy has been described as a 'nascent theme' of Labour policy since at least the 1960s (Stedward, 2001, 169–71). Finally, the neo-revisionist, John Mackintosh, was one of the first to advocate giving parents the chance to choose to which school to send their children, in the hope this would improve standards in unpopular institutions (Marquand, 1982, 84–6).

During the 1980s Conservative ministers explored many of these insights and gave them their own particular emphasis. Most importantly, they focused on the principle of parental 'choice'; established a national curriculum and tests for children at set ages; and constructed league tables to help parent-consumers decide where to send their children. The extent to which all parents benefited from choice, especially in deprived areas, was doubted; but once conceded, many wanted it extended (Brighouse, 2001, 19–20). Enthusiasm was greatest amongst the middle class and the 'aspirational' working class, those whose votes Labour most needed if it was to return to office. Such parents considered the ability to influence where their children were educated to be a crucial influence on their development. They also saw an over-riding virtue in the pursuit of standards (Tomlinson, 1998).

Long before 1994, Labour accepted the need to strengthen the link between education and employability; and by 1992 the leadership had also endorsed the importance of nationally monitored standards (Labour Party, 1992, 17–18; McCaig, 2001, 200). Yet there remained a solid body of opinion within the party that believed parental choice was simply a means by which the middle class could grab extra resources for their children at the expense of those from poorer backgrounds. The freedom to choose in education, it was argued, therefore increased inequality (Hattersley, 1987, 143–4). Blair, however, realized the popularity of his opponents' stress on choice and encouraged Blunket to embrace this theme fully. This Blunkett did with alacrity, and also echoed the need for more prescription and monitoring in regard to standards. Given the high proportion of teachers in Labour's ranks and the extent to which they felt stigmatized for the perceived failures of state education, this reorientation of policy and rhetoric provoked much irritation.

The related questions of choice and selection were consequently highly controversial within the Labour Party. The comprehensive principle was dear to many party members who, like Crosland, saw it as an important means of promoting equality by including children from a range of backgrounds in the same institution. This would not only encourage the development of an equality of regard between the classes, but also prevent children who failed the grammar school entrance exam from being condemned as failures at the early age of eleven. Consequently, the party initially opposed the Conservatives' creation of quasi-independent grant-maintained schools that were permitted to select a proportion of their intake. This was seen as an attempt to reintroduce grammar schools by the back door, a policy that would only benefit middle-class children. As late as 1992 Labour was pledged to end all forms of selection, and in 1995 Blunkett promised there would be 'no selection' at all under a 'New' Labour government. A year later, however, with an election on the horizon, he was forced to qualify his statement by indicating that there would be 'no further selection' (McCaig, 2001, 192).

Despite the impression encouraged by some rhetoric, 'New' Labour did not attack the comprehensive principle. Wholesale selection at the age of eleven was considered unjustifiable, while the full participation of middle-class children in state education was encouraged. The leadership moreover opposed Conservative plans to restore grammar schools as outlined before the 1997 General Election because they could only benefit a minority. Blair was happy to concede that in the suburbs, rural areas and small towns comprehensives enjoyed an exemplary record. The focus of Blair's criticism was instead concentrated on the performance of comprehensive schools in the most deprived urban areas where residential segregation meant they were exclusively comprised of children from the poorest backgrounds. He particularly disparaged some teachers' low expectations: by not adhering to high standards they adversely affected the chances of children from poor backgrounds making the most of themselves. In such places, he believed, comprehensive education clearly required improvement (Blair, 1996, 173–6; Mandelson and Liddle, 1996, 92–5). Where necessary, this might involve the private sector running state-funded schools.

Thus, if Labour in power did not abolish selection, its growth was in one sense restricted. Blunkett devised a process that made it possible, but not exactly easy, for ballots of local parents to force existing grammar schools to become comprehensives. As a result, of the 166 grammar schools in existence in 1997, there were only two less in 2001. However, in other respects choice and selection were considered useful means of promoting higher standards. The Education White Paper published after Blair's re-election confirmed his government's desire to enhance choice and limited selection within state-administered secondary schools. Critics considered this a further betrayal of the comprehensive principle, but it met with popular approval (*The Guardian*, 6 September 2001).

If selection was thought to benefit only children from affluent backgrounds, Labour ministers also introduced schemes designed to help under-privileged children make the most of their education. In particular, the government drafted measures to reduce truancy as part of its strategy to reduce social exclusion. In addition, Education Action Zones were established to allow the authorities to focus on areas with consistently under-performing children, invariably located in the inner cities. With the party's critics undoubtedly in mind Estelle Morris, Blunkett's successor at education, claimed she would put at the 'core' of government policy 'an absolute determination' to raise standards amongst the disadvantaged children and to close the gap between them and children of the better-off (*The Guardian*, 2 January 2002).

Higher Education

In Opposition Labour committed itself to increasing the proportion of those enrolling in higher education from one-third to half of 18–30 year olds. Consistent with its desire to increase access to education, the party was especially keen to raise the number of students from less privileged backgrounds: this group had long been under-represented in universities. The leadership, however, did not want to finance such expansion through general taxation. Thus, once in government, Blunkett introduced a system that obliged students themselves to pay £1,000 per year in tuition fees. As this had been first mooted under Smith, it was not a specifically 'New' Labour policy; indeed, it is highly likely that, had they been re-elected, the Conservatives would have introduced a similar scheme (McCaig, 2001, 190).

While students were offered low-interest loans to pay for this new burden, many educationalists argued that increasing their level of debt would deter potential students from working-class backgrounds, the very people Labour hoped to attract. As many institutions specializing in recruiting such students immediately suffered acute recruitment problems, this prediction appeared to have been accurate. Moreover, the money raised through tuition fees was modest and would only scratch the surface of long-standing university under-funding. In response, Blunkett argued that those who went to university earned more than those who did not, so they should finance that from which they benefited. Furthermore, as the scheme was means-tested, students from low-income families would not pay tuition fees; even those subject to fees would only repay their loans after they had started to earn a set income. Blunkett did not highlight the mildly redistributive impact of his controversial policy, presumably for electoral reasons, for the ultimate effect of tuition fees was that middle-class students effectively contributed to higher government spending on those universities promoting access to socially deprived groups (McCaig, 2001, 194–5).

In truth, the Blair government achieved little of note in higher education. By the end of its first term, the proportion of young people in higher education had not increased: students remained disproportionately middle class. Moreover, if ministers put an end to the Conservative practice of habitually cutting funding to higher education, they did not raise it much: those institutions that served poorer students were more badly hit by this neglect. Such matters were left to the second term. Indeed, effectively acknowledging the failure of his government in this area, soon after being re-elected the Prime Minister announced that tuition fees would be abolished, possibly in favour of a graduate tax.

Further Education

Much more surprisingly, Labour's first term saw little improvement to further education after the age of sixteen, while skills training remained a backwater. In Opposition the party had stressed how vital it considered development in these areas to be, due to their supposed effect on improving workers' ability to prosper in the modern labour market. It should moreover be recalled the extent to which Brown's vision of a 'recurrent' equality of opportunity relied on improvements to school leavers' access to education and training (Labour Party, 1996; Hillman, 1998). If 'New' Labour's interest echoed that of the Wilson governments of the 1960s, this was only because British workers had long been thought less skilled than their European counterparts. Employers simply did not take the matter seriously. The precise economic impact of this indifference was difficult to calculate, but it undoubtedly impeded efficiency (Robertson, 1997).

The need to enhance access to training was something Kinnock had stressed, and to that end had advocated a compulsory training levy to be imposed on employers, as they were the ones who would benefit from any improvements. Prior to the 1980s Labour had adopted a more voluntarist approach to this problem, and in 1996 'New' Labour reverted to largely non-compulsory methods, partly due to fears of appearing anti-business (King and Wickham-Jones, 1998). In its place the party proposed creating Individual Learning Accounts through which government and employers would subsidize workers' training or education. According to one Labour document this 'put opportunity in the hands of the individual': if it did place a greater onus on the workers' desire for self-improvement, it also let the employer off the hook (Labour Party, 1996). In 1999 the government announced it wanted to create one million such accounts: by 2001 over 2.5 million had been created. Unfortunately, the system by which such accounts could be established was vulnerable to fraud, so the scheme was suspended soon after Labour's re-election. If learning accounts attracted the interest of undesirable criminal elements, the scheme failed to appeal to legitimate (if short-sighted) employers. This lack of significant demand had thwarted policy-makers in the past, and without some form of compulsion it looked unlikely that business would take the matter at all seriously (Stedward, 2001, 173–5; Wood, 2001, 50–3, 55–7).

Prior to the 2001 election, the Learning and Skills Council was formed, given a budget of £6 billion and charged with the strategic direction of further education and training. If this marked a potential new start for government policy, this body would have to work hard to live up to 'New' Labour's pre-1997 rhetoric and make up the time lost during Blair's first term.

The New Deal

The centrepiece of 'New' Labour's case that the welfare state could promote employability was what it referred to as the New Deal. Despite some suspicions on the left, this was more than a ruse to take people off the unemployed register for six months. In fact, due to the significance attached to the scheme by ministers, had it demonstrably failed to help participants into work 'New' Labour's credibility would have been severely damaged. If the New Deal had floundered, voter cynicism about collective help for the unemployed would only have been reinforced and this would probably have prevented the government mounting further initiatives.

The scheme's rationale was that the unemployed needed help to secure work which the majority were in fact keen to do. As Brown stated, there were many whose 'motivation and ambition' had been so 'eroded' under the Conservatives they needed the sort of help only government could provide (*The Independent*, 16 July 1997). Critics claimed, however, that the New Deal was neither new nor much of a deal as it largely echoed an earlier Conservative initiative. Launched in 1994, the JSA had made unemployment benefit dependent on the recipient actively seeking work, to which end the authorities provided modest assistance. Failure to conform resulted in individuals having part of their benefit revoked. While the New Deal shared some similarities with this scheme, the extent to which its distinctiveness lay, as one authority has asserted, 'more in packaging than substance', is debatable (Tonge, 1999, 230).

The main difference between the New Deal and the JSA was that the former was backed by the investment of £3.6 billion raised from the government's windfall utilities tax. This meant the scheme could be far more ambitious than its predecessor: initially intended to assist the young unemployed, it was soon extended to the older long-term unemployed, partners of the unemployed, lone parents, and the disabled. By 2001 all unemployed adults were obliged to fully participate in the scheme, the exceptions being lone parents and the disabled who were still expected to attend an initial interview. The windfall monies also allowed the help offered to participants to be of a very high order. Those on the scheme entered a 'gateway' lasting four months during which time their needs were appraised; at this point they were given appropriate counselling by a dedicated personal adviser who would see them through the entire process. Thus during the 'gateway' period those with particular difficulties (such as illiteracy or innumeracy, drug or alcohol problems) were identified and offered assistance. Simply as a result of the help given at this preliminary stage about half the participants found work. After the assessment period had been completed the remainder were offered six months' employment; a sixth-month placement with a voluntary organization or environmental task force; or an educational course which could last up to a year. Should none of these lead to a full-time job, individuals were offered further guidance from their adviser.

The controversial aspect to the scheme – and the one that drew particular parallels with the JSA – was that all claimants were obliged to take one of the options offered or lose their benefit for two weeks. A second refusal would merit the loss of four weeks' benefit. This was the most prominent example of Blair's belief that rights required responsibilities. In particular, if they had the right to expect that government would provide them with opportunities to train so as to become better able to find work, the unemployed had a responsibility to take advantage of such openings: a life on benefit was not an option (Labour Party, 1997b; *The Guardian*, 25 April 1997). Initially, the punitive nature of the sanction had been enthusiastically underlined so as to appeal to those voters who saw any form of aid to the unemployed as encouraging 'scroungers'. Thus one anonymous 'insider' described the threatened withdrawal of benefit as amounting to an 'attack on the work shy' (Lister, 2000, 12). That not many more than 32,000 people had their benefits suspended during the first term puts this rhetoric into perspective: most of the unemployed were more than willing to take advantage of the opportunities offered (Oppenheim, 2001, 81).

Other Inequalities

Historically, Labour tended to conceive of the pursuit of equality in relation to class-based disparities; this was also true of 'New' Labour. However, the contemporary party paid greater attention to gender issues than in the past, particularly the problem of lone parents and part-time workers who were overwhelmingly female.

The rising number of lone mothers living on benefit had been the catalyst for a transatlantic debate on the rise of welfare 'dependency' and the decline of 'family values' that came to the fore during the early 1990s. Such women seemed to embody all that Conservatives thought wrong with the welfare state: between 1979 and 1990 the proportion of families headed by lone mothers doubled to 19 per cent, while their reliance on state benefits increased. Single mothers consequently found themselves stigmatized by Conservative ministers for their moral and economic shortcomings. At the same time, the Major government developed policies designed to encourage lone mothers into work (Lewis, 1998, 4–13).

If 'New' Labour sometimes seemed to echo the Conservatives' hostile rhetoric while proposing initiatives that also looked familiar, the party's approach was, however, subtly different. While some Labour leaders thought the 'traditional' family preferable to any alternative, policy nonetheless treated other family types as equally valid (Lewis, 2001, 489–91, 503–4). This thinking was undoubtedly influenced by the fact that in 1997 no fewer than 101 Labour MPs were women, and an increasing proportion found themselves in ministerial positions as Parliament progressed. Within a few months of winning office, however, the new government appeared to go out of its way to prove it was no different to its predecessor when it implemented a Conservative-inspired cut in lone parent benefit. This resulted in a substantial revolt amongst Labour MPs, while many of those voting with the government did so with deep misgivings (Purdy, 2001, 190–1). It is unlikely the cut expressed the government's true attitude to lone parents. Indeed, measures introduced in the following Budget more than restored what had been lost. Instead, it was a symbolic gesture to reassure key voters that Labour was not 'soft' on welfare; once that had been made, ministers became free to pursue policies from which lone parents gained particular advantage.

As Dawn Primarolo, Financial Secretary to the Treasury, stated, the government wanted women to take their place as 'economic equals to men' while still supporting them in their accustomed nurturing role. To better assess what help was being given, the Treasury even introduced a 'gender impact' analysis of budgetary policy (Robinson, 1998, 27–8). The government's ultimate object was to encourage as many single parents as possible to enter the labour market. They were, therefore, expected to attend at least one New Deal interview and benefited disproportionately from measures designed to make low-paid work more remunerative. In particular, help with childcare was meant to eliminate the most common reason why lone parents could not look for work (Lewis, 2001, 498–503; Stedward, 2001, 172–3).

For women in work, the government promoted family-friendly policies but for the most part disavowed legislation. Employers were encouraged to see that such policies were in their own self-interest, although few seemed to. The government extended statutory paid maternity leave so it could last 26 weeks, in contrast to the nine weeks they inherited in 1997. As part of its employment reforms, Labour also gave part-time workers the same rights as full-time employees, such as access to paid holidays and pensions. Yet, despite being the party that introduced the Equal Pay Act in 1970, Labour did little to address the fact that 30 years later women in full-time work were still paid one–fifth less than men. Once again, the government was inhibited by its reluctance to compel employers to act in ways they clearly opposed.

The government took modest but significant steps towards fostering greater equality between the majority population and ethnic minorities. Some ministers considered legislation meant to guarantee equality was limited, and recognized the continued existence of discrimination in the labour market (Hodge, 2000, 38). Nonetheless, little was done to address this issue. Even so, when he was Home Secretary, Jack Straw did establish an inquiry into the reasons behind the failure of the Metropolitan Police to prosecute those guilty of the apparently racist murder of the black teenager, Stephen Lawrence. This case had become a *cause célèbre* and was taken to indicate a more general failure of the police to protect black citizens. The Lawrence inquiry concluded that the capital's police force was institutionally racist. In response, Straw extended the Race Relations Act to all police forces and other public employers, something which even the famously liberal Labour Home Secretary Roy Jenkins had failed to do. Afterwards there was a rise in the reporting of racially motivated crimes, indicative less of an increase in such crimes and more representative of a greater confidence amongst ethnic minorities that their complaints would now be taken seriously by the police (Toynbee and Walker, 2001, 172–3).

In terms of inequalities based on differences of sexuality, the main bugbear was the continued existence of Section 28 of the Local Government Act which forbade the 'promotion' of homosexuality in schools. This was largely a totemic issue but no less powerful for that: it had been drafted by the Conservatives to address a problem which did not exist, while no teacher had ever been prosecuted under its provisions. Labour's attempt to repeal the measure was, however, frustrated by vigorous opposition in the Lords. In contrast, the government overcame hostility in the Upper House to the equalization of the age of consent for all sexual orientations to 16 years of age. The presence of a number of openly gay Cabinet ministers – some reluctantly so – did not influence such policies, despite insinuations in the *Sun* that the Cabinet was governed by a 'gay mafia'. Instead these policies were a mark of the party's social liberalism, in contrast to the more authoritarian Conservatives. Indeed, such was the difference between the parties that 'New' Labour's commitment to gay rights was used to justify the defection of a number of liberal-leaning Conservatives, such as Ivan Massow and Shaun Woodward.

The Impact of Policy

Enough time has not yet elapsed to allow for a complete analysis of the impact of Labour's first term on inequality as it takes many years before the full effect of policies in this field can be felt. Moreover, during its first two years the government was hamstrung by its spending promise so little could be done: the full effect of extra 'investment' cannot yet be assessed.

It is nonetheless generally agreed that the quality of state education was enhanced: as measured by exam results and national tests, pupil performance has demonstrably improved since 1997. However, while standards appear to be rising, the ability of education to aid the country's economic performance has yet to be established. Furthermore, some believe 'New' Labour's endorsement of choice and limited selection means that education now promotes more, not less, inequality. This is because choice gives 'aspirational' parents the chance to secure greater relative advantage for their charges compared to the children of the poor. Thus, regardless of whether overall standards improve, the children of the better-off will continue to move ahead of those below them (Tomlinson, 1998, 28–35; Smithers, 2001, 411–13).

It is in addition presently hard to distinguish between the effect of government policy and the performance of an economy that continued to grow on poverty and inequality. Crucially, it was unclear how far the government was responsible for the fall in unemployment (in May 2001 this had been reduced to well under a million, its lowest point since 1976). Ministers were naturally keen to stress the role of the New Deal. They could point to the fact that in September 2000 the scheme had met its initial target of taking 250,000 people aged between 18 and 24 away from benefits and into work; by August 2001 this figure reached 300,000. Others speculated that had the New Deal not existed, matters would have been little worse. One authority nonetheless suggested that youth unemployment was 40 per cent lower than it might have been had the scheme not existed (Glennester, 2001, 387). While some considered it accounted for no more than half that figure, they still conceded the New Deal probably promoted the 'employability' even of those who found work by more conventional means (Riley and Young, 2001). The New Deal might have also had another, less tangible but still positive, impact by challenging the fatalism of the long-term unemployed. That one-third of those participating in the scheme had never held a job suggests it reached people who would otherwise have continued to be strangers to the world of work.

Only the most insensate Labour spin-doctor could consider the New Deal flawless. That nearly 40 per cent of those graduating from the scheme became unemployed within thirteen weeks indicated that further refinement was required. Moreover, many of those lone parents who moved from benefit into work only found employment in low-paid, part-time work with few prospects and little in-house training. If they were in employment, such conditions undermined their ability to move further out of poverty (Casebourne, 2001, 16–19). In light of this, ministers conceded that simply getting people into work was no longer enough: if dead-end low skilled jobs were better than nothing, they did not exactly represent a quantum leap up the social ladder (Hodge, 2000, 37). Moreover, if unemployment in general fell, there remained disadvantaged parts of the country that were largely untouched by government action. To help such areas, the government created Employment Zones which sought local solutions to lack of work opportunities. Some also wondered how vulnerable were any gains made by the New Deal to a recession: if the demand for jobs declined, it was doubtful that a more 'employable' profile would prevent unemployment from rising (Purdy, 2001, 187–9).

In terms of inequality and poverty the statistics are limited but suggestive. Thus, according to the Institute for Fiscal Studies (IFS), on the basis of Labour's tax and benefit reforms announced since 1997 and which will be effective by April 2003, all households should have gained from the party's first term (Clark and Dilnot, 2001, 28–36, 37–46). Most crucially, the poorest 10 per cent of households should be 13 per cent better off, the richest 10 per cent only marginally so. The poor gained most due to the substantial rise in key benefits, particularly those available to pensioners and households with children. Indeed, Andrew Dilnot of the IFS declared that benefits under Labour had 'produced very significant increases in generosity at a level we haven't seen in many, many years' (*The Financial Times*, 8 August 2001). These are, however, only estimates. Not all those eligible to claim benefits do so (in the case of some, up to a quarter do not), while certain consumption taxes, in particular that levied on cigarettes, disproportionately hit the poor. Nonetheless, despite these caveats, Labour's measures were progressive in their effect.

The force of the government's fiscal reforms did not, however, prevent a further rise in inequality during the first half of its first term. Largely as a result of economic expansion, net disposable incomes for all sections of the population rose between 1996/7 and 1999/2000, the only period for which figures are presently available. Incomes for the rich rose faster than those for the poor: it is not uncommon for workers with scarce skills and talents to take better advantage of a tight labour market than the unskilled. However, in 1999/2000 such inequality began to decline, most likely as a result of the fall in unemployment and the government's own welfare measures. Moreover, in contrast to inequality, it has been estimated that poverty fell during the course of Labour's first term but remained much higher than it was before 1979. Those who benefited most from this process were, once again, pensioners and families with children. Indeed, it was calculated that one million children had been lifted out of poverty by end of Labour's first term, although others estimated that only half that number had been (Piachaud, 2001; *The Independent*, 12 April 2002).

Conclusion

Many of those who consider that 'New' Labour marks a break with the party's past often idealize the party's previous disposition and achievements (Bevir, 2000). Thus while true that, if measured against its record on equality 'New' Labour's period in power was imperfect, this put it in good company: many of the party's keenest supporters criticized Labour ministers during the 1960s and 1970s for not tackling inequality to what they considered a sufficient degree (Townsend and Bosanquet, 1972; Bosanquet and Townsend, 1980). If historians of the Wilson and Callaghan governments have taken a more sympathetic view by pointing out the numerous constraints confronted by ministers, even they rarely conclude that Labour advanced equality by anything more than a modest amount (Ponting, 1989, 390–3; Gillie, 1991, 229–47; Ellison, 1994, 339–48). Moreover, as suggested in Chapter 3, 'New' Labour's pursuit of an equality that lay somewhere between outcome and opportunity – but probably closer to the latter than the former – was similar to that that envisaged by the party's post-war revisionists.

Ministers claimed that, while still committed to the welfare state and public services, they had to be reformed for the modern era. For some 'reform' was a synonym for retrenchment. Thus, Labour's first term saw it pursue a welfare policy based on what has been termed 'selective universality'. The key universal services of health and education were given increasing amounts of public funds. However, benefits – either in the form of cash or tax credit – were targeted at those believed to need help most: that is, the working poor with children and pensioners. Nonetheless, the erosion of universally available benefits began well before Blair – and Thatcher – had assumed office. Under 'New' Labour, though, access to certain benefits was undoubtedly made more conditional. Thus money that might have been spent on increasing unemployment benefit was instead devoted to the New Deal. For many claimants, access to state cash depended on their participation in this scheme. According to some, the liberty of income-tax payers to retain more of their earnings was bought through the erosion of the freedom of those forced to exist on benefit. Nonetheless, if the New Deal built on an earlier Conservative initiative, it merely made explicit something latent in the post-war welfare state: that social rights should be met by certain responsibilities.

Another result of 'reform' was that the private sector enjoyed a greater role in the delivery of health and education, although these services remained financed through taxation and free to all. Public sector trade unions saw this as a pernicious development, although they viewed it from the perspective of provider rather than consumer. Had the public sector delivered an efficient service in the past there would have been no need for 'New' Labour ministers to seek out alternatives. In any case, reform embraced more than simply private sector involvement: the move away from the top-down approaches made state-funded provision more responsive to local needs and those of the individual (Annesley, 2001, 214).

If the government appeared to think it unnecessary to raise spending on the welfare state as a proportion of the GDP by as much as some critics on the left demanded, the Conservatives would undoubtedly have reduced it. Thus, on that basis alone, Blair's approach was distinguished from that of his opponents on the right. Moreover, working within existing tax constraints and accepting the assumptions of many of the Conservatives' reforms, Blair's government reshaped the latter to refocus attention on the poorest and increase spending on key services. The reduction of poverty and, to a lesser extent, inequality was an (at times) deliberately obscured priority. Having moved from the early desire to be seen as more Thatcherite than it actually was, 'New' Labour became more aggressive about the virtues of public spending and the need for better-funded public services to reduce poverty and increase equality (Hewitt, 2001b). Current figures suggest that during Labour's first term the Thatcher-inspired increase in poverty and inequality has at least been halted, and may even have been reversed for certain groups (Annesley, 2001, 217–18; Glennester, 2001, 402). On this basis, it should be concluded that 'New' Labour's approach to poverty and equality remains comparable with that of both its predecessors and its counterparts in contemporary European social democracy.

Conclusion: The Death of 'New' Labour?

The purpose of this conclusion is threefold. First, it will draw together the most significant points raised in the preceeding chapters and thereby make more explicit some of the key underlying assumptions that formed the basis of this attempt to place Labour's recent progress into historical perspective. The chapter will next analyse the result of the 2001 campaign and consider what it tells us about the nature of 'New' Labour's achievement. It will draw to a close by critically assessing the claim (made by numerous commentators) that some time after 2000 'New' Labour shuffled off this mortal coil.

The Argument Underlined

The basic contention of this work is that we are presently forced to refer to the Labour party as 'New' Labour due to the widespread acceptance of a rhetorical device designed to improve its chances of gaining national office. In particular, it was meant to win the support of relatively affluent Conservative-inclined voters who associated the party with extremism, division, economic incompetence, militant trade unions and the poor. Prefixing Labour with 'New' was part of a simple but audacious electoral strategy that required Tony Blair and his cohorts to stress their apparent accommodation with what is normally described as Thatcherism and downplay their adherence to Labour's more established ideas and practices.

While this tactic succeeded in winning over numerous wavering voters it also alienated many within Labour's ranks, fuelling their belief that Blair aimed to betray the party's traditions. It should be noted in passing that many of those holding to this latter view felt the same about Neil Kinnock and most of his predecessors: to them any move away from the policies contained in the 1983 manifesto amounted to treason. Indeed, it is tempting to believe that both those who embraced and opposed change within the party found 'New' Labour, and its necessary antithesis, 'Old' Labour, highly convenient terms, for they dramatized in an especially acute form a division in the party's ranks that had festered for many decades. The past could now be explicitly presented as a golden age to which the party should return or a dystopia, comprised of grave errors never to be repeated. The present account proceeds from the belief that this dichotomy (and the widely held characterizations contained in Table C.1 that have been generated by it), while aiding contemporary political knock-about, seriously distorts any proper understanding of the party's present relationship to its own history.

Those closely attending to the words of the Labour leader and others, such as Gordon Brown, would have discerned that they were in any case attempting something subtler than simply asserting Labour's newness. It is certainly true, however, that for the benefit of less sophisticated electors Blair and Brown appeared to draw a stark line between themselves and the party before 1994. Yet, at the same time (albeit in a lower key) they argued that if 'New' Labour sought to change the means by which the party's established ends were to be achieved, it remained firmly committed to those ends. Even so, their dominant message was one of radical and irreversible change which led Blair to sometimes gratuitously disparage much of Labour's past. Thus he described 'Old' Labour as obsessed with 'tax and spend', preoccupied with state intervention for its own sake and too much in awe of the unions to run the economy efficiently. If genuinely believed by some in the leadership it was nonetheless a wilful distortion of history and eviscerated many of those underlying continuities that linked 'New' Labour to the party's past.

This is not to say that beneath the glossy surface of 'New' Labour substantive change had not occurred. Blair was not Clement Attlee with slightly more hair or Harold Wilson with fewer jokes: the social and economic context in which both led the party had changed significantly by the 1990s; yet neither was Blair a less aggressive version of Margaret

Table C.1 Popular characterizations of 'Old' and 'New' Labour

	'Old' Labour	*'New' Labour*
Attitude to Liberals	oppose	cooperate or merge
Ideology	dogmatic/principled	pragmatic/unprincipled
Electoral appeal	to the working class	to middle class/everybody
Organization	democratic/ union-dominated	autocratic/one member, one vote
Fiscal policy	redistribution/ 'tax and spend'	'prudence'/low tax and spend
Economic bias	state and unions	market and business
Type of equality favoured	outcome	opportunity

Thatcher as reform occurred within a recognizably social democratic frame of reference. Indeed, many of the changes 'New' Labour was designed to highlight had been prefigured not just by Kinnock's late 1980s Policy Review, but by 1970s neo-revisionists and some of the actions – if not quite all the thoughts – of the Callaghan government that lost power in 1979. In fact, the roots of 'New' Labour's basic orientation can be traced at least as far back as the opinions expressed by the party's post-war revisionists. Thus what we describe as 'New' Labour was part of a well-established tendency with strong roots in the party, in fact one that had been dominant for most of its history.

Consequently, the 'modernization' of the party ostensibly initiated by Kinnock and continued by Blair actually marked the resumption of a process rudely interrupted by the party's historically aberrant move left. Yet it would be wrong to think that 'New' Labour was in some way the inevitable product of a process of change determined by iron laws of causality. It is certainly possible, for example, that had James Callaghan called an election in 1978 prior to the 'winter of discontent' Labour might have just about retained power, thereby preventing a Thatcher victory and stalling the party's own shift leftwards. In such circumstances it is not inconceivable that a Labour government would have followed the instincts of its neo-revisionists and gradually introduced its own (albeit more modest) privatization programme and fostered other reforms which the British in their parochial way describe as Thatcherite. There were after all plenty of social democratic governments elsewhere in the world that did as much during the 1980s and 1990s. Like all historical counter-factual scenarios this is mere speculation and some may consider its assumptions laughable: in any case events did not take such a course. The 'winter of discontent' was followed by Thatcher's assumption of office, Labour's unprecedented embrace of left-wing policies, the defection of certain leading neo-revisionists in 1981 and the 1983 disaster, all of which entrenched a deeply negative view of the party in many voters' minds.

The point to be stressed here is that the assertion of 'New' Labour was an extreme reaction to the dire position in which the party found itself by the early 1990s. To the likes of Blair and Brown it appeared the only way the party could end a run of four back-to-back election defeats. This meant applying a radical version of the party's long-standing accommodate-to-shape strategy as outlined in Chapter 4. Hence some of the basest prejudices of key voters were placed at the heart of policy, while the need to assuage the sometimes wholly unreasonable doubts of international speculators were given unprecedented primacy. At least, that was the impression many were meant to draw. If by 1997 Labour had been subject to many significant organizational and policy changes, their scale was deliberately exaggerated. Blair's revision of clause four in 1995 exemplifies this very well. Widely hailed as 'New' Labour's defining moment, this involved deleting from the party's constitution words that enjoyed nothing more than a questionable relevance. They were moreover replaced by another set of words that still allowed for the possibility of state ownership. Furthermore, while the new clause endorsed the market, that was something party leaders had done decades before. Consequently, if the revision of clause four was the ultimate expression of 'New' Labour, then 'New' Labour was nothing new.

It is, however, true that under Blair the party continued to revise its position on a number of policies, most prominently those relating to the role of the state. Yet revision should not be seen to indicate 'New' Labour's deviation from social democracy: revisionism was at the heart of European social democracy's dominant tradition. As most social democrats have done in the past, Blair sought to keep his party in step with what he considered to be contemporary developments in capitalism. At the start of the twenty-first century this meant taking heed of globalization and acknowledging the past failures of common ownership and the apparent success of the market. At mid-century it had meant attempting to reconcile what were generally regarded to be the strengths of public ownership with a vigorous but apparently tempered post-war capitalism. Earlier in the century, the market was assumed to be irredeemably inefficient and doomed to collapse, while state ownership was thought the only solution to each and every problem. Eduard Bernstein challenged aspects of this latter view through his analysis of the direction of capitalist development. This led him to draw conclusions uncomfortable to many contemporaries. Nonetheless, since the 1890s all social democrats aspiring to hold office and thereby improve the lives of their supporters sought to come to terms with what they thought capitalism made possible. In that respect, certain national peculiarities aside, 'New' Labour remained true to mainstream social democracy.

If 'New' Labour really is recognizably social democratic, some might wonder why so many critics within the party consider Blair has committed apostasy. Censure of this sort from the likes of Tony Benn was to be expected: a Labour leader not greeted by cries of betrayal from that quarter would indeed have been exceptional. However, condemnation from old revisionists such as Roy Hattersley, Kinnock's deputy and self-proclaimed advocate of the ideas of Anthony Crosland, does require explanation. This appears to be the result of a combination of generational and cultural influences. For the most part such detractors take what they imagine to have been the form assumed by social democracy half-way through the twentieth century – which often is the time in which they came to political maturity – to be its final and perfect expression. This is part of a wider modernist fallacy, which considered that the years following the end of the Second World War saw civilization reach its ultimate manifestation. Labour's revisionists shared this illusion along with many other thinkers at the time, believing the 'golden age' of full employment was effectively the end of history. Moreover, such critics appear to assume that Keynesianism and limited state control of the economy worked well, while the form assumed by the welfare state after 1945 could not be improved upon. They also seem to imagine that the time-bound social relations and assumptions that gave rise to these practices and institutions could somehow be kept in aspic. Ironically, in their regard for what they take to be the past, they are guilty of that which Crosland warned against: they have confused means with end.

Since the ending of the 'golden age', others of a more right-wing disposition than the revisionists concluded that history had come to an end, this time in 1989 with the collapse of communism (Fukuyama, 1992). They encouraged the belief that the free market had finally triumphed over all other forms of economic management. As we should know by now, history does not end but constantly develops (as must those who wish to influence its direction). Thus, in the hands of Blair and Brown, the assertion of 'New' Labour was but the latest (if most hard-nosed) means by which Labour leaders have sought to make their party appear relevant to the times in which they lived.

The 2001 General Election

Labour's relevance to contemporary Britons was tested by the 2001 General Election, for central to the assertion of 'New' Labour was the belief that only it could improve the party's chances of winning power. This strategy proved to be exceptionally successful in as much as it produced an unprecedented Commons majority in 1997 and one almost as large in 2001 (Norris, 2001; Butler and Kavanagh, 2002; Geddes and Tonge, 2002). Yet, many suspected that in 1997 Labour only won because, while key voters rejected the Conservative Party, they believed Blair offered them a competent but watered-down version of Thatcherism. That the party did not win on its own merits was, it seemed, the logical result of the entire 'New' Labour strategy. Similarly, victory in 2001 was tempered by a dramatic decline in the turn out; from an already poor share of 71.5 per cent in 1997, the proportion who voted in 2001 amounted to only 59.4 per cent of those qualified so to do. This meant that the number of non-voters actually exceeded Labour's own tally. Moreover, Labour's share of votes that were cast was, at 40.7 per cent, very meagre for a winning party. 'New' Labour's deliberate emulation of established Conservative policy was blamed for the widespread lack of motivation to go to the polls.

Declining participation in established politics was a trend that embraced most other advanced societies, while non-voting has always been higher amongst the working class than the middle class. The year 2001 saw this process reach an acute point and was of particular concern to Labour, given that it was most obvious within the party's heartlands. There were, then, many possible explanations other than 'New' Labour's putative Thatcherism, but the precipitate drop in turn-out was widely believed to vindicate the fears of those such as Peter Kilfoyle. Even during Blair's earliest days as leader they had argued that because 'New' Labour appeared to attend to the needs of middle-class voters at the expense of those in the working class, the latter would become alienated from the political system. The evidence generated by the 2001 election suggests this belief was more than plausible (Whiteley *et al.*, 2001). Indeed, such was their alienation from mainstream politics that in a few especially disadvantaged seats some working-class voters did more than stay at home: they supported the neo-Nazi British National Party.

Certainly, the popular impression was that 'New' Labour, in contrast to 'Old' Labour, was increasingly bourgeois. An ICM exit poll discovered that those who voted in 2001 considered Blair's party to be predominantly concerned with middle-class interests. In 1987 Labour was thought to look after working-class interests by 89 per cent of those polled; 14 years later only 57 per cent thought this. In contrast, those believing Labour looked after middle-class interests had increased from 58 to 68 per cent. The apparent deproletarianization of Labour's vote established by the pattern of non-voting was reproduced in the changing distribution of the party's support amongst those who actually voted. For, while the party experienced a small national swing against it, in northern England and Wales Labour suffered the most, in the affluent South East the movement towards the Conservatives was almost imperceptible. Survey evidence confirmed that in 2001 Labour support fell most heavily amongst council tenants, trade unionists and unskilled manual workers, heartlands voters all (see Table C.2).

Table C.2   Percentage of electorate supporting
'New' Labour in 2001 by social category

Category	%
All	42 (−2)
Men	42 (−3)
Women	42 (−2)
AB	30 (−1)
C1	38 (−1)
C2	49 (−1)
DE	55 (−4)
18–24	41 (−8)
25–34	51 (+2)
35–44	45 (−3)
45–54	41 (0)
55–64	37 (−2)
65+	39 (−2)
Home owners	32 (0)
Council tenants	60 (−4)
Trade unionists	50 (−7)

Note: Change from 1997 in brackets.
Source: Butler and Kavanagh (2002), 257.

Such movements undoubtedly reflected the Blair government's priorities, something that in turn echoed the essential aim of 'New' Labour. As Blair candidly admitted in February 2001, his first period in government was about 'reassurance' and that principally meant reassuring Middle England by sticking to Conservative spending limits for two years and not raising income tax (Blair, 2001a). By making this admission, Blair was effectively drawing the first phase of 'New' Labour's development to a close. For 'reassurance' read 'accommodation': it was now time to shape the voters' preferences. Nonetheless, the government's support for higher investment in the public services, increasingly enthusiastic after the 2000 Comprehensive Spending Review (CSR), came too late to have much of an effect on the result. For while ministers' rhetoric shifted leftwards and departmental spending plans were upgraded, significant improvements to health care and educational provision (and also the reduction of inequality) need years before they can be felt. Moreover, any impact that might have been registered by 2001 was obscured by ministers' unwillingness to admit that higher personal taxation might have to finance future progress. In addition, Blair's talk of allowing a greater role for private companies in the public services appeared to threaten the conditions of already low-paid public employees. This won few friends in the unionized heartlands.

Even so, if many poor-working class voters had yet to feel much of an improvement to their lives as a result of Labour's first term – and saw little reason to believe matters would get better as a result of a second – an increasing number of commentators believed that a transformation had occurred. Indeed, some began to talk of the 'death' of 'New' Labour.

The Death of 'New' Labour?

After the announcement of the 2000 CSR 'New' Labour rhetoric was in marked contrast to that employed prior to the 1997 General Election: then the leadership gave every impression of being implacably opposed to the 'tax and spend' ethos. Significantly, it was Stephen Byers, one of Blair's most faithful Cabinet colleagues, who stated that as there was no need for the caution of 1997, the forthcoming election provided Labour with a 'once-in-a-generation opportunity to change our country fundamentally' (*The Independent*, 4 January 2001).

Promises to spend unprecedented amounts of tax-payers' money on health, education and transport prompted many commentators to consider that 'New' Labour was transforming itself before their very eyes. Hattersley had spent most of Blair's first term attacking the Prime Minister for what he supposed was a lack of social democratic principle. Even he considered 'New' Labour was now returning to his definition of Labour's proper ideological bearings. Consistent with his view of 'New' Labour as the product of an elite conspiracy, Hattersley ascribed this change of course to Peter Mandelson's second resignation from the Cabinet (*The Guardian*, 29 January 2001). A friendlier critic, Michael Jacobs of the Fabian Society, dismissed the importance of Mandelson's departure to what he termed the 'death' of 'New' Labour. This was, he believed, instead due to the government's careful management of the economy, which had lain to rest the party's reputation for extremism, incompetence and division, leaving it free to advance a more conventional social democratic agenda (*The Independent*, 12 February 2001). Such was the perceived scale of transformation that Stephen Pollard, a commentator once close to 'New' Labour, declared that Blair's was now a 'traditional tax-and-spend' government (*The Sunday Telegraph*, 11 March 2001).

The 2001 campaign marked an uncertain stage in this process: a leadership schooled in electoral defeat was not inclined to take risks with public opinion when votes were so obviously at stake. Nonetheless, Labour's manifesto still marked a move back to the left compared to the one issued in 1997, although it remained some distance to the right of even Kinnock's 1992 programme (Bara and Budge, 2001, 28). Reflecting the contradictions inherent in popular opinion, the leadership was now happy to promise extra spending but unwilling to indicate that taxes might also have to rise. Blair insisted on repeating the 1997 pledge not to raise income tax; and during the campaign Brown fought hard to avoid saying whether he would increase National Insurance contributions for the better off. Blair's insistence that extra 'investment' in the public services had to be accompanied by 'reform' was also part of his attempt to ensure Middle England did not believe Labour would simply pour their taxes into often-inefficient organizations. It was nonetheless construed by public sector trade unionists and other interested parties as a call for their privatization.

After Labour was returned to office, such was the hostility of the unions to the government's apparent intentions that ministers were forced to clarify. In so doing they gave a better indication of the particular policies the leadership now considered appropriate to the Third Way. The Prime Minister in particular denied that he thought the private sector was a panacea, although 'in certain circumstances, cooperation with it can work, and if it works to the benefit of the patient or the pupil or the user of a public service, do it'. 'If it doesn't', he stated, 'don't' (*The Guardian* website, 12 September 2001). Most concern was expressed about what 'reform' meant for the National Health Service (NHS). Alan Milburn, the Minister of Health, outlined his desire to break with the 'centralist' legacy of Aneurin Bevan's original 1940s conception of the NHS. However, he was insistent that the NHS would remain a universal service, funded and operated within the public domain. 'Reform' did not mean privatization but might imply giving those Milburn described as successful 'public sector entrepreneurs' greater autonomy (*The Guardian*, 26 June and 24 October 2001). If some were shocked by such suggestions, they should not have been. During debates about how best to create a public health service, Clement Attlee's deputy, Herbert Morrison, had fought hard to retain a role for autonomous municipal and voluntary provision. Morrison lost the argument in 1945 but his was a respectable social democratic alternative to the form eventually assumed by the NHS (Morgan, 1984, 154–6).

If many union leaders remained unconvinced their members would not suffer as a result of 'reform', ministers such as Margaret Hodge nonetheless made a case for the 'central importance of public institutions controlling public services' and praised the 'moral underpinning to the public realm' (*The Guardian*, 6 September 2001). Patricia Hewitt went so far as to declare that the public services offered a welcome space

beyond the rules of the market, a place where 'centre left values of justice, solidarity, community and co-operation can take root' (Hewitt,
2001b, 124). After his experience with Railtrack, Byers even had the
temerity to state that the Third Way was too uncritical (or, as he put it,
'flaky') in its attitude to the private sector and needed to be firmed up
(*The Guardian*, 14 January 2002). Thus, while remaining overtly pragmatic about means, 'New' Labour's leading lights drew clearer bound-
aries between what functions the state and market could legitimately
perform. As a result, it became obvious that if deemed more efficient,
alternatives to centrally directed provision would be entertained,
although all services would remain free at the point of delivery and
under public supervision (Giddens, 2002).

To many observers, even talk of public sector 'reform' smacked of
Thatcherism. Hattersley in particular reversed his earlier judgement and
claimed that those who controlled 'New' Labour remained the enemies of
social democracy (*The Observer*, 24 June 2001). Nonetheless, others
continued to believe the CSR marked a significant phase in the development of New' Labour, if not its actual death. They saw the early stages of
Blair's second term, in particular the enforced demise of Railtrack, as further evidence that ministers were moving back to the left (*The Guardian*,
30 October 2001). This latter opinion was reinforced by Brown's
November pre-Budget statement. Referring to the interim findings of the
Wanless report into NHS funding, the Chancellor asserted that the public
sector had suffered from decades of under-investment. Moreover, the
most efficient means of reversing the trend was to finance the shortfall
through general taxation. Nobody, least of all Brown, actually stated that
income taxes would have to rise, but the implication of his statement that
a 'significantly higher share' of national income should be devoted to the
public services was clear enough (BBC website, 28 November 2001). At
the same time as he delivered this message, Brown confirmed that in
2003 his innovative tax credit system would be simplified and extended
to include pensioners with modest savings and working families without
children. Help for working families with children was also set to be
entrenched to enable the government to further reduce the number of
children in poverty by the end of its second term.

According to many of Blair's critics on the centre-left such announcements amounted to the 'end of an era'; the Labour leadership's accommodation of Thatcherism had been concluded and this was now a
'post-New Labour era' (*New Statesman*, 3 December 2001; *The Guardian*,
14 December 2001). Those who continued to see merit in giving the
market its head looked on Brown's emphasis as a reversion to 'Old'
Labour. To them it looked as if ministers would give the public services

more money in return for very feeble reforms that would not upset the unions (*Economist*, 1 December 2001).

These positions were entrenched in April 2002 after Brown announced plans to further increase investment in the NHS. *The Daily Mail* led the charge from the right, with a front-page headline that accused the Chancellor of 'Wringing the Middle Class', subsequently asserting his proposals marked 'The Return of Old Labour' (*The Daily Mail*, 18 April 2002). For, Brown had cast aside the dissembling that marked some of his contributions to Labour's 2001 campaign and bluntly stated that additional improvements to the NHS would have to be financed from a rise in National Insurance contributions. As these payments were linked to income, it meant the better off would make a disproportionate contribution. Thus, while staying true to Blair's pledge not to raise income tax, Brown had nonetheless increased a tax on incomes, effecting a modest redistribution of wealth. If some saw this as confirming that 'tax and spend' was back, Blair denied it. Brown's 2002 Budget was, he claimed, no turning point; it was, instead, 'another stage of New Labour as a progressive centre-left government'. 'We have', he stated, 'never been anything else' (*The Independent*, 13 April 2002).

Conclusion

Whether one considers 'New' Labour had died, was transformed or simply continued to develop its Thatcherite enthusiasms after 2000 depends very much on how one conceptualizes 'New' Labour. Colin Crouch usefully clarified matters by suggesting that 'New' Labour could be one of three phenomena: a form of social democracy forced to make concessions to powerful neo-liberal interests; a development of neo-liberalism obliged to make concessions to the party's social democratic heritage; or an unresolved mix of the two. Conceding that it was too early to be definitive, Crouch nonetheless considered – like Hattersley – that 'New' Labour was primarily a neo-liberal force occasionally compelled to make social democratic gestures (Crouch, 2001, 104–7; *The Guardian*, 3 December 2001).

In contrast to what Crouch and others might think, Blair claimed that raising taxes to pay for increased public spending was a logical development for his party (*The Independent on Sunday*, 2 December 2001). This new emphasis certainly had all the appearance of the second stage of the Prime Minister's extreme version of the 'accommodate-to-shape' strategy. It nonetheless remained a cautious revelation of the party's continued social democratic character, and one attuned to the times in which Labour now operated. As a result, it took full account of the frail nature of voter loyalties and their confused attitude to the role of taxation in financing public services. As Blair's influential adviser, Philip Gould, stated, 'New' Labour was a 'fluid evolving movement, made up of a cross-current of opinions, views and values'; it was, he claimed, 'always changing' (Gould, 2001). While exaggerating the point, at its heart Gould's was an unremarkable statement, for all successful parties have evolved as circumstances dictated and amended certain of their assumptions to allow them to operate successfully in the new environment. As a result, Labour's past is one of unremitting transformation and adaptation: its history only appears static in retrospect.

As suggested at various points in this work, the categories of 'Old' and 'New' Labour distort our understanding of the party's present development and its relationship to its past. Labour's contemporary course has certainly been influenced by the environment in which it operates, one defined by the declining salience of collective identities, a more market-orientated economy and a popular scepticism about government's ability to achieve good. In this sense, therefore, Labour is 'new': but then all major parties are constantly forced to renew themselves. The extent to which Blair abandoned the party's past preoccupations in the process of this adaptation remains, of course, highly controversial. The basic contention here is that, based on a reading of Labour's history which is intended to avoid reproducing old myths and creating new ones, Blair remained remarkably faithful to Labour's past. The party at the start of the twenty-first century may be a highly cautious social democratic organization; but recognizably social democratic it remains. If the state has advanced modestly and in novel ways since 1997 Labour's purpose in office is the same as it ever was: to reform capitalism so that it may better serve the interests of the majority. The government even managed to start to reverse two decades of Conservative-inspired increasing inequality.

Talk of the 'death' of 'New' Labour should be taken with the same number of pinches of salt as came with the notion that it ever existed in the first place. Moreover, the return of 'Old' Labour is unlikely, if only because, just like 'New' Labour, as constructed by most contemporaries it bore little relation to reality. Thus, if this book has one message it is that these two categories should be dispensed with as soon as possible, for they prevent us properly understanding the past and present course of what we should now simply refer to as the 'Labour Party'.

Guide to Further Reading

Introduction: What is 'New' Labour?

A useful introduction to some of the trickier issues raised by the 'New' Labour debate has been supplied by Kenny and Smith (2001), while the question of when 'New' Labour can – or cannot – be said to have begun has been helpfully clarified by Lent (1997). Hay (1999) and Heffernan (2000) are prominent exponents of the opinion that 'New' Labour represents the party's accommodation with Thatcherism. Slightly at odds with this view is that of Driver and Martell (1998) who suggest that Tony Blair's party should be considered 'post-Thatcherite' in as much as it is critical of both contemporary Conservative and 'Old' Labour thinking. In stark contrast, albeit in different ways, are Coates (1996), Bale (1999b) and Rubinstein (2000) who believe that 'New' Labour marks a clear continuum with the party's past. Jones (1996) in particular makes the connection between Blair and post-war revisionism while Ludlam (2001b) provides evidence for seeing the 1974–9 Wilson–Callaghan governments as an important influence. Assuming a wider perspective, both Sassoon (1996) and Callaghan (2000) locate 'New' Labour in the overall evolution of European social democracy.

1 Historicizing 'New' Labour

Those wishing to gain a firm grounding in Labour's basic chronology, facts and figures could do a lot worse than consult Hamer (1999). While Thorpe (2001) provides the best single volume narrative account of the party's development, Tanner, Thane and Tiratsoo (2000) contains a series of interpretive essays by some of the leading historians of the party. Of those accounts of Labour's past that draw their inspiration from the 'Old'/'New' Labour divide, Gould (1998) is probably the most developed 'New' Labour view while Harrison (1996) is a fairly representative example of the 'Old' Labour perspective. Of those rival attempts to encapsulate the party's history, Miliband (1972) is the prototypical socialist account, Marquand (1999) the pre-eminent social democratic example while Fielding, Thompson and Tiratsoo (1995) is characteristic of work by adherents of the constraints school.

2 The Liberal Connection

Remarkably little has been written about Labour's relationship with the Liberals so it was perhaps no surprise that Blair's support for greater cooperation appeared novel to many. Laver (1997) and Schofield (1993) have established a theoretical framework for understanding coalition-building although this does not give a definitive means of appreciating the particularities of the Labour–Liberal dynamic. Fortunately Joyce (1999) has supplied a solid historical account of this relationship while Clarke (1978) and Freeden (1978) have highlighted the intellectual assumptions of early social democrats and New Liberals, many of which remain relevant today. The diary entries contained in Ashdown (2000 and 2001) provide an invaluable insider account and fully illustrate Blair's day-by-day uncertainty regarding reuniting the centre-left. Just when the prospect had again fallen into the shadows, Lawson and Sherlock (2001) produced an insight into the hopes of those in both parties who wished to see their leaders construct a closer relationship.

3 From Clause Four to Third Way: Labour's Ideological Journey

An accessible and stimulating approach to understanding political ideologies has been provided by Freeden (1996). Foote (1997) has written a more specific account of Labour's political thought, one complemented by Thompson (1996) who surveys the party's political economy. The nature of 'New' Labour's ideology has been analysed from a critical perspective by Bevir (2000) and from a more friendly position by Plant (2001). It is always useful to read for oneself what the major protagonists have to say about any issue: Blair (1998b), along with Blair and Schroeder (2000), outline Blair's vision of the Third Way. Giddens (1998 and 2000) has supplied a sympathetic elaboration of Blair's themes and responds to some of the Prime Minister's many critics.

4 Accommodating or Shaping? Labour's Electoral Dilemma

Tiratsoo (2000) has concisely put Labour's problematic relationship with the electorate into historical perspective while Heath, Jowell and Curtice (2001) focus on those issues relevant to the creation of 'New' Labour. Crewe (1988) and Rentoul (1989) have each questioned the extent to which Thatcherism affected voters' attitudes. Anybody wishing to gain a detailed insight into the state of popular opinion – Thatcher-influenced or not – prior to Blair becoming Labour leader should consult Radice (1992) and Radice and Pollard (1993 and 1994). 'New Labour's impact on the 1997 General Election has been analysed by Butler and Kavanagh (1997), Geddes and Tonge (1997) and Evans and Norris (1999). Bromley and Curtice (1999), along with Hedges and Bromley (2001), illustrate the limited impact of Labour's 1997–2001 government on perceptions of issues such as the Third Way and income tax. The cautious radicalism that emerged after the 2000 Comprehensive Spending Review and under-pinned Labour's 2001 campaign is highlighted in Fielding (2002).

5   Becoming Blair's Party? Labour Organization

Tanner (2000) has provided a succinct assessment of the leadership's strained relationship with party members; this is supplemented by Fielding (2001a), who has outlined the character of the party's membership for much of the post-war period. We are deeply indented to the work of Minkin (1978 and 1992) whose comprehensive accounts of the workings of Labour's conference and the nature of the party's union link in the pre-'New' Labour era leave little else to say. Whiteley (1983) and Seyd (1987) have produced analyses of the party's move to the left and the loss of leadership autonomy that occurred during the early 1980s. Mair (1994) and Katz and Mair (1995) have sketched out a comparative theoretical framework for understanding the internal reforms introduced since 1983. Assessments of the post-1997 regime tend to be very critical: Davies (2001), along with Sturgeon and Hurley (2001), gives a sense of what a number of the party's active members think. In contrast, Shaw (2001b) and Morgan and Mungham (2000) have supplied more balanced accounts of the often-disputatious process of candidate selection.

6   Managing the Economy

Tomlinson (2000) gives an admirably condensed historical account of the party's attitude to the economy. Stephens (2001) and Gamble and Kelly (2001) encapsulate the debate about 'New' Labour's economic policy, the former presenting it as a sharp break with the past whereas the latter detect a greater degree of continuity. Contrasting positions with regard to the existence or otherwise of 'globalization' are represented by the 'hyperglobalist' Ohmae (1995), the sceptical Hirst and Thompson (1999) and Held *et al.* (1999) who consider it a reality albeit of a more limited nature than some enthusiasts. 'New' Labour's approach to the economy is best considered in light of Brown (1994) and Blair (1996). MacIntyre (1999) gives a full account of Peter Mandelson's time at the Department of Trade and Industry whereas Taylor (2001) and Ludlam (2001a) provide authoritative accounts of the progress of the Fairness at Work legislation. Clark and Dilnot (2001) have gathered together non-partisan and comprehensive assessments of the impact of the Blair administration's policies on the British economy.

7   Advancing Equality?

Bobbio (1996) provides an appreciation of the continued importance of reducing inequality to all parties of the left while Ellison (1994) assesses Labour's historical attitude to welfare. An understanding of 'New' Labour's approach to welfare and equality can be gleaned from the Commission on Social Justice (1994), Brown (1996) and Mandelson (1997). Those policies relevant to welfare and the pursuit of equality introduced since 1997 have been capably surveyed by Johnson (2001), Annesley (2001) and Glennester (2001); the vital matters of education and training are in addition tackled by Wood (2001), Smithers (2001), Stedward (2001) and McCaig (2001). Establishing the impact of any government on inequality is a fraught business but Clark and Dilnot (2001) appear to have the figures to back up their claim that the 1997–2001 government engineered a modest redistribution of wealth.

Conclusion: The Death of 'New' Labour?

The significance of the 2001 election to the development of 'New' Labour is well covered in Butler and Kavanagh (2002), Geddes and Tonge (2002) and Norris (2001). Useful post-Comprehensive Spending Review clarifications of 'New' Labour themes number Blair (2001b), Hewitt (2001b) and Giddens (2002). The continued debate regarding the future direction of 'New' Labour – if indeed it has a future – is best followed in *Political Quarterly*, *Renewal* and *New Statesman*.

References

Addison, P. (1975) *The Road to 1945*, London, Quartet.

Alcock, P. (1992) 'The Labour party and the welfare state', in Smith, M.J. and Spear, J. (eds), *The Changing Labour Party*, London, Routledge.

Alexander, K.J.W. and Hobbs, A. (1967) 'What influences Labour MPs?', in Rose, R. (ed.), *Studies in British Politics*, London, Macmillan – now Palgrave.

Allen, Michael (1998) 'British trade unionism's quiet revolution', *Renewal*, 6(4).

Althusser, L. (1977) *For Marx*, London, Verso.

Anderson, P. (1965) 'Origins of the present crisis' in Anderson, P. (ed.), *Towards Socialism*, London, Fontana.

Anderson, P. (1987) 'The figures of descent', *New Left Review*, 161.

Annesley, C. (2001) New Labour and welfare', in Ludlam, S. and Smith, M.J. (eds), *New Labour in Government*, London, Macmillan – now Palgrave.

Artis, M. and Cobham, D. (eds) (1991) *Labour's Economic Policies, 1974–9*, Manchester, Manchester University Press.

Ashdown, P. (2000) *The Ashdown Diaries. Volume One, 1988–1997*, Harmondsworth, Penguin.

Ashdown, P. (2001) *The Ashdown Diaries. Volume Two, 1997–1999*, Harmondsworth, Penguin.

Attlee, C. (1937) *The Labour Party in Perspective*, London, Gollancz.

Bale, T. (1999a) *Sacred Cows and Common Sense*, Aldershot, Ashgate.

Bale, T. (1999b) 'The logic of no alternative? Political scientists, historians and the politics of Labour's past', *British Journal of Politics & International Relations*, 1(2).

Bara, J. and Budge, I. (2001), 'Party policy and ideology: still New Labour?', in Norris, P. (ed.), *Britain Votes 2001*, Oxford, Oxford University Press.

Barker, R. (1972) *Education and Politics, 1900–1951*, Oxford, Oxford University Press.

Barrow, L. and Bullock, I. (1996), *Democratic Ideas and the British Labour Movement, 1880–1914*, Cambridge, Cambridge University Press.

Bartolini, S. (1983) 'The European left since World War One; size, composition and patterns of electoral development', in Daalder, H. and Mair, P. (eds), *West European Party Systems*, Beverly Hills, CA, Sage.

BBC website www.bbc.co.uk/politics.

Bealey, F. and Pelling, H. (1958) *Labour and Politics, 1900–1906*, London, Macmillan – now Palgrave.

Bealey, F., Blondel, J. and McCann, W.P. (1965) *Constituency Politics. A Study of Newcastle-under-Lyme*, London, Faber & Faber.

Beer, S.H. (2001) 'New Labour: Old Liberalism', in White, S. (ed.), *New Labour. The Progressive Future?*, London, Palgrave.

Benn, M. (2000) 'New Labour and social exclusion', *Political Quarterly*, 71(3).

222

Benn, T. (1983) 'The Labour Party as an alliance for progress', in Lansman, J. and Meale, A. (eds), *Beyond Thatcherism*, London, Junction.
Benn, T. (1994) *The End of an Era. Diaries, 1980–90*, London, Arrow.
Berger, S. (1994) *The British Labour Party and the German Social Democrats, 1900–31*, Oxford, Oxford University Press.
Berger, S. (1995) 'European labour movements and the European working class in comparative perspective', in Berger, S. and Broughton, D. (eds), *The Force of Labour*, Oxford, Berg.
Bernstein, E. (1961) *Evolutionary Socialism*, New York, Schocken.
Bevan, A. (1952) *In Place of Fear*, London, Heinemann.
Bevir, M. (2000) 'New Labour: a study in ideology', *British Journal of Politics & International Relations*, 2(3).
Blaazer, D. (1992) *The Popular Front and the Progressive Tradition*, Cambridge, Cambridge University Press.
Black, A. (1996) 'Labour Reform: distraction or necessity?', *Chartist*, May–June.
Black, A. (2000) *Labour Reform Members' Newsletter*, September.
Blair, T. (1993) 'Foreword', in Bryant, C. (ed.), *Reclaiming the Ground. Christianity and Socialism*, London, Spire.
Blair, T. (1994) 'Socialism', *Fabian Pamphlet*, 565.
Blair, T. (1996) *New Britain. My Vision of a Young Country*, London, Fourth Estate.
Blair, T. (1998a) Speech to the French National Assembly, 24 March, www. number-10.gov.uk.
Blair, T. (1998b) 'The Third Way', *Fabian Pamphlet*, 588.
Blair, T. (2001a) Speech at a North London Comprehensive, 8 February, www.number-10.gov.uk.
Blair, T. (2001b) 'Third Way, phase two', *Prospect*, March.
Blair, T. and Schroeder, G. (2000) 'Europe: the Third Way/Neue Mitte', in Hombach, B., *The Politics of the New Centre*, Cambridge, Polity.
Bobbio, N. (1996) *Left and Right. The Significance of a Political Distinction*, Cambridge, Polity.
Bogdanor, V. (1983) 'The Liberal Party and constitutional reform', in Bogdanor, V. (ed.), *Liberal Party Politics*, Oxford, Oxford University Press.
Bogdanor, V. (2001) 'Constitutional reform', in Seldon, A. (ed.), *The Blair Effect*, London, Little, Brown.
Boggs, C. (1995) *The Socialist Tradition from Crisis to Decline*, London, Routledge.
Bosanquet, N. and Townsend, P. (eds) (1980) *Labour and Equality*, London, Heinemann.
Bradshaw, B. (2000), 'False choices', in Bradshaw, B. and others, *Must Labour Choose?*, London, Progress.
Breuilly, J. (1992) *Labour and Liberalism in Nineteenth Century Europe*, Manchester, Manchester University Press.
Brighouse, T. (2001) 'New Labour and education; could do better', *Political Quarterly*, 72(1).
Brivati, B. (1996) *Hugh Gaitskell*, London, Cohen.
Bromley, C. and Curtice, J. (1999) 'Is there a Third Way?', in Jowell, R., Curtice, J., Park, A. and Thomson, K. (eds), *British Social Attitudes. The 16th Report*, Aldershot, Ashgate.

Brown, C. (1997) *Fighting Talk. The Biography of John Prescott*, London, Pocket Books.

Brown, G. (1994) 'The politics of potential: a new agenda for Labour', in Miliband, D. (ed.), *Reinventing the Left*, Cambridge, Polity.

Brown, G. (1996) 'Tough decisions', *Fabian Review*, 108(3).

Brown, G. (2000a) James Meade memorial lecture, 8 May, www.hm-treasury.gov.uk/press/2000.

Brown, G. (2000b) Speech to the British-American Chamber of Commerce, 22 February, www.hm-treasury.gov.uk/press/2000.

Brown, G. (2000c) Speech to the National Council of One Parent Families, 5 December, www.hm-treasury.gov.uk/press/2000.

Brown, G. (2001a) Speech to the Child Poverty Action Group, 15 May, www.hm-treasury.gov.uk/press/2001.

Brown, G. (2001b) Speech to the Transport and General Workers' Union conference, 5 July, www.hm-treasury.gov.uk/press/2001.

Budge, I. (1999) 'Party policy and ideology: reversing the 1950s?', in Evans, G. and Norris, P. (eds), *Critical Elections*, London, Sage.

Bulmer, S. (2001) 'European policy: fresh dawn or false start?', in Coates, D. and Lawler, P. (eds), *New Labour in Power*, Manchester, Manchester University Press.

Butler, D. and Kavanagh, D. (1997) *The British General Election of 1997*, London, Macmillan – now Palgrave.

Butler, D. and Kavanagh, D. (2002) *The British General Election of 2001*, London, Palgrave.

Butler, D. and Stokes, D. (1969) *Political Change in Britain*, Harmondsworth, Penguin.

Cairncross, A. (1985) *Years of Recovery. British Economic Policy, 1945–51*, London, Methuen.

Callaghan, J. (2000) *The Retreat of Social Democracy*, Manchester, Manchester University Press.

Carr, E.H. (1964) *What is History?*, Harmondsworth, Penguin.

Casebourne, J. (2001) 'When work isn't working', *Fabian Review*, 113(1).

Chapple, B. and Sutton, J. (1999) 'The agony and the ecstasy', *Modern Labour*, October.

Clark, T. and Dilnot, A. (eds) (2001) *Election Briefing 2001*, London, Institute for Fiscal Studies.

Clarke, C. (2000) 'Delivering change' in Bradshaw, B. and others, *Must Labour Choose?*, London, Progress.

Clarke, P. (1971) *Lancashire and the New Liberalism*, Cambridge, Cambridge University Press.

Clarke, P. (1978) *Liberals and Social Democrats*, Cambridge, Cambridge University Press.

Clarke, P. (1983) 'Liberals and social democrats in historical perspective', in Bogdanor, V. (ed.), *Liberal Party Politics*, Oxford, Oxford University Press.

Clift, B. (2001a) 'New Labour's Third Way and social democracy', in Ludlam, S. and Smith, M.J. (eds), *New Labour in Government*, London, Macmillan – now Palgrave.

Clift, B. (2001b) 'The Jospin way', *Political Quarterly*, 72(2).

Clifton, D. (1994) 'The death of the mass party', *Renewal*, 2(2).

Coates, D. (1975) *The Labour Party and the Struggle for Socialism*, Cambridge, Cambridge University Press.

Coates, D. (1980) *Labour in Power? A Study of the Labour Government, 1974–1979*, London, Longman.

Coates, D. (1996) 'Labour governments: old constraints and new parameters', *New Left Review*, 291.

Coates, D. (1999) 'Models of capitalism in the New World Order: the UK case', *Political Studies*, 47(4).

Coates, D. (2001a) 'Capitalist models and social democracy: the case of New Labour', *British Journal of Politics & International Relations*, 3(3).

Coates, D. (2001b) 'New Labour's industrial and employment policy', in Coates, D. and Lawler, P. (eds), *New Labour in Power*, Manchester, Manchester University Press.

Coates, K. and others (1999) 'New Labour, New Democracy', *Independent Labour Network Pamphlet*.

Commission on Public Private Partnerships (2001) *Building Better Partnerships*, London, Institute for Public Policy Research.

Commission on Social Justice (1994), *Social Justice. Strategies for National Renewal*, London, Vintage.

Commission on Taxation and Citizenship (2001) *Paying for Progress. A New Politics of Tax for Public Spending*, London, Fabian Society.

Coopey, R., Fielding, S. and Tiratsoo, N. (eds) (1993) *The Wilson Governments, 1964–1970*, London, Pinter.

Crewe, I. (1988), 'Has the electorate become Thatcherite?', in Skidelsky, R. (ed.), *Thatcherism*, Oxford, Basil Blackwell.

Crewe, I. (2001) 'Elections and public opinion', in Seldon, A. (ed.), *The Blair Effect*, London, Little, Brown.

Crewe, I. and King, A. (1995) *SDP. The Birth, Life and Death of the Social Democratic Party*, Oxford, Oxford University Press.

Crewe, I. and Sarlvik, B. (1987) *Decade of Dealignment*, Cambridge, Cambridge University Press.

Crewe, I. and Thompson, K. (1999) 'Party loyalties: realignment or dealignment?', in Evans, G. and Norris, P. (eds), *Critical Elections*, London, Sage.

Crosland, A. (1956) *The Future of Socialism*, London, Cape.

Crosland, A. (1962) *The Conservative Enemy*, London, Cape.

Crosland, A. (1974) *Socialism Now*, London, Cape.

Crouch, C. (1999) 'The parabola of working-class politics', in Gamble, A. and Wright, T. (eds), *The New Social Democracy*, Oxford, Basil Blackwell.

Crouch, C. (2001) 'A third way in industrial relations?', in White, S. (ed.), *New Labour: the Progressive Future?*, London, Palgrave.

D'Arcy, M. and MacLean, R. (2000) *Nightmare! The Race to become London's Mayor*, London, Politico's.

Davey, A. (1996) 'Who are Blair's babes?', *Red Pepper*, February.

Davies, L. (2001) *Through the Looking Glass*, London, Verso.

Deighton, A. (2001) 'European Union policy', in Seldon, A (ed.), *The Blair Effect*, London, Little, Brown.

Dell, E. (1991) *A Hard Pounding. Politics and Economic Crisis, 1974–76*, Oxford, Oxford University Press.

Desai, R. (1994) *Intellectuals and Socialism. 'Social Democrats' and the Labour Party*, London, Lawrence & Wishart.

Dixon, J. (2001) 'Health care: modernising the Leviathan', *Political Quarterly*, 72(1).

Donoughue, B. and Jones, G.W. (1973) *Herbert Morrison*, London, Weidenfeld & Nicolson.

Downs, A. (1957) *An Economic Theory of Democracy*, New York, Harper & Row.

Draper, D. (1997) *Blair's Hundred Days*, London, Faber & Faber.

Driver, S. and Martell, L. (1998) *New Labour. Politics after Thatcherism*, Polity, Cambridge.

Driver, S. and Martell, L. (2001) 'From Old Labour to New Labour: a comment on Rubinstein', *Politics*, 21(1).

Drucker, H.M. (1979) *Doctrine and Ethos in the Labour Party*, London, Allen & Unwin.

Drucker, H.M. (1991) 'The influence of the trade unions on the ethos of the Labour Party', in Pimlott, B. and Cook, C. (eds), *Trade Unions in British Politics*, London, Longman.

DTI (2001) Press release, 26 July, www.dti.gov.uk.

Dunleavy, P. and Husbands, C. (1985) *British Democracy at the Crossroads*, London, Allen & Unwin.

Dunleavy P. with Ward, H. (1991) 'Party competition – the preference-shaping model', in Dunleavy, P., *Democracy, Bureaucracy and Public Choice*, Brighton, Harvester.

Duverger, M. (1964) *Political Parties*, London, Methuen.

Ellison, N. (1994) *Egalitarian Thought and Labour Politics*, London, Routledge.

Evans, E.J. (1997) *Thatcher and Thatcherism*, London, Routledge.

Evans, G. (2000) 'The working class and New Labour: a parting of the ways', in Jowell, R., Curtice, J., Park, A., Thomson, K., Jarvis, L., Bromley, C. and Stratford, N. (eds), *British Social Attitudes. The 17th Report. Focusing on Diversity*, London, Sage.

Evans, G. and Norris, P. (eds) (1999) *Critical Elections*, London, Sage.

Evans, G., Heath, A. and Payne, C. (1999) 'Class: Labour as a catch-all party?', in Evans, G. and Norris, P. (eds), *Critical Elections*, London, Sage.

Exworthy M. and Berney, L. (2000) 'What counts and what works? Evaluating policies to tackle health inequalities', *Renewal*, 8(4).

Fatchett, D. and Hain, P. (1997) 'A Stakeholder Party', *Tribune Pamphlet*.

Farrell, D.M. and Webb, P. (2000) 'Political parties as campaigning organizations', in Dalton, R.J. and Wattenberg, M.P. (eds), *Parties without Partisans. Political Change in Advanced Industrial Democracies*, Oxford, Oxford University Press.

Field, F. (1996) *Stakeholder Welfare*, London, Institute of Economic Affairs.

Fielding, S. (1992) 'Labourism in the 1940s', *Twentieth Century British History*, 3(2).

Fielding, S. (1993) ' "White heat" and white collars: the evolution of "Wilsonism" ', in Coopey, R., Fielding, S. and Tiratsoo, N. (eds), *The Wilson Governments, 1964–70*, London, Pinter.

Fielding, S. (1997a) 'Labour's path to power', in Geddes, A. and Tonge, J. (eds), *Labour's Landslide*, Manchester, Manchester University Press.

Fielding, S. (1997b) 'The good war: 1939–45', in Tiratsoo, N. (ed.), *From Blitz to Blair*, London, Weidenfeld & Nicolson.

Fielding, S. (1997c) *The Labour Party since 1951. 'Socialism' and Society*, Manchester, Manchester University Press.

Fielding, S. (2000a) 'A new politics?', in Dunleavy, P., Gamble, A., Holliday, I. and Peele, G. (eds), *Developments in British Politics 6*, London, Macmillan – now Palgrave.

Fielding, S. (2000b) 'New Labour and its past', in Tanner, D., Thane, P. and Tiratsoo, N. (eds), *A Centenary History of the Labour Party*, Cambridge, Cambridge University Press.

Fielding, S. (2000c) 'The "penny farthing machine" revisited: Labour Party members and participation in the 1950s and 1960s', in Pierson, C. and Tormey, S. (eds), *Politics at the Edge*, London, Macmillan – now Palgrave.

Fielding, S. (2001a) 'Activists against "affluence": Labour party culture during the "Golden Age", c. 1950–1970', *Journal of British Studies*, 40(2).

Fielding, S. (2001b) ' "But westward, look, the land is bright!" Labour's revisionists and the imagining of America, c. 1945–64', in Hollowell. J. (ed.), *Twentieth-Century Anglo–American Relations*, London, Palgrave.

Fielding, S. (2002) "No-one else to vote for"? Labour's campaign', in Geddes, A. and Tonge, J. (eds), *Labour's Second Landslide*, Manchester, Manchester University Press.

Fielding, S. and McHugh, D. (2001) 'The social democratic interpretation of the Labour party', Political Studies Association Labour Movement Studies Group conference.

Fielding, S. and Tonge, J. (1999) 'Economic and industrial policy', in Kelly, R. (ed.), *Changing Party Policy in Britain*, Oxford, Basil Blackwell.

Fielding, S., Thompson, P. and Tiratsoo, N. (1995) *'England Arise!' The Labour Party and Popular Politics in 1940s Britain*, Manchester, Manchester University Press.

Financial Times website www.ft.com.

Finlayson, A. (1999) 'Third Way theory', *Political Quarterly*, 70(3).

Fisher, T. (1994) 'What's the strategy?', *Chartist*, May–June.

Fisher, T. (1996) 'Labour's democratic deficit', *Chartist*, July–August.

Flynn, P. (1999) *Dragons Led by Poodles*, London, Politico's.

Foley, M. (2000) *The British Presidency*, Manchester, Manchester University Press.

Foote, G. (1997) *The Labour Party's Political Thought*, London, Macmillan – now Palgrave.

Foster, C. (2001) 'Transport policy', in Seldon, A. (ed.), *The Blair Effect*, London, Little, Brown.

Freeden, M. (1978) *The New Liberalism*, Oxford, Oxford University Press.

Freeden, M. (1986) *Liberalism Divided*, Oxford, Oxford University Press.

Freeden, M. (1996) *Ideologies and Political Theory*, Oxford, Oxford University Press.

Fukuyama, F. (1992) *The End of History and the Last Man*, London, Hamish Hamilton.

Gaitskell, H. (1955) 'Public ownership and equality', *Socialist Commentary*, 19.

Gaitskell, H. (1956) 'Socialism and Nationalisation', *Fabian Tract*, 300.

Gallup Poll (1976) 'Voting Behaviour in Britain, 1945–1974', in Rose, R. (ed.), *Studies in British Politics*, London, Macmillan – now Palgrave.

Gamble, A. (1988) *The Free Economy and the Strong State. The Politics of Thatcherism*, London, Macmillan – now Palgrave.

Gamble, A. (1992) 'The Labour party and economic management', in Smith, M.J. and Spear, J. (eds), *The Changing Labour Party*, London, Routledge.

Gamble, A. and Kelly, G. (2001) 'New Labour's economics', in Ludlam, S. and Smith, M.J. (eds), *New Labour in Government*, London, Macmillan – now Palgrave.

Garrard, J. (2002) *Democratisation in Britain, 1800–1950*, London, Palgrave.

Garrett, G. (1998) *Partisan Politics in the Global Economy*, Cambridge, Cambridge University Press.

Gay, P. (1952) *The Dilemma of Democratic Socialism*, New York, Collier.

Geddes, A. and Tonge, J. (eds) (1997) *Labour's Landslide*, Manchester, Manchester University Press.

Geddes, A. and Tonge, J. (eds) (2002) *Labour's Second Landslide*, Manchester, Manchester University Press.

George, S. and Rosamond, B. (1992) 'The European Community', in Smith, M.J. and Spear, J. (eds), *The Changing Labour Party*, London, Routledge.

Giddens, A. (1994) *Beyond Left and Right*, Cambridge, Polity.

Giddens, A. (1998) *The Third Way*, Cambridge, Polity.

Giddens, A. (2000) *The Third Way and its Critics*, Cambridge, Polity.

Giddens, A. (2002) *Where Now for New Labour?*, Cambridge, Polity.

Gillie, A. (1991) 'Redistribution', in Artis, M. and Cobham, D. (eds), *Labour Economic Policies 1974–79*, Manchester, Manchester University Press.

Glennester, H. (2001) 'Social policy', in Seldon, A. (ed.), *The Blair Effect*, London, Little, Brown.

Goldthorpe, J.H., Lockwood, D., Bechhofer, F. and Platt, J. (1968) *The Affluent Worker: Political Attitudes and Behaviour*, Cambridge, Cambridge University Press.

Gould, B. (1989) *A Future for Socialism*, London, Cape.

Gould, P. (1998) *The Unfinished Revolution*, London, Little, Brown.

Gould, P. (2001) 'The Labour strategy', paper presented to the Elections, Public Opinion and Parties in Britain annual conference.

Gray, J. and Willetts, D. (1997) *Is Conservatism Dead?*, London, Profile.

Guardian website www.guardian.co.uk.

Hain, P. (1999) 'A Welsh Third Way?', *Tribune Pamphlet*.

Hall, S. (1983) 'The great moving Right show', in Hall, S. and Jacques, M. (eds), *The Politics of Thatcherism*, London, Lawrence & Wishart.

Hall, S. and Jacques, M. (eds) (1983) *The Politics of Thatcherism*, London, Lawrence & Wishart.

Hall, S. and Jacques, M. (eds) (1990) *New Times*, London, Lawrence & Wishart.

Halsey, A.H. (1974) 'Government against poverty in school and community', in Wedderburn, D. (ed.), *Poverty and Inequality and Class Structure*, Cambridge, Cambridge University Press.

Hamer, H. (1999) *The Longman Companion to the Labour Party, 1900–1998*, London, Longman.

Hanley, D. (forthcoming) 'Managing the plural left: implications for the party system', in Evans, J. (ed.), *The French Party System: Continuity and Change*, Manchester, Manchester University Press.

Harrison, R. (1971) 'The War Emergency Workers' National Committee, 1914–20', in Briggs, A. and Saville, J. (eds), *Essays in Labour History*, London, Macmillan – now Palgrave.

Harrison, R. (1996) 'New Labour as Past History', *Socialist Renewal Pamphlet*.

Hatfield, M. (1978) *The House the Left Built*, London, Gollancz.

Hattersley, R. (1987) *Choose Freedom*, London, Michael Joseph.

Hay, C. (1994) 'Labour's Thatcherite revisionism: playing the "Politics of Catch-up"', *Political Studies*, 42(4).

Hay, C. (1999) *The Political Economy of New Labour*, Manchester, Manchester University Press.

Heath, A., Jowell R. and Curtice, J. (1994) 'Can Labour win?', in Heath, A., Jowell R. and Curtice, J. with Taylor, B. (eds), *Labour's Last Chance? The 1992 Election and Beyond*, Aldershot, Dartmouth.

Heath, A., Jowell R. and Curtice, J. (2001) *The Rise of New Labour*, Oxford, Oxford University Press.

Heath, A., Jowell, R., Curtice, J., Evans, G., Field, J. and Witherspoon, S. (1991) *Understanding Political Change*, Oxford, Pergamon.

Hedges, A. and Bromley, C. (2001) *Public Attitudes towards Taxation*, London, Fabian Society.

Heffernan, R. (1998) 'Labour's transformation: a staged process', *Politics*, 18(2).

Heffernan, R. (2000) *New Labour and Thatcherism*, London, Macmillan – now Palgrave.

Heffernan, R. and Marqusee, M. (1992) *Defeat from the Jaws of Victory*, London, Verso.

Held, D. McGrew, A., Goldblatt, D. and Perraton, J. (1999) *Global Transformations: Politics, Economics and Culture*, Cambridge, Polity.

Hewitt, P. (2001a) Speech to the *Guardian* and *Observer* conference, 9 July, www.dti.gov.uk/ministers/speeches.

Hewitt, P. (2001b) 'The principled society', *Renewal*, 9(2/3).

Hillman, J. (1998) 'The Labour government and lifelong learning', *Renewal*, 6(2).

Hills, J. and Lelkes, O. (1999) 'Social security, selective universalism and patchwork redistribution', in Jowell, R., Curtice, J., Park, A. and Thomson, K. (eds), *British Social Attitudes. The 16th Report*, Aldershot, Ashgate.

Hirst, P. (2000) 'The knowledge economy: fact or fiction', *Renewal*, 8(2).

Hirst, P. and Thompson, G. (1999) *Globalisation in Question*, Cambridge, Polity.

Hobsbawm, E. (1981) 'The forward march of labour halted?', in Mulhern, F. and Jacques, M. (eds), *The Forward March of Labour Halted?*, London, Lawrence & Wishart.

Hobsbawm, E. (1995) *The Age of Extremes*, London, Michael Joseph.

Hodge, M. (2000) 'Equality and New Labour', *Renewal*, 8(3).

Holmes, M. (1985) *The Labour Government, 1974–79*, London, Macmillan – now Palgrave.

Howarth, C. (2001) 'Winning friends and influencing people', *Fabian Review*, 113(1).

Howell, David (1980) *British Social Democracy*, London, Croom Helm.

Hughes, C. and Wintour, P. (1990) *Labour Rebuilt*, London, Fourth Estate.

Jacobs, M. (2001) 'Narrative', in Harvey, A. (ed.), 'Transforming Britain. Labour's Second Term', *Fabian Pamphlet*, 599.

Jeffery, T. (1989) 'The suburban nation. Politics and class in Lewisham', in Feldman, D. and Stedman Jones, G. (eds), *Metropolis. London. Histories and Representations since 1800*, London, Routledge.

Jenkins, R. (1970) 'Equality', in Crossman, R.H.S. (ed.), *New Fabian Essays*, London, Dent.

Jenkins, R. (1972) *What Matters Now*, London, Fontana.

Johnson, P. (2001) 'New Labour: a distinctive vision of welfare policy?', in White, S. (ed.), *New Labour, The Progressive Future?*, London, Palgrave.

Jones, J. (1999) *Labour of Love. The 'Partly-Political' Diary of a Cabinet Minister's Wife*, London, Politico's.

Jones, H. (1999) '"New Conservatism"? The Industrial Charter, modernity and the reconstruction of British Conservatism after the war', in Conekin, B., Mort, F. and Waters, C. (eds), *Moments of Modernity. Reconstructing Britain, 1945–1964*, London, Rivers Oram.

Jones, N. (2001) *The Control Freaks*, London, Politico's.

Jones, T. (1996) *Remaking the Labour Party*, London, Routledge.

Jospin, L. (1999) 'Modern Socialism', *Fabian Pamphlet*, 592.

Joyce, P. (1999) *Realignment of the Left? A History of the Relationship between the Liberal Democrat and Labour Parties*, London, Macmillan – now Palgrave.

Kampfner, J. (1998) *Robin Cook*, London, Phoenix.

Katz, R. and Mair, P. (1995) 'Changing models of party organization and party democracy: the emergence of the cartel party', *Party Politics*, 1(1).

Kavanagh, D. (1987) *Thatcherism and British Politics*, Oxford, Oxford University Press.

Kavanagh, D. (1991) 'Why political science needs history', *Political Studies*, 39(3).

Kelly, G. and Oppenheim, C. (1998) 'Working with New Labour', *Renewal*, 6(3).

Kelly, R. (1989) *Conservative Party Conferences*, Manchester, Manchester University Press.

Kenny, M. and Smith, M.J. (2001) 'Interpreting New Labour: constraints, dilemmas and political agency', in Ludlam, S. and Smith, M.J. (eds), *New Labour in Government*, London, Macmillan – now Palgrave.

Kilfoyle, P. (2000) *Left Behind*, London, Politico's.

King, A. (1993) 'Preface', in King, A. and others, *Britain at the Polls 1992*, Chatham, NJ, Chatham House.

King, D. and Wickham-Jones, M. (1998) 'Training without the state? New Labour and labour markets', *Policy & Politics*, 26(4).

Kinnock, N. (1994) 'Reforming the Labour party', *Contemporary Record*, 8(3).

Kitschelt, H. (1994) *The Transformation of European Social Democracy*, Cambridge, Cambridge University Press.

Labour Co-Ordinating Committee (1982) *Labour and Mass Politics*, London, Labour Co-Ordinating Committee.

Labour Co-Ordinating Committee (1996) *New Labour: A Stakeholders' Party*, London, Labour Co-Ordinating Committee.

Labour Party (1955) *Interim Report of the Sub-Committee on Party Organisation*, London, Labour Party.

Labour Party (1956a) *Personal Freedom*, London, Labour Party.

Labour Party (1956b) *Towards Equality*, London, Labour Party.
Labour Party (1957) *Industry and Society*, London, Labour Party.
Labour Party (1959) *Annual Conference Report*, London, Labour Party.
Labour Party (1970) *Annual Conference Report*, London, Labour Party.
Labour Party (1976) *Annual Conference Report*, London, Labour Party.
Labour Party (1983) *Annual Conference Report*, London, Labour Party.
Labour Party (1988) *Democratic Socialist Aims and Values*, London, Labour Party.
Labour Party (1989) *Meet the Challenge, Make the Change*, London, Labour Party.
Labour Party (1990) *Looking to the Future*, London, Labour Party.
Labour Party (1992) *It's Time to Get Britain Moving Again*, London, Labour Party.
Labour Party (1996) *Learn as You Earn*, London, Labour Party.
Labour Party (1997a) *Labour into Power*, London, Labour Party.
Labour Party (1997b) *New Deal for a New Britain*, London, Labour Party.
Labour Party (1997c) *New Labour. Because Britain Deserves Better*, London, Labour Party.
Labour Party (1997d) *Partnership in Power*, London, Labour Party.
Labour Party (1999) *21st Century Party*, London, Labour Party.
Labour Party (2001) *Ambitions for Britain*, London, Labour Party.
Larkin, P. (2001) 'New Labour in perspective: a comment on Rubinstein', *Politics*, 21(1).
Laver, M. (1997) *Private Desires, Political Action*, London, Sage.
Lawrence, J. and Taylor, M. (1997) 'Introduction', in Lawrence, J. and Taylor, M. (eds), *Party, State and Society*, Aldershot, Scolar.
Lawson, N. and Sherlock, N. (2001) 'The progressive century: ours to make', in Lawson, N. and Sherlock, N. (eds), *The Progressive Century*, London, Palgrave.
Leadbeater, C. (1999) *Living on Thin Air*, Harmondsworth, Penguin.
Leaman, A. (1998) 'Ending equidistance', *Political Quarterly*, 69(2).
Lent, A. (1997) 'Labour's transformation: searching for the point of origin', *Politics*, 17(1).
Leonard, D. (1981) 'Labour and the voters', in Lipsey, D. and Leonard, D. (eds), *The Socialist Agenda. Crosland's Legacy*, London, Cape.
Leonard, M. (2000) 'Introduction', Hombach, B., *The Politics of the New Centre*, Cambridge, Polity.
Leventhal, F.M. (1989) *Arthur Henderson*, Manchester, Manchester University Press.
Lewis, J. (1998) ' "Work", "welfare" and lone mothers', *Political Quarterly*, 69(1).
Lewis, J. (2001) 'Women, men and the family', in Seldon, A. (ed.), *The Blair Effect*, London, Little, Brown.
Lister, R. (1997) 'From fractured Britain to one nation? The policy options for welfare reform', *Renewal*, 5(3/4).
Lister, R. (2000) 'To Rio via the Third Way. New Labour's "welfare" reform agenda', *Renewal*, 8(4).
Little, R. and Wickham-Jones, M. (eds) (2000), *New Labour's Foreign Policy*, Manchester, Manchester University Press.
Lovecy, J. (2001) New Labour and the "left that is left" in western Europe', in Coates, D. and Lawler, P. (eds), *New Labour in Power*, Manchester, Manchester University Press.
Ludlam, S. (2000) 'New Labour: what's published is what counts', *British Journal of Politics & International Relations*, 2(2).

Ludlam, S. (2001a) 'New Labour and the unions: the end of the contentious alliance?' in in Ludlam, S. and Smith, M.J. (eds), *New Labour in Government*, London, Macmillan – now Palgrave.

Ludlam, S. (2001b) 'The making of New Labour', in Ludlam, S. and Smith, M.J. (eds), *New Labour in Government*, London, Macmillan – now Palgrave.

Ludlam, S. (2001c) 'The union–party link: divorce papers withdrawn?', paper presented to the Political Studies Association annual conference.

McCaig, C. (2001) 'New Labour and education, education, education', in Ludlam, S. and Smith, M.J. (eds), *New Labour in Government*, London, Macmillan – now Palgrave.

McCormick, J. (2001) 'Welfare and well-being', *Political Quarterly*, 72(1).

MacDonald, C. and Arnold-Foster, J. (1995) 'Working Together: Joint Administrations in Local Government', *LINC Pamphlet*, 1.

MacDonald, R. (1929) *Socialism: Critical and Constructive*, London, Cassell.

McHugh, D. (2001) 'A "mass" party frustrated? The development of the Labour party in Manchester, 1918–31', PhD thesis, University of Salford.

MacKenzie, R. (1964) *British Political Parties*, London, Heinemann.

McKibbin, R. (1974) *The Evolution of the Labour Party, 1910–1924*, Oxford, Oxford University Press.

McKibbin, R. (1990) *The Ideologies of Class. Social Relations in Britain, 1880–1950*, Oxford, Oxford University Press.

McKibbin, Ross (1998) *Classes and Cultures. England 1918–1951*, Oxford, Oxford University Press.

McKibbin, Ross (2000) 'Treading water?', *New Left Review*, 4.

Mackintosh, J.P. (1978) 'Has social democracy failed in Britain?', *Political Quarterly*, 49(3).

MacIntyre, D. (1999) *Mandelson. The Biography*, London, HarperCollins.

MacIntyre, S. (1980) *A Proletarian Science. Marxism in Britain, 1917–1933*, Cambridge, Cambridge University Press.

McSmith, A. (1993) *John Smith*, London, Mandarin.

Mair, P. (1994) 'Party organizations: from civil society to state', in Katz, R. and Mair, P. (eds), *How Parties Organize*, London, Sage.

Mair, P. (2000) 'Partyless democracy', *New Left Review*, 2.

Mandelson, P. (1997) 'Labour's next steps: tackling social exclusion', *Fabian Pamphlet*, 581.

Mandelson, P. (1998a) Speech to the British-American Chamber of Commerce, 13 October, www.dti.gov.uk/ministers/speeches.

Mandelson, P. (1998b) Speech to CBI conference, 2 November, www.dti.gov.uk/ministers/speeches.

Mandelson, P. and Liddle, R. (1996) *The Blair Revolution*, London, Faber & Faber.

Marquand, D. (1979) 'Inquest on a movement: Labour's defeat and its consequences', *Encounter*, July.

Marquand, D. (ed.) (1982) *John P. Mackintosh on Parliament and Social Democracy*, London, Longman.

Marquand, D. (1988) *The Unprincipled Society*, London, Fontana.

Marquand, D. (1997) *Ramsay MacDonald*, London, Cohen.

Marquand, D. (1998), 'Must Labour Win?', *Fabian Pamphlet*, 589.

Marquand, D. (1999) *The Progressive Dilemma. From Lloyd George to Blair*, London, Phoenix.

Marquand, D. and Wright, A. (1995) 'Commentary', *Political Quarterly*, 66(3).
Marqusee, M. (1997) 'New Labour and its discontents', *New Left Review*, 224.
Marsh, D. and others (1999) *Postwar British Politics in Perspective*, Polity, Cambridge.
Marx, K. (1975) *Early Writings*, Penguin, Harmondsworth.
Mercer, H. (1991) 'The Labour governments of 1945–51 and private industry', in Tiratsoo N. (ed.) *The Attlee Years*, London, Pinter.
Mercer, H. (1992) 'Anti-monopoly policy', in Mercer, H., Rollings, N. and Tomlinson, J. (eds), *Labour Governments and Private Industry. The Experience of 1945–51*, Edinburgh, Edinburgh University Press.
Mercer, H., Rollings, N. and Tomlinson, J. (1992) 'Introduction', in Mercer, H., Rollings, N. and Tomlinson, J. (eds), *Labour Governments and Private Industry. The Experience of 1945–51*, Edinburgh, Edinburgh University Press.
Metcalf, D. (1999) 'The British minimum wage', *British Journal of Industrial Relations*, 37(2).
Michels, R. (1962) *Political Parties*, New York, Free Press.
Miliband, R. (1972) *Parliamentary Socialism*, London, Merlin.
Minkin, L. (1978) *The Labour Party Conference. Trade Unions and the Labour Party*, Harmondsworth, Penguin.
Minkin, L. (1992) *The Contentious Alliance*, Edinburgh, Edinburgh University Press.
Monks, J. (2000) 'Trade unions and the second term', *Renewal*, 8(3).
Moran, M. and Alexander, E. (2001) 'The economic policy of New Labour', in Coates, D. and Lawler, P. (eds), *New Labour in Power*, Manchester, Manchester University Press.
Morgan, K. and Mungham, G. (2000) *Redesigning Democracy. The Making of the Welsh Assembly*, Bridgend, Seren.
Morgan, K.O. (1984) *Labour in Power, 1945–1951*, Oxford, Oxford University Press.
Morgan, K.O. (1997), *Callaghan. A Life*, Oxford, Oxford University Press.
Mortimer, J. (1997) 'PiP: the management of criticism', *Labour Left Briefing*, September.
Mulgan, G. (1994) *Politics in an Anti-Political Age*, Cambridge, Polity.
Munby, S. (1998) 'Welfare reform', *Renewal*, 6(3).
Nairn, T. (1965) 'The nature of the Labour party', in Anderson, P. (ed.), *Towards Socialism*, London, Fontana.
Naughtie, J. (2001) *The Rivals. The Intimate Story of a Political Marriage*, London, Fourth Estate.
New Statesman & Society/Tribune (1995) 'Rewriting Clause Four: the Debate', London, *New Statesman & Society/Tribune*.
Norris, P. (ed.) (2001) *Britain Votes 2001*, Oxford, Oxford University Press.
Norris, P. and Evans, G. (1999) 'Conclusion: was 1997 a critical election?', in Evans, G. and Norris, P. (eds), *Critical Elections*, London, Sage.
Ohmae, K. (1995) *The End of the Nation State*, New York, Free Press.
Oppenheim, C. (2001) 'Enabling participation? New Labour's welfare-to-work policies', in White, S. (ed.), *New Labour. The Progressive Future?*, London, Palgrave.
Owen, D. (1981) *Face the Future*, Oxford, Oxford University Press.
Owen, D. (1984) *A Future that Will Work*, Harmondsworth, Penguin.

Owen, D. (1986) *A United Kingdom*, Harmondsworth, Penguin.

Owen, G. (2001) 'Industry', in Seldon, A. (ed.), *The Blair Effect*, London, Little, Brown.

Panebianco, A. (1988) *Political Parties: Organization and Power*, Cambridge, Cambridge University Press.

Panitch, L. (1976) *Social Democracy and Industrial Militancy*, Cambridge, Cambridge University Press.

Pattie, C. (2001) 'New Labour and the electorate', in Ludlam, S. and Smith, M.J. (eds), *New Labour in Government*, London, Macmillan – now Palgrave.

Pelling, H. (1965) *Origins of the Labour Party, 1880–1900*, Oxford, Oxford University Press.

Piachaud, D. (2001), 'Child poverty, opportunities and quality of life', *Political Quarterly*, 72(4).

Pimlott, B. (1977) *Labour and the Left in the 1930s*, Cambridge, Cambridge University Press.

Plant, R. (1981) 'Democratic socialism and equality', in Lipsey, D. and Leonard, D. (eds), *The Socialist Agenda. Crosland's Legacy*, London, Cape.

Plant, R. (2001) 'Blair and ideology', in Seldon, A. (ed.), *The Blair Effect*, London, Little, Brown.

Ponting, C. (1989) *Breach of Promise. Labour in Power, 1964–1970*, London, Hamish Hamilton.

Przeworski, A. (1985) *Capitalism and Social Democracy*, Cambridge, Cambridge University Press.

Purdy, D. (2001) 'New Labour and welfare reform', in Coates, D. and Lawler, P. (eds), *New Labour in Power*, Manchester, Manchester University Press.

Putnam, R. (2000) *Bowling Alone. The Collapse and Revival of American Community*, New York, Simon & Schuster.

Radice, G. (1992) 'Southern Discomfort', *Fabian Pamphlet*, 555.

Radice, G. and Pollard, S. (1993) 'More Southern Discomfort', *Fabian Pamphlet*, 560.

Radice, G. and Pollard, S. (1994), 'Any Southern Discomfort?', *Fabian Pamphlet*, 568.

Rentoul, J. (1989) *Me and Mine*, London, Unwin.

Rentoul, J. (2001) *Tony Blair. Prime Minister*, London, Little, Brown.

Richards, P. (1998) 'The permanent revolution of New Labour', in Coddington, A. and Perryman, M. (eds), *The Modernizer's Dilemma*, London, Lawrence & Wishart.

Riddell, N. (1999) *Labour in Crisis. The Second Labour Government, 1929–31*, Manchester, Manchester University Press.

Riley, R. and Young, G. (2001) 'The Macroeconomic Impact of the New Deal for Young People', *National Institute for Economic and Social Research, Discussion Paper*, 184.

Robertson, D. (1997) 'Lifelong learning: can Labour deliver the unifying strategy we need?', *Renewal*, 5(3/4).

Robinson, S. (ed.) (1998) *The Purse or the Wallet?*, London, Women's Budget Group.

Robinson, T. and Turner, R. website (2001) www.unofficialnec.co.uk.

Rothstein, T. (1983) *From Chartism to Labourism. Historical Sketches of the English Working Class Movement*, London, Lawrence & Wishart.

Routledge, P. (1999) *Mandy. The Unauthorised Biography of Peter Mandelson*, London, Simon & Schuster.
Rubinstein, D. (2000) 'A new look at New Labour', *Politics*, 20(3).
Ruhemann, P. (1995) 'Where's the Beef? Labour and Liberal Democrat Policies Compared', *LINC Pamphlet*, 2.
Sainsbury, D. (1996) 'A competitive economy', in Radice, G. (ed.), *What Needs to Change*, London, HarperCollins.
Salmon, H. (1998) 'Ending social exclusion: can Labour deliver?', *Renewal*, 6(3).
Saville, J. (1967) 'Labourism and the Labour Government', in Miliband, R. and Saville, J. (eds), *The Socialist Register 1967*, London, Merlin.
Saville, J. (1973) 'The ideology of labourism', in Benewick, R., Berki, R.N. and Parekh, B. (eds), *Knowledge and Belief in Politics*, London, Allen & Unwin.
Sassoon, D. (1996) *One Hundred Years of Socialism*, London, I.B. Tauris.
Sassoon, D. (ed.) (1997) *Looking Left. European Socialism after the Cold War*, London, I.B. Tauris.
Scarrow, S.E. (1996) *Parties and Their Members*, Oxford, Oxford University Press.
Scarrow, S.E. (2000) 'Parties without members?', in Dalton, R.J. and Wattenberg, M.P. (eds), *Parties Without Partisans. Political Change in Advanced Industrial Democracies*, Oxford, Oxford University Press.
Scarrow, S.E., Webb, P. and Farrell, D.F. (2000) 'From social integration to electoral contestation. The changing distribution of power within political parties', in Dalton, R.J. and Wattenberg, M.P. (eds), *Parties Without Partisans. Political Change in Advanced Industrial Democracies*, Oxford, Oxford University Press.
Scharpf, F.W. (1991) *Crisis and Choice in European Social Democracy*, New York, Cornell University Press.
Schofield, N. (1993) 'Political competition and multiparty coalition governments', *European Journal of Political Research*, 23(1).
Seyd, P. (1987) *The Rise and Fall of the Labour Left*, London, Macmillan – now Palgrave.
Seyd, P. and Whiteley, P. (1998) 'New Labour – a new grass roots party?', paper presented to the Political Studies Association annual conference.
Seyd, P. and Whiteley, P. (2001) 'New Labour and the party: members and organization', in Ludlam, S. and Smith, M.J. (eds), *New Labour in Government*, London, Macmillan – now Palgrave.
Shaw, E. (1994), *The Labour Party Since 1979*, London, Routledge.
Shaw, E. (2001a) 'British social democracy: expiring or reviving?', *Parliamentary Affairs*, 54(1).
Shaw, E. (2001b) 'New Labour: new pathways to Parliament', *Parliamentary Affairs*, 54(1).
Short, C. (1999) 'Globalisation and poverty', *Renewal*, 7(3).
Smith, M.J. (1992) 'A return to revisionism? The Labour party's Policy Review', in Smith, M.J. and Spear, J. (eds), *The Changing Labour Party*, London, Routledge.
Smith, M.J. (1994) 'Understanding the "politics of catch-up": the modernization of the Labour party', *Political Studies*, 42(4).
Smithers, A. (2001) 'Education policy', in Seldon, A. (ed.), *The Blair Effect*, London, Little, Brown.
Smyth, G. (1996) ' "The centre of my political life": Tony Blair's Sedgefield', in Perryman, M. (ed.), *The Blair Agenda*, London, Lawrence & Wishart.

Social Exclusion Unit (1998) *Bringing Britain Together: A National Strategy for Neighbourhood Renewal*, London, Stationery Office.
Socialist Labour Party website (2001) www.socialist-labour-party.org.uk.
Stedman Jones, G. (1983) 'Why is the Labour party in a mess?', in Stedman Jones, G., *Languages of Class*, Cambridge, Cambridge University Press.
Stedward, G. (2001) 'Labour's education policy', in Coates, D. and Lawler, P. (eds), *New Labour in Power*, Manchester, Manchester University Press.
Stephens, P. (2001) 'The Treasury under Labour', in Seldon, A. (ed.), *The Blair Effect*, London, Little, Brown.
Straw, J. (1993) *Policy and Ideology*, Blackburn, Blackburn Labour Party.
Sturgeon, S. and Hurley, J. (eds) (2001) *Reforming Labour. Reclaiming the People's Party*, King's Lynn, Polemic Books.
Tanner, D. (1991) 'Ideological debate in Edwardian Labour politics: radicalism, revisionism and socialism', in Reid, A. and Biagini, E. (eds) *Currents of Radicalism. Popular Radicalism, Organized Labour and Party Politics in Britain, 1850–1914*, Cambridge, Cambridge University Press.
Tanner, D. (2000) 'Labour and its membership', in Tanner, D., Thane, P. and Tiratsoo, N. (eds), *Labour's First Century*, Cambridge, Cambridge University Press.
Tanner, D., Thane, P. and Tiratsoo, N. (eds) (2000) *Labour's First Century*, Cambridge, Cambridge University Press.
Taylor, G. (1993) 'Changing conference: embracing an illusion of democracy', *Renewal*, 1(4).
Taylor, M. (2000) 'Labour and the constitution', in Tanner, D., Thane, P. and Tiratsoo, N. (eds), *Labour's First Century*, Cambridge, Cambridge University Press.
Taylor, R. (2001) 'Employment relations policy', in Seldon, A. (ed.), *The Blair Effect*, London, Little, Brown.
Thompson, E.P. (1978), 'The peculiarities of the English', in Thompson, E.P., *The Poverty of Theory*, London, Merlin.
Thompson, N. (1996) *Political Economy and the Labour Party*, London, University College Press.
Thorpe, A. (2001) *A History of the British Labour Party*, London, Palgrave.
Tiratsoo, N. (1990) *Reconstruction, Affluence and Labour Politics: Coventry, 1945–60*, London, Routledge.
Tiratsoo, N. (ed.) (1991) *The Attlee Years*, London, Pinter.
Tiratsoo, N. (1993) 'Labour and its critics: the case of the May Day Manifesto Group', in Coopey, R., Fielding, S. and Tiratsoo, N. (eds), *The Wilson Governments, 1964–1970*, London, Pinter.
Tiratsoo, N. (1997) ' "Never had it so bad"? Britain in the 1970s', in Tiratsoo, N. (ed.), *From Blitz to Blair*, London, Weidenfeld & Nicolson.
Tiratsoo, N. (2000) 'Labour and the electorate', in Tanner, D., Thane, P. and Tiratsoo, N. (eds), *Labour's First Century*, Cambridge, Cambridge University Press.
Tiratsoo, N. and Tomlinson, J. (1993) *Industrial Efficiency and State Intervention. Labour 1939–51*, London, Routledge.
Tomlinson, J. (1997) *Democratic Socialism and Economic Policy. The Attlee Years, 1945–51*, Cambridge, Cambridge University Press.

Tomlinson, J. (2000) 'Labour and the economy', in Tanner, D., Thane, P. and Tiratsoo, N. (eds), *Labour's First Century*, Cambridge, Cambridge University Press.

Tomlinson, S. (1998) 'Educational dilemmas in a post-welfare age', *Renewal*, 6(3).

Tonge, J. (1999) 'New packaging, old deal? New Labour and employment policy innovation', *Critical Social Policy*, 19(2).

Townsend, P. and Bosanquet, N. (eds) (1972) *Labour and Inequality*, London, Fabian Society.

Toynbee, P. and Walker, D. (2001) *Did Things Get Better?*, Harmondsworth, Penguin.

TUC (2001) Press release, 22 June, www.tuc.org.uk.

Wallace, D.I. (1976), *The Radical Center: Middle Americans and the Politics of Alienation*, Notre Dame, Indiana, University of Notre Dame Press.

Ward, S. (2002) 'Environment and transport policy: a conspiracy of silence?', in Geddes, A. and Tonge, J. (eds), *Labour's Second Landslide*, Manchester, Manchester University Press.

Webb, P. (1994) 'Party organizational change in Britain: the iron law of centralisation', in Katz, R. and Mair, P. (eds), *How Parties Organize*, London, Sage.

Webb, P. (2000) *The Modern British Party System*, London, Sage.

Webb, P. and Farrell, D.M. (1999) 'Party members and ideological change', in Evans, G. and Norris, P. (eds), *Critical Elections*, London, Sage.

Weiss, L. (1998) *The Myth of the Powerless State*, Cambridge, Polity.

Westlake, M. (2001) *Kinnock. The Biography*, London, Little, Brown.

Wheeler, P. (1995) 'Politics in a cold climate', *Renewal*, 3(1).

White, S. (2001) 'The ambiguities of the Third Way', in White, S. (ed.), *New Labour. The Progressive Future?*, London, Palgrave.

Whitehead, A. (2000) 'Cleaning up the dogma doings: Labour and the market', *Renewal*, 8(4).

Whiteley, P. (1983) *The Labour Party in Crisis*, London, Methuen.

Whiteley, P., Clarke, H., Sanders, D. and Stewart, M. (2001), 'Turnout', in Norris, P. (ed.), *Britain Votes 2001*, Oxford, Oxford University Press.

Wickham-Jones, M. (1996) *Economic Strategy and the Labour Party*, London, Macmillan – now Palgrave.

Wickham-Jones, M. (2000) 'New Labour and the global economy: partisan politics and the social democratic model', *British Journal of Politics & International Relations*, 2(1).

Wilkinson, E. (1935) 'Socialism and the problem of the middle classes', in Caitlin, G.E.G (ed.), *New Trends in Socialism*, London, Lorat, Dickson and Thompson.

Wilkinson, R. (2001) 'New Labour and the global economy', in Coates, D. and Lawler, P. (eds), *New Labour in Power*, Manchester, Manchester University Press.

Willetts, D. (1992) *Modern Conservatism*, Harmondsworth, Penguin.

Williams, P.M. (1982) *Hugh Gaitskell*, Oxford, Oxford University Press.

Williams, R. (ed.) (1968), *The May Day Manifesto*, Harmondsworth, Penguin.

Wincott, D. (2001) 'The next nature/nurture debate; or should Labour place mothers and infants at the heart of public policy?', *Political Quarterly*, 72(2).

Winter, J.M. (1972) 'Arthur Henderson, the Russian revolution and the reconstruction of the Labour party', *Historical Journal*, 4(15).

Wollmar, C. (2001) 'Working for two masters? The future of the railway industry after Hatfield', *Renewal*, 9(1).

Wood, S. (2001) 'Education and training: tensions at the heart of the British Third Way', in White, S. (ed.), *New Labour. The Progressive Future?*, London, Palgrave.

Young, M. (1961) *The Rise of the Meritocracy*, Harmondsworth, Penguin.

Young, M., Henn, M. and Hill, N. (1997) 'Labour renewal under Blair? A local membership study in Middelham', paper presented to the Political Studies Association annual conference.

Index